MW00596776

Small Acts

of

Courage

Also by Ali Velshi

The Trump Indictments

How to Speak Money (with Christine Romans)

Gimme My Money Back

Small Acts
of
Courage

A Legacy of Endurance and
the Fight for Democracy

Ali Velshi

ST. MARTIN'S PRESS
NEW YORK

First published in the United States by St. Martin's Press, an imprint of St. Martin's Publishing Group

SMALL ACTS OF COURAGE. Copyright © 2024 by Ali Velshi. All rights reserved. Printed in the United States of America. For information, address St. Martin's Publishing Group, 120 Broadway, New York, NY 10271.

www.stmartins.com

Designed by Gabriel Guma

The Library of Congress Cataloging-in-Publication Data is available upon request.

ISBN 978-1-250-28885-1 (hardcover)
ISBN 978-1-250-28886-8 (ebook)

Our books may be purchased in bulk for promotional, educational, or business use. Please contact your local bookseller or the Macmillan Corporate and Premium Sales Department at 1-800-221-7945, extension 5442, or by email at MacmillanSpecialMarkets@macmillan.com.

First Edition: 2024

10 9 8 7 6 5 4 3 2 1

To the remarkable women who have shaped my journey in life:

My late paternal grandmother, Jena, who passed both the wisdom of Gandhi and her own traditions on to my sister and me.

My late maternal grandmother, Koolsam, who fixed the world with countless small acts of courage while almost single-handedly raising twelve children and keeping a small business going.

My mother, Mila, without whom our nuclear family's involvement in politics could never have happened—and who gave up her own career in politics to make the courageous choice to prioritize her family in a time of need.

My sister, Ishrath, for whom I'll vote every time I'm given the chance (but only once per election).

My daughter, Erica, who fights injustice not just with courage but also with the ferocity of Rajabali Velshi.

And my wife, Lori, who never bargained for a ride into the thick of this fight but who has embraced it, not just as my copilot and strongest champion but also in her own work toward the empowerment of women throughout their careers.

Contents

Small Acts
of
Courage

Prologue

How to Become an American Citizen in Three Easy Steps

On May 30, 2020, I got shot in Minneapolis, Minnesota. I don't know who it was who shot me. It could have been an officer of the Minneapolis police or the Minnesota State Police, or it could have been a member of the National Guard. All I know for certain is that I got shot in the leg, with a rubber bullet. Obviously, getting shot with a rubber bullet is not the same as getting shot with a real bullet, but it *hurts*. We're not talking about a Nerf gun. And if you have the misfortune to take a rubber bullet someplace more sensitive than your leg—like, for instance, your face—it can cause serious injury, up to and including death.

Also, the rubber bullet isn't really the point here. The point is that a law enforcement officer, likely aware of the fact that I was a journalist covering a peaceful march, raised up a gun, took aim, and pulled the trigger. It matters less what was in the chamber when the trigger was pulled and more that someone felt they had the right to pull it in the first place. That is what makes May 30, 2020, such an important day for me, because it is the day I finally understood what it meant to be a citizen of the United States of America.

The path I took to becoming an American citizen was long, circuitous, and not especially intentional. It took me eighteen years, nine months, and seventeen days. But I won't waste your time recounting every part of the journey. I can save us countless hours by doing what I try to do with complex issues on television every day: boiling the story down to its essence.

I became an American citizen in three steps—three distinct, indelible moments. The first of these moments was the day I showed up, which is true for every American citizen, whether they arrived in a hospital maternity ward or the international terminal at JFK. My arrival was only unique in its timing, which by total coincidence came on September 13, 2001. That was the day I arrived here to stay, crossing the Canada-US border with a faxed copy of my O-1 visa, riding my Honda Hawk 750cc motorcycle across the George Washington Bridge into New York City, with lower Manhattan still in flames in the distance.

At that point, I became a resident of America, but I wasn't an American. I certainly didn't *feel* American, and unlike many immigrants, I hadn't come here out of a desire to *become* an American. Canadians have always had a complicated relationship with our impossibly powerful neighbor. We're defensive and protective of our own identity, but at the same time, we can't help but gaze south in awe of what America has to offer. Whether you're a journalist, an actor, or a businessperson, America gives you a bigger stage, a bigger opportunity, a bigger everything.

So when America called, I came. I worked first for CNN, then for Al Jazeera, and finally for MSNBC. I got married, raised a family, and my wife, Lori, and I made America our home. Even then, I didn't give the idea of citizenship much thought. Because of my family's long and seminomadic history, I already had more citizenships than I knew what to do with. Since my family's journey began in India a century before, as a member of the Indian diaspora I carry an Overseas Citizens of India (OCI) card, which doesn't give you all the rights and privileges of being an Indian citizen but does act as a passport that allows you visa-free entry to the country. Then, fleeing from starvation and debt under the British Raj in their native land, my forebears landed in South Africa, where they lived and worked under that country's racist regime for decades—with my grandfather living with Mahatma Gandhi as the youngest pupil on his ashram, Tolstoy Farm; my father running a bakery that served the Black townships of Pretoria; my uncle fighting Apartheid in the streets alongside Nelson Mandela. When democracy finally arrived in that country in the 1990s, the full rights of citizenship they'd long been denied were finally granted to them and, through them, to me. Driven out of South Africa for their family's political activism, my parents then made their way to Kenya, the country where I was born—so, naturally, I was able to claim citizenship there. Then, when life in Kenya proved to be politically untenable for them, they moved once again, to Canada, where we were all welcomed with open arms and granted citizenship in fairly short order.

For my parents, a passport was never a mere travel document. For them, a passport was freedom. It was security. It was evidence of their right to belong. I never needed a passport for that. When it came to my Canadian citizenship, I was secure enough and privileged enough to take it for granted. For me, at the time, having a passport was no different than having a driver's license, and with four passports in my desk drawer, I was already the Jason Bourne of cable news anchors. Going for American citizenship on top of all that felt unnecessary.

Sometime around 2012, while I was still at CNN, I popped into the office of my colleague Ashleigh Banfield for a quick chat. A fellow journalist and a fellow Canadian, Ashleigh and I had been good friends for years. So I was leaning in her doorway and she was sitting at her desk, and somehow the subject of American citizenship came up. She asked me why I hadn't become one yet. I tossed off some dumb joke about not wanting to deal with jury duty, fully expecting her to take the comment in the lighthearted and offhanded manner I intended. But that is not what happened. Her whole demeanor and expression changed, and she lit into me—and I mean she gave me a hell of a lecture. "Being a citizen of this country is not something to be taken lightly," she said. "You live in this country. You benefit from its services and infrastructure, and if you're planning to stay here, that comes with rights and responsibilities. This is not a joking matter." And she was right. Citizenship in a democracy is something millions around the globe would die for, yet I'd become so blasé about it that I'd started thinking of it in terms of how it would inconvenience me. But if you want to enjoy the benefits of living in a free society, jury duty is just that: a duty.

In 2015, having left CNN for Al Jazeera, I finally started the process, beginning with an in-person interview and a test. The in-person interview was a nonevent, a short matter in downtown Manhattan. The test wasn't much harder. I was worried it would include things that I hadn't learned as a kid. So I studied. But it was mostly pretty basic stuff. "What are the three branches of government?" and so forth.

After I passed and completed the standard waiting period, they sent me a letter telling me my swearing-in ceremony would be on September 25. Up to that point, I'd been treating the whole process with about the same level of enthusiasm as a trip to the DMV. But when I arrived for the swearing-in ceremony at the Thurgood Marshall United States Courthouse on Foley Square in downtown Manhattan, something changed. Seeing the other soon-to-be citizens made me stop and open my eyes. I travel all the time. For me, flying in an airplane is like riding a crosstown bus. There's no romance left to it. But whenever I fly, I try to remember that this might be somebody's first trip, maybe a vacation they've saved up for or maybe a reunion with family they haven't seen for years. Even though it's just a commute for me, to somebody else it might be the most important moment of their lives.

I had that same feeling arriving that morning. I had covered many major financial trials from outside that courthouse, but I had never once been inside. When I went through the metal detector and into this beautiful, ornate chamber where the oath was to be administered, I saw all the other people, most of whom were not white. Watching as they filtered in and took their seats, I started to think about their stories the same way I would passengers on an airplane. Maybe the document they were about to get was their Golden Ticket. Maybe that man was a refugee from a war-torn homeland he'd never see again. Maybe that woman spent years slogging through the immigration bureaucracy to finally be with the spouse she loved. Seeing how special this moment was for all these other people, I finally realized how special it was for me.

That fact was driven home even further over the next two hours as I sat and waited for the ceremony to begin. We'd all had to surrender our phones back at the metal detector, so with nothing to do and having brought nothing of my own to read, I picked up the only printed material available: a copy of the United States Constitution. Sitting in that chamber, on the cusp of becoming a citizen, I read the Constitution three times, start to finish. There's no doubt that it was written by people who were doing heinous things at the time, and it's undeniable that the country has too often failed to live up to its ideals in the years since. Still, I was genuinely moved by the intent behind the document, to create a more perfect union and to enumerate specific rights and liberties that were revolutionary at the time, and now those rights and those liberties were being conferred on me.

Two hours later, when I swore my oath of citizenship, I meant it. Still, other than being able to vote and being eligible for jury duty, my day-to-day life wasn't greatly transformed. I would say that as a result of the oath, I'd been given a greater awareness of the rights and privileges of citizenship, but I wasn't any more concerned with the responsibilities and obligations of citizenship.

Then I got shot by an armed agent of the state.

In the last week of May 2020, with so much of the real world still in lockdown from COVID-19, a lot of the big news grabbing people's attention derived from whatever was happening online. The first story to go viral that week was a video taken by Christian Cooper, a birdwatcher in Central Park, who'd recorded a white woman threatening to call the police on him as retaliation for his asking her to leash her dog. Which, given that Cooper is Black, had all kinds of unpleasant implications. The morning after that story broke, I was on a conference call with my senior producer, Jared Blake, and other senior staff. We discussed trying to book Cooper about the Central Park story, but then Jared said something to the effect of "I think this Minneapolis thing is a bigger deal. Have you seen the video?"

I hadn't. The video hadn't quite percolated up yet. So I went on my phone, pulled it up, and watched as Minneapolis police officer Derek Chauvin, for nine and a half agonizing minutes, kept his knee on George Floyd's neck, even as the man choked and gasped and kept saying, "I can't breathe." My reaction was the same as every other human being who saw the footage, which was a mix of horror, revulsion, and outrage.

By that afternoon, the streets of Minneapolis had begun to erupt in protests and the police had brought out the tear gas and the riot gear. Once that happened, I knew I was on my way to Minnesota. I tend to be that guy at MSNBC, the guy who goes to hurricanes, and shootings, and hot zones. When I landed, I was met by Evan Minogue, a former NYPD lieutenant who had recently been hired by our security department. His job was to escort my crew and me through the city and to keep us safe. After giving us a quick debrief, the first thing he asked was if I'd brought a bulletproof vest and a gas mask. I'd brought a vest; I own a few, for the trips I've taken to cover conflict zones overseas. But I told him I didn't have a gas mask, so he procured one for me with two attachable gas-filter canisters.

Up to that point in my career as a broadcaster, I'd been to several events with the Committee to Protect Journalists, black-tie events at the Waldorf Astoria. The honorees were almost always reporters who had to walk around their own countries in flak jackets and helmets because they were being targeted by their own governments. There were also awards being given in absentia, because the recipients were either imprisoned, missing, or dead or forbidden to leave their own countries. It had never occurred to me before that night that I would need to don a bulletproof vest in my own country. Yet here I was in Minneapolis, doing exactly that. I wore the vest under my shirt and carried the mask at the ready.

Once Evan had us all set to go, I got on camera more or less immediately and stayed there, broadcasting live, for the next several days. That Thursday night, three days after Floyd had been killed, I was on air with Brian Williams, who was hosting his nightly MSNBC show back in New York. We'd been broadcasting nonstop all evening. Minnesota's governor had activated the National Guard. Derek Chauvin would not be arrested and charged with third-degree murder for another day. President Trump had gone on Twitter and called the protesters "thugs." And on this night, Minneapolis's Third Precinct—the precinct at which the cops who'd arrested Floyd were based—had been overrun. The protesters had Molotov cocktails and rocks, the police had bean bag shot guns and flash-bangs and rubber bullets and tear gas, and there was a live battle that went on for hours. There were several active fires in the neighborhood, including one in the liquor store behind me. I could see a fire truck a couple of blocks away, but there was no way that truck was going to come in because they can't ride themselves into a riot unprotected; so, these buildings were going to be left to burn.

It was quite a thing to see—and that was the problem. In television news, the camera distorts as much as it reveals, and the spectacle of what was going on at the police station was giving a skewed view of everything that was happening around it, which was far less devastating than it appeared to be onscreen. Minneapolis as a whole was quiet. The vast majority of the protests were peaceful vigils, but on TV, the way we set up shots draws focus to the most visually striking elements of the story. So I finally said to Brian Williams, "I want to be clear on how I characterize this. This is mostly a protest. It is not, generally speaking, unruly." Because it wasn't. Outside of a small group of violent agitators, most of the people out that night were engaging in the act of being citizens in a democracy, voicing their protests over an egregious crime committed by the police of their city, one that had been clearly and unambiguously captured on video.

In the days that followed, I walked with those protesters everywhere they went. Then, that Saturday evening, because the Third Precinct had been closed off, everyone had gathered around the barricades outside the Fifth Precinct, a little over two miles away. I was in the middle of the crowd, reporting on it. There was a curfew in effect for 8:00 p.m. that night, and right before the appointed hour, announcements started coming over loudspeakers from the police: "There is a curfew in effect. Anybody who is gathered here after that will be in violation of the curfew." Everyone's phones then started to ping as texts popped up saying the same thing:

EMERGENCY ALERT

The city of Minneapolis is under a strict curfew, beginning at 8 pm. Go home or to a safe location. Avoid the outdoors. The curfew is enforceable by law.

At that point, the entire crowd, which was thousands of people, sat down en masse. It felt very Gandhian, an immediate manifestation of nonviolent resistance. People were saying, "You will have to arrest us and drag us out sitting down, and we will not help you."

By 9:00 p.m., the curfew had been in effect for an hour, but people weren't going home. The announcements continued, and at a certain point, the whole crowd stood up again and started moving. It wasn't even a march, really. It was more of a walk. There were chants rippling through the crowd, and the people next to me were talking and waving their Bernie Sanders signs. It felt light. Unlike a couple of nights earlier, there were no violent overtones to it. It was just a walk.

The crowd stretched several blocks, and I was two-thirds of the way toward the back. We walked for about twenty-five, thirty minutes, and then we reached an intersection. Suddenly, people started making noise. We looked up and saw lights and heard sirens, and then out of nowhere the police and National Guard raced into the intersection ahead of us, splitting the crowd in half. Then, completely unprovoked, they started firing tear gas and rubber bullets into the crowd. It was remarkable. Again, I can't emphasize enough how peaceful this gathering was. People were singing tunes and walking. But the police weren't waiting for something violent to happen. They just started firing.

Because most people didn't have gas masks, the crowd split. Half the people ran south, and the other half ran north. Having been mostly in the back of the crowd, I was now closest to the police. As a result, we now had live footage of the cops and National Guard shooting into the crowd. Then they started firing in our direction. Evan, himself a twenty-six-year veteran police officer, couldn't believe it. You could hear him on the broadcast saying, "They're *shooting* at us?!" as he pulled me backward to try to get me out of the way.

At that point, most of the crowd was gone. It should have been easy for the authorities to identify that we were media. My cameraman Miguel Toran is an exceptionally tall guy. He's about six-foot-three, and he carries a big camera on his shoulder. The people who were firing at us were, theoretically, using scopes, so it seems almost impossible that they wouldn't have known we were journalists, which means they likely were targeting us *because* we were journalists.

As we backed up, walking slowly away from the authorities, I was live on TV the whole time. The guy next to me got shot by something, and moments after I reported the fact that he'd been shot, I got shot. I took the bullet in my left leg, right in my shin. I stayed standing but hobbled and limped to the side of the street, in shock at what had happened, trying to keep my composure and report on the story even as I became a part of the story. We walked to the next intersection, only to find that the police had converged there as well. Having just been shot at, we all put up our hands and said, "We're media!" Somebody from the police side yelled back, "We don't care!" Then they started shooting at us. Luckily, this time they didn't hit anyone, but the sense of impunity with which they were firing was astonishing. We weren't doing anything except quietly backing away from them, but they shot at us all the same.

That was the third step. That was the moment when I finally became a citizen in the deepest sense of the word, because that was the day I understood how invested in this place I truly need to be. One day I'll find out who shot me, and when I do, I'll go and I'll thank them, because what they did was open my eyes. They woke me up. They changed my entire outlook on democracy. That rubber bullet told me, "You're in this fight. You're not watching it anymore. You're in it, whether you want to be or not."

And that epiphany, in turn, is what led to this book.

———————————

Over the course of the next few days, we learned that earlier that week, the police had been called to the scene to investigate an alleged crime. The shopkeeper at a store called Cup Foods thought George Floyd might have tried to pass a counterfeit twenty-dollar bill. The fact that the shopkeeper made the call was understandable, but the punishment for maybe passing a bogus twenty isn't death. And in a democracy founded on the rule of law, no punishment can be administered without the presumption of innocence, a fair trial, and an opportunity to mount your own defense. In this case, the cops had skipped right to an extrajudicial sentencing, which meant you had to call this killing what it was: a lynching.

The same had been true for Ahmaud Arbery, Philando Castile, Walter Scott, Sandra Bland, Breonna Taylor, and so many other Black people killed indiscriminately in recent years, either for trivial infractions or without any provocation at all. In most of those cases, the only reason their families saw even the slightest measure of justice was because the killings were caught on video and went viral.

As the facts around George Floyd's murder slowly came to light, I couldn't help but think about the moment I'd shared with a young Black man in the streets of Minneapolis the night before I'd been shot with that rubber bullet. As my crew and I were watching a liquor store burn down, this guy came over to me and struck up a conversation. His name was Ja'Mal Green, and it turned out that he was a Black Lives Matter activist and former Chicago mayoral candidate. At that point, there had been no arrests and no one had been charged, and this was three days after George Floyd was killed on video. Nodding toward the fire, Green said to me, "People are angry, and their reaction, you can't be mad at them for it, because what does justice look like? Why do I have to play by somebody's rules if there's no justice?" He was saying that the rules that had been set up for society didn't work for everyone, so why did those people have to live within those rules, especially if those rules don't protect them from getting killed. The people rioting couldn't respect the police because the police didn't respect them. They felt no obligation to the system, because it wasn't their system.

Green hadn't been looting or setting fires himself. He was simply explaining to me why this was happening, that everything I was watching around me stemmed from the fact that Black people were not getting justice. They were not getting protection from the law. When they saw the police, they saw only a threat. I understood where he was coming from. I had never faced the same systemic racism and prejudice that he had endured, but for most of my family's history, my parents, grandparents, and great-grandparents had lived a life not so different from his. They, too, had lived inside of systems that actively disrespected them. They, too, fought against regimes that didn't protect them. To this day, my parents and many of my aunts and uncles still break out in a cold sweat whenever they get stopped by the police. In Canada, spot checks for drunk driving are common. Whenever we used to get pulled over, my father, who is possibly the most mild-mannered human on the planet, who has never even thought about breaking any traffic law anywhere, would always feel his heart start to race, and that's because he grew up thinking that when the law comes for you, you're going to end up on the wrong side of it if your skin isn't the right color. (Naturally, he always passed, and they would give him a commemorative ice scraper as a reward for not driving drunk, which is a typically Canadian thing to do.)

Long before the cushy life that allowed me to take my citizenship for granted, my family had endured what the protesters in Minneapolis had endured. They had suffered economic hardship, political persecution, and state-sponsored violence as well. Yet through it all they had never succumbed to hopelessness or despair. They had never resigned themselves to the idea that their actions were futile or that they had no agency in determining their own path in life. At every critical juncture, often in defiance of the governments that oppressed and disenfranchised them, they had chosen to use what little resources they had to make the biggest difference they could, sometimes for the sake of their own survival, but often for the good of their community and the larger society around them. And what started as a life of total deprivation and servitude under the British Raj in India culminated in my father becoming the first Muslim and first South Asian to be elected to public office in Canada. Over the course of four generations, their small acts of courage amounted to an astonishing, unprecedented achievement.

Leaving Minneapolis, I found myself not only in an entirely new place in my life but also on an entirely new journey in my career. Two journeys, in fact. The first played out on the air at MSNBC. In the history of hurting America's democracy, cable news has played no small part, with social media coming up behind to finish the job. Understanding the degree to which cable news has often sensationalized the wrong issues and actively impeded efforts to have a constructive dialogue, I decided to use my show as a tool to fix democracy rather than tear it down. I've got the same tools that every other television journalist has. I've got freedom of speech and access and an audience and a platform, and I decided to make a conscious effort to use them for good to focus on issues around democracy. My team and I started to program and curate my show to do more to inform people who, like me, generally see themselves as being on the side of social justice but don't understand firsthand how high the stakes are for millions of others in this country.

We changed the representation of guests on the show as well, bringing in people who would probably be considered outside the cable news norm in terms of who typically gets on TV to talk about politics. I centered racial justice in my show to the extent that I talked about it from economic perspectives and policing perspectives. Where I'd spoken to maybe a handful of historians on my show in the twenty-five years prior to that, each week was now a master class, putting the moment that America was going through into context.

I realized that I needed to bring my own family history in as well. I realized that, in this instance, journalistic objectivity was less useful to me than the perspective I could bring from my own lived experience. I started to write monologues and introductions to stories that spoke to my own personal history with politics and elections. For the first time in my career, my story became relevant to the story of the world that we were telling, and I decided I needed to be open about it.

That decision, in turn, is what led me to the second part of my journey, which is what you now hold in your hands with this book—a book that, incidentally, is not about me, or not entirely or even mostly about me. I had always known the broad outlines of my family's history, but once I set out to write about it, I realized how much of it I only remembered through the limited perspective of a young boy who'd heard small bits of it here and there. I knew part of the what, where, and when, but I lacked any real grasp of the why.

Very soon I came to the realization that my story is but one link in a chain, a chain that stretches back over a hundred years across five countries on three continents, and I wanted to understand where I fit in that chain. So I put on my reporter's cap and I started traveling and I started digging, going through letters and papers and archives, interviewing family members, revisiting the places we'd lived across the decades. What I knew from the beginning was that my family had been on a lifelong search for the betterment of their own lot in life, for a place where they could live safely, securely, and above all freely. What I wanted to understand is how the quest for the betterment of one's own situation can, and must, lead to the betterment of society as a whole. I wanted to know how we can get to a place where I never again have to wear a bulletproof vest and a gas mask in my own country.

The senseless murder of George Floyd had taken me to Minneapolis, but I left thinking more and more about the young man I'd met while watching that liquor store burn down. He and I were two sides of the same coin. Despite the vast difference in our lived experiences, we were both legal citizens of the United States. Up until the point I got shot, I wasn't fully invested in that citizenship because I didn't have to be. I was fortunate and privileged enough to be able to take it for granted. Meanwhile, he was not fully invested in his citizenship because he felt that it had failed to provide him with the rights and protections that he deserved. What I know now, after three years of traveling, researching, and writing, is that if we want to prevent the murder of the next George Floyd, it will require more than just reforming the way we police. It will require us to build a society where the rights, privileges, and protections of citizenship—and the responsibilities of citizenship—are shared by all.

As my family's hundred-year journey illustrates, for far too many people, achieving true citizenship and belonging in a new country is no easy endeavor. It can be long, arduous, and beset by discouraging setbacks at every turn. And for all of us as a society to work together to build a shared notion of citizenship, to build a truly united country on a bedrock of universal principles and common values, that is the truly difficult task that we face. It takes at least a generation. Sometimes two, and maybe even three. But it can be done, and for the sake of our children and their future, it must be done.

1

Why Does Anyone Leave Anywhere?

In March 2012, in addition to normal reporting and anchoring for CNN, I was also the cohost for *World Business Today* on CNN International. It aired at 9:00 a.m. eastern time, right when the markets opened, which made it something of a must-watch for traders in Hong Kong, India, and across Asia. As a result, I started enjoying a bit of notoriety in those places, and someone at CNN arranged for me to speak at an event in New Delhi.

By the time I was born, my family had been out of India for close to one hundred years. My connection to that place and that identity is tenuous at best. Most of my life, if you'd asked me what I am or where I was from, I would have said, "I'm Canadian." It wouldn't have even occurred to me to say that I was Indian. I suppose the most accurate way to describe me is that I'm a member of the Indian diaspora, which is its own thing, both very Indian and not exactly Indian at the same time.

The sense of unity among the Indian diaspora is strong. As a person of Indian extraction who shows up on television, I'm regularly invited to American India Foundation banquets and things like that, and what's interesting is that nobody at these things seems to care that I didn't come from India and that my life is quite removed from India. Even though the organizers behind these events are overwhelmingly Hindu, they don't seem to care that I'm Muslim. And because I'm Muslim, people from Pakistan tend to embrace me as well, even though I have zero connection to Pakistan whatsoever. The regional and factional politics in India can get quite heated, even violent, but those tensions become muted in the diaspora. Generally speaking, brown people from the Indian subcontinent, even when they have legitimate religious, political, and cultural differences, tend to identify with each other. There's a kinship—which is precisely how I feel about it.

India was at the vanguard of postcolonial independence and has been the world's largest democracy for some time. Sadly, under Narendra Modi, the current prime minister, it is taking a sharply antidemocratic turn. It still has the vote, but the shift toward autocracy has made it increasingly dangerous for both members of the political opposition and the journalists who report on the regime. So while I don't love India's current political trajectory, I love the *idea* that I'm Indian. And I like the food.

As a child, I enjoyed going to Indian movies with my sari-wearing, Gujarati-speaking grandmother. Other than that, India for me was just the place we had left. My parents had visited. They enjoyed it, but India never became a larger part of our ethos or legend. I truly didn't know where Gujarat was. The only thing my father ever said of my Indian ancestors was "Thank God they left." Because it wasn't clear what opportunities we would have had if they hadn't.

Up to that point in my life, I'd never felt any need to go back, to make some sort of pilgrimage to the homeland. I'd never even considered it. It wasn't on my bucket list. But with a speaking gig as a pretext for going, it seemed I would be undertaking a pilgrimage after all. My wife, Lori, and I started planning what would become a two-week holiday to see the country.

At that point, I thought I knew India well or, at least, better than the average person. I had my ancestral connection to the place and my family's stories. I had the official status afforded by my Overseas Citizens of India card. Plus, through my show on CNN, I'd been covering India a great deal. The offshoring of jobs from America to the subcontinent was one of the big, ongoing stories of the day, and I'd covered it extensively from every angle. So I thought I knew pretty well what to expect. Then I stepped out of the airport terminal in Mumbai, and I realized I knew nothing.

India is an assault on the senses. Given what I do for a living, I'm accustomed to my senses being assaulted. I've dropped into plenty of hot zones around the world to report on them. I'm used to processing tons of new people and new information all at once. But on the day we arrived in Mumbai, India overwhelmed me completely. It was impossible to digest all of it at the same time—the smells, the sounds, the cows and donkeys and horses and sheep in the streets, entire families riding on a motorcycle, four or five of them clinging precariously to the sides.

The other thing you can't help but gawk at is the stark proximity and yet stark divide between the very rich and the very poor. We'd walk into these fancy brand-new five-, six-, and seven-star hotels where every surface was gleaming. Then we'd go ten feet out the front door, and we'd be in squalor, with gangs of children begging at every street corner. There's homelessness and poverty everywhere. At no point does it stop, and nothing really works the way that you expect it to in the Western world, either. As we skipped across the country from Mumbai to Jaipur to Delhi to Bangalore, one of our airlines up and declared bankruptcy, so we had to change airlines and find another flight.

The side trip to visit my family's ancestral home started with a bumpy flight into Rajkot, one of the larger cities in the state of Gujarat, which sits on the Kathiawar peninsula on the western coast of India. Gujarat is not only a state. It's a people, it's its own language, it's a cuisine—all of those things. Gujarati is the language my parents would use at home when they didn't what me to know what they were talking about. (Though when they suspected that my grandmother was teaching me Gujarati, they then switched to speaking in Afrikaans.)

Outside of India, if you've even heard of Gujarat, it's probably for the fact that it's the birthplace of Mahatma Gandhi. Today, the province's most recent claim to fame is that it's where Prime Minister Narendra Modi is from. With a population of around 70 million and bustling port cities on the Arabian Sea, it's one of India's more prosperous states, with a per capita GDP one and a half times higher than the nation's average. That's true for parts of it, at any rate. My family is from a different part.

In Rajkot, we were met by a driver, someone my mother, a travel agent, had arranged for us. He picked us up at the airport and drove us the forty-five kilometers east to Chotila, my family's village. It's a cheap journalistic cliché to describe a trip to a desolate, undeveloped place as "like traveling back in time." But it's overused because often it's just true. I've been to rural places in America that made me feel like I was going back to the 1930s or 1940s, but driving along that road to Chotila was something else entirely. The landscape was barren and dry. The few people and huts we saw looked like the past hundred years had passed them by—except for the cell phones everyone carried, of course, and the satellite dishes grafted onto the rooftops of the ancient dwellings. But other than that, it felt like nothing must have changed since the time my great-grandparents left it behind at the end of the nineteenth century.

My family's journey out of Chotila and out of India starts with my great-great-grandfather, Keshavjee Ramji Murji, known in our family as KeshavjeeBapa, the suffix *Bapa* meaning "father." Together with his wife, my great-great-grandmother Mithima, he had six children: two daughters, Manek and Santok, and four sons. Of the sons, Jivan was the eldest. Next came Naran; then my paternal great-grandfather Velshi, whose first name would eventually become my last name; and then the youngest, my maternal great-grandfather Manjee. (Yes, my great-grandfathers were brothers. It sounds taboo to modern ears, but when you grew up as my parents did in South Africa, in a tiny segregated ghetto where intermarriage with outsiders was literally against the law, second and third cousins getting married was actually quite common.)

All four of the sons worked for KeshavjeeBapa in the family business, and their family business was, well, business, which was typical for the area. Some parts of India are known for agriculture. If you're from Bangalore these days, it's all tech. But Gujarat is known, even within India, as the place where businesspeople come from. They're merchants, traders, shopkeepers. In Gujarati tradition, other than farming, being a small, self-employed merchant has long been considered the most honorable path in life. It's an idea rooted in a deep cultural belief that grace only comes to those who have their own basket into which God can place bounty; being someone else's employee deprives you of the opportunity to set your own path.

KeshavjeeBapa was a prominent businessman in the region. He owned both farmland and properties in town, including a couple of warehouses and some small shops that sold necessities like flour and rice and spices and ghee—all of which made him relatively prosperous, particularly when compared with the dire poverty that surrounded him. He was also religious, and for Ismaili Muslims, making money is never an end in itself. It is simply a means to living a moral life. You should work hard, be entrepreneurial, and do well, but always remember that any money you make brings certain obligations to care for your family, to look after the poor, to care for the environment, and to ensure that you play a positive role in civil society. KeshavjeeBapa lived in accordance with those ideals, and he used his money to build the well that had brought fresh water to the village in the 1850s, and also to finance the *jamatkhana*, the local mosque, far and away the nicest building in town.

Despite his relative good fortune, KeshavjeeBapa had the great misfortune of living in India in the mid- to late nineteenth century, which meant living under complete subjugation and exploitation, first under the ownership of the East India Company and then, later, after Queen Victoria claimed control of the colony, under the British Raj. At the peak of its power, the United Kingdom ruled over a quarter of the land and people on the entire planet, justifying its economic plundering of foreign lands as a God-given imperative to uplift and

"civilize" all the backward, benighted brown peoples of the world—
what Rudyard Kipling would later term "the white man's burden."
The reality is that for this tiny island to keep a quarter of the world's
population under its thumb required a level of brutality that is hard
to even fathom: the torture and massacre of dissidents from Ireland
to Jamaica to Palestine; letting tens of thousands die in concentration camps in South Africa and Kenya; the partition of India and
Pakistan, which left over a million dead in sectarian violence; millions of persons stolen off their native soil and sold off in the international slave trade. The list goes on. But even as the worst abuses of
colonialism have been exhaustively documented and brought to light,
there are those who still maintain a sort of "yes, but" defense of Great
Britain's imperial project: that it was worthwhile because, in the end,
the British left their former subjects with the rule of law and better
railroads and "Western values."

We now know that the opposite is true, particularly in India.
Before the British arrived, India had a successful, self-sustaining,
and prosperous economy. Left to its own devices, it might be one
of the most powerful countries in the world today. Colonialism de-
nuded the Indian subcontinent, stripped it bare. Instead of traditional craftsmen producing finished goods and services for the local
population, India's economy was put in the service of creating raw
materials to feed the British industrial machine, which produced the
goods that India's people were then forced to reimport at an exorbi-
tant markup because their economy no longer existed to serve the
people who toiled in it. In addition to wrecking local economies, the
British levied punitive land taxes on Indian farmers. When they were
unable to pay, their lands were confiscated according to laws passed
by British courts. The Mughal princes who'd ruled India before the

British arrived were stripped of their real power and became, in essence, political cronies of the colonial government, complicit in the exploitation of their own people. Britain's venerated "rule of law" was essentially a fig leaf, covering up a system rife with kickbacks, corruption, and nepotism.

Shashi Tharoor, an Indian politician who also served as an undersecretary general at the United Nations, has achieved a great deal of notoriety in recent years for his writings and lectures, the gist of which boils down to "Yeah, actually the Brits just wrecked the place." In his two books, *An Era of Darkness: The British Empire in India* and *Inglorious Empire: What the British Did to India*, Tharoor has outlined all the ways in which the economic and cultural trajectory of India before the British arrived had been outstanding and that the effect of colonialism was not to improve that record but to decimate it. At the start of British rule in India, for example, the Indian share of the global economy was 23 percent. By the time the Brits finally left in 1947, it had plummeted to less than 4 percent. As of 2022, it's now around 7.5 percent. Being the "crown jewel" of the empire was so devastating to the jewel itself that, even seventy-five years after the empire fell, it's still going to be quite some time before India fully recovers its true potential and wealth.

The catalyst for our family's departure came, as it did for millions of other Indians, in the mid- to late nineteenth century. After the British had finally succeeded in running India into the ground, the ill effects of colonialism were compounded by environmental catastrophe. Waves of drought parched and devastated the land, wiping out whole crops and herds of livestock, leading to mass starvation. In the first half of the nineteenth century there were seven famines that killed, by conservative estimates, around eight hundred thousand people. The second half of the nineteenth century was worse, bringing seven additional famines that killed over 15 million. All the while, tons of Indian wheat were being exported to feed the British back home, and the money and resources that might have eased the devastation caused by famine had gone elsewhere, taken by the British and used to support their various military adventures overseas. The starving people of India were left with no choice but to go elsewhere themselves. Between 1830 and 1870, nearly 2 million workers left the country in search of better prospects. That was the Big Bang. The Indian diaspora was born.

The world created by that diaspora, the world in which we now live, where my parents were born in one country and I was born in another country and we immigrated to a third country and I now live in a fourth country, that's normal for us. It wasn't normal at the time. The way of the world at that time was that you went to work on the same farm or in the same trade as your grandfather. Your parents found you someone to marry, you married them, and you stayed put, following the same tried-and-tested customs that your family had followed for generations. You didn't even leave for the next village thirty miles up the road, never mind boarding a ship to cross the ocean to live on a separate continent where who knows what was in store. But the conditions in India in the late 1800s were that dire.

Unlike the emigrants fleeing deprivation and political unrest in mainland Europe, Indians by and large did not make their way to North America. That door was not open to them. All they could do was follow the trade routes that left from Bombay and India's other major ports. Because those trade routes were controlled by the

British, the places they led were out into the farther reaches of the empire. The resources that had been plundered from India were being used to build railways and farms and factories in China, in the Middle East, and primarily in Africa. That's where the jobs were and that's where the boats were going, so that's where Indians went. In a cruel twist of fate, they left their homes and their families to toil on behalf of the same empire that had devastated their native land and forced them onto the open seas in the first place.

Although slavery had been formally outlawed in the British Empire in 1834, the worldwide demand for slave labor hadn't slackened one bit. So the practice carried on more or less as it had before, only now it was under the guise of indentured labor. The first wave of Indians fleeing Gujarat and the other impoverished regions of India were too poor to afford even the boat fare to leave. Eager to take advantage of this were slick, smooth-talking recruiters who offered them free passage to Africa and false promises of the prosperity on distant shores. In exchange for the price of a ticket, the Indians agreed to become indentured workers, signing five-year contracts that bound them to their future employers on onerous terms.

Once at sea, they quickly learned of the bait and switch. The journey meant weeks on rusty, stinking ships infested with cockroaches and rats. Thousands died at sea from malnutrition and disease. Those who didn't were subject to brutal beatings and rape at the hands of the crews. Then, once they arrived at their destination, the false promise of prosperity quickly evaporated, revealing the harsh reality of what it was: slavery by another name. Even still, in the decades that followed, millions continued to sign on, simply because conditions in India were that much worse.

Today you'll find enclaves of the nineteenth-century Indian diaspora in every corner of every continent. Most of the migration was to
Africa, to places like Natal and Mombasa, Zanzibar and Dar es Sa-
laam, Mauritius and Madagascar. Some of it went farther into Asia
and the South Pacific, to Malaysia and to Fiji, and a fair amount
even went as far as the New World, to newly formed colonies in
Guyana and Trinidad. There the indentured Indians became known
as "coolies," a pejorative term for menial, subsistence workers from
the Far East. (Millions of Chinese laborers, also known as coolies,
suffered the same fate.)

Wherever these new Indian populations took root, they soon created a demand for the necessities of life. They needed shops from
which to buy dry goods and clothes. They needed restaurants and
bakeries to make food. And they needed merchants to run them. This
demand gave rise to a second wave of emigration, the shopkeepers
and businessmen who would become known as "passenger Indians,"
so named because they could afford to pay their own passage to their
destination.

By the 1890s, the twin devastations of colonialism and famine
had wiped out even the small, relative prosperity enjoyed by my great-
great-grandfather's family in Chotila. With the land decimated by
drought and the farming economy decimated by the tax policies of
the British, fewer and fewer goods were being brought to Chotila
for trade. As the middleman who made his living buying and ware-
housing and selling those goods, KeshavjeeBapa watched as his business slowly crumbled. In Gujarati culture at the time, to be in debt
carried a huge social stigma; it was considered a disease worse than
leprosy. But KeshavjeeBapa soon found himself with no choice. He
was forced to borrow large sums to keep his family afloat, leaving him

in a crippling downward spiral of debt from which there appeared to be no way out.

As the family's situation in Chotila continued to deteriorate, the first generation of passenger Indians was establishing a beachhead overseas, and news of their efforts began to trickle back home. The reality was that most passenger Indians fared little better than their indentured countrymen. They lived as second-class citizens, a disenfranchised underclass, confined to ghettoes where they scratched out a living running small shops (if they were lucky) or more likely selling goods and trinkets door to door or from a handcart.

Still, a few did manage to prosper, particularly in South Africa. Between the colony's bountiful plantation farms and the discovery of its rich gold, diamond, and mineral deposits, there was so much wealth coming out of the ground that even the lowly passenger Indians managed to muscle a small share. They built up shops and enterprises that generated enough income to send money to relatives back home—one had even managed to purchase a shipping company, with boats ferrying goods and passengers between Durban and Bombay. This handful of success stories was all it took to make it sound as if the streets in Africa were paved with gold.

As KeshavjeeBapa grew older, his eldest son, Jivan, had begun taking charge of the family's day-to-day affairs. Watching the local economy slide from miserable to unsustainable, Jivan saw his family's future prospects grow smaller by the day. Their standing in the community was imperiled, and their standing in the community was everything to them. Jivan began to consider the stories coming back from South Africa, particularly from his friend Cassam, whose relatives had apparently done well there. Cassam was adamant that they journey to Africa together in search of opportunity and fortune.

I imagine Jivan looking at his brothers and saying something like, "If we stay here we'll starve to death. In Africa, we've at least got a chance."

The way the story gets told, Jivan's mother, my great-great-grandmother Mithima, was opposed to his leaving. They had always been a close, tight-knit family, and his departure would mean losing her eldest son, with a good chance she would never see him again. Leaving for Africa, she argued, would create a rupture in the community and traditions and culture that they held dear.

But her husband looked at the situation more pragmatically. "We have to let him go," KeshavjeeBapa said. "If we tie him down, we will be limiting the destiny of our children and their children and their children. We have no hope in Gujarat. Look at me, I am like a dead man because I can't pay my debts. My honor has been tainted. Let's be courageous and let him go. Allah will take care of him."

So, in 1894, Jivan and his friend Cassam left Chotila in a hired cart, their few belongings packed in a small wooden trunk. The whole village gathered to see them off. Mithima placed a coconut under one of the cart's wheels, the cracking of which would give her son and his friend a smooth trip and success on the road ahead. They set off for Thaan, thirty miles to the north, arriving there around midnight, and from there boarded the train for Bombay, packing themselves into third-class passenger cars alongside dozens of other young men on the same journey to what they hoped would be a better life. They reached Bombay at dawn and then made their way down to the piers of the Apollo Bunder area at the coast of the Arabian Sea, where a flotilla of old, rusted-out steamer ships awaited.

High up in the hills above the docks were the beautiful villas of the British sahibs, all built with the riches extracted from India's soil and its people, with their big, wide-open verandas looking out over the Arabian Sea. Below them, the young men boarded the cramped and filthy ships that would carry them to all the corners of the empire.

Once Jivan was established in Pretoria, he would send for his siblings, including my great-grandfathers Velshi and Manjee. They would make a new life together in the strange land, starting a new branch on our family tree, one that would eventually have over a thousand relatives spread across six continents, strangers in foreign lands, all of whom would one day look around and ask themselves, "How the hell did I end up here?"

Making my return trip 118 years later, as Lori and I were driven across the barren landscape between Rajkot and Chotila, I was curious what this ancestral home of mine was going to be like. Finally pulling into the center of town, I found it to be not really a town at all but more of a settlement. Think of an American country road in the middle of West Texas where you find an intersection with a gas station and a general store and a cluster of houses. The whole place probably took up less than a square mile, end to end.

Once we were out of the car and walking around, I was struck by how urban it felt despite how small it was. The center of the village itself was close-packed quarters and windy little streets, some of them barely wide enough for a cart, none of them particularly level or smooth. The buildings weren't what you would call modern construction by any stretch; most of them were fashioned out of whitewashed cinderblock and corrugated metal sheeting. Some places looked a bit more sophisticated, like the medical center—and I use the word *center* loosely. It was basically a storefront. The lone exception was the *jamatkhana*. If you stood fifty feet back from it, you'd say, "Wow. That's a beautiful building." But the streets were so narrow you couldn't stand fifty feet back from anything. Everything was on top of everything, and it didn't look like there was a right angle anywhere in the whole town. It was all ramshackle and disorderly and somewhat medieval, only not in the attractive Disneyfied Prague sort of way.

The streets were busy, filled with people. Stringy cats and dogs darted about as bikes and cars and pedestrians all jostled to get past one another. What really stood out in Chotila is the degree to which the whole economy seemed to be composed of people selling stuff to each other and buying each other's stuff in return. You can't walk anywhere without passing rows of pushcarts and stands and hearing, "Hey! Come here! We have this at such a cheap price today! We've got green chilies! This is fresh stuff!" These guys were selling everything you could imagine. There was food, like nuts and dates and spices and peppers and mangoes and the odd chicken here and there, but there were also tchotchkes and souvenirs and all manner of stuff. The whole place was like a general store, only nobody appeared to have a whole lot of money. As a business journalist who's covered markets from Saskatchewan to Singapore, I was completely befuddled by how the whole thing sustained itself.

We did manage to meet up with an old man who'd agreed to help show us around. His name was HassanChaCha, *ChaCha* meaning "uncle." He wasn't my uncle, but he was somebody's uncle and was one of those old guys who's so old you can't tell how old he actually is. He could have been seventy. He could have been a hundred. It was my uncle Mohammad, my mother's brother, who'd found Hassan-ChaCha initially, as a source for researching our family's history.

HassanChaCha wasn't a formal tour guide. He was just "the old man in the village who knows the stories." He was a very prominent member of the community. He'd been the mayor and a city councilor at different points over the years, and if you wanted to know anything about Chotila, he was pretty much the guy you went to. From talking to him, it was clear he'd done this tour before.

Hassan first took us to his house and introduced us to his family. It was modest living, for sure. In typical Indian fashion, the house was not well decorated, mostly bare walls painted in a dark green. But it was clean and they appeared to be what you'd call middle or upper-middle class by the standards of that town. There were three generations living there: Hassan, his son, and his son's children. We all sat in close quarters, and they brought us snacks and bottled water and Thums Up, which is their version of Coke.

After we chatted in his home for a while, he took us to lunch at a small restaurant, which wasn't like anything that you would generally call a restaurant. It was more like a room built onto a low-slung building that may or may not have been some kind of boardinghouse or hostel. It was fairly large inside with several tables. I don't recall there being much of a menu, but we got our food, which in Gujarat is served on a *thali*, a metal plate with dividers, like an old-fashioned TV dinner but with six or seven sections, each one filled with a curry or lentil, with some bread and some chutneys around it.

They brought Lori some milk, which was really buttermilk. When they put the glass down in front of her, she stared at it for a moment and then glanced over to me.

"Do you think it's pasteurized?" she asked.

"It probably came from the cow out back," I replied.

At which point, Lori very creatively made me think that she was drinking it, but really she'd just given herself a tiny buttermilk mustache to make it look like she was drinking when actually she wasn't drinking at all. But the people were kind, their hospitality was tremendous, and they couldn't quite make out why we seemed to be struggling to consume the food. Lori got away with it without seeming rude because she's a tiny person. But I'm a big guy. I don't look like someone who eats sparingly, and at a certain point you just give up because there's nothing you can do. So I dug in and luckily didn't get sick, so it was all fine.

After lunch, Hassan took us on a tour around the village and way back into the history of my family, which he knew chapter and verse, and he wasn't the only one. Any blood relatives I had in Chotila had long since died or moved away, but everybody there seemed to know our story. Everybody we met seemed to know who we were and why we were there, and they were all excited to meet us. We were Chotila's big success story: the family that had moved away and made good. As Hassan walked us around, he pointed out all the landmarks connected with my forebears, all the shops and houses and warehouses that KeshavjeeBapa had owned—and that we, for the most part, still technically own to this day, though no one has collected rent on them in over a hundred years.

Interestingly, for the most part, Hassan spoke of our family not in the past tense but in the present. "Your uncle's place is here. This is the mosque that your family built. This is your family's property." The descendants of KeshavjeeBapa had also continued to play a prominent role in the village in the decades since we'd left, sending money back to support the mosque and even to dig a new well when the old one stopped working. And that seemed to be KeshavjeeBapa's biggest legacy: he did just well enough for his children to leave.

Soon, it was time for Lori and me to do the same. We zipped around the village with Hassan, listening to his stories for a couple more hours, but we didn't spend the night. Not that you could spend the night there without considerable discomfort if you wanted to. If I was doing it today, it would be a different trip. But back then I was preoccupied with work, and my overly rushed attitude was "OK, show me this. Show me this. Show me this. Have you showed everything I have to see? Great. Now we have to get in the car and get on the plane." I wasn't in the mindset to fully appreciate a pilgrimage to my homeland the way one should.

We left for the airport in Rajkot about an hour before sundown so as to not be on the road after dark in case the car broke down. As we drove, looking out at the dry and desiccated nothing all around, Lori turned to me and, echoing my own father's sentiments, said, "Your great-grandfather made a good decision to get out of here." I couldn't think of a single reason why she was wrong. The way people were living in Chotila, I wouldn't call it poverty, because that's imposing an outside standard on a place that seemed to be doing fine. Everyone we met was thoughtful and kind. No one seemed to be making much money, but everybody had a shelter and a couch. And for the most part everyone seemed happy. Still, the way in which they lived seemed inescapable. There wasn't critical mass in Chotila for it to become a thriving place. There was little chance that living in this village was going to lead to prosperity for anyone. I don't know how Chotila might have been different if it had been left alone by colonialism and India had been able to develop on its own track, but as it was, like my wife and my dad, I was hard-pressed to come up with any reason why my forebears should have stayed.

Flying out of Rajkot that evening, Lori and I returned to Mumbai, made a few more stops, and soon caught our flight home to JFK. At the time, I didn't really register the trip as a pilgrimage of any sort. It had just been a trip, albeit an interesting one. It was just odd, being in a place where everyone looked like me and yet were all so different from me, and it left me with a funny feeling of belonging and yet not belonging. I didn't come away feeling any kinship with the people whom I met there. I felt something, but it wasn't a kinship—or, at least, no more of a kinship than I feel with Indians and Pakistanis in general. I left realizing I probably identify more with India when I'm eating Indian food at Indian events with other Indians in America than I did when I was actually in India itself— which makes sense, I suppose, because I'm not actually Indian. I'm Canadian and now, also, American.

It was only much later, after the events that pushed me to begin thinking about what would become this book, that I started to reflect on what it all meant and what my family's story said about our place in history. The main thought I kept coming back to was "What if they hadn't left? Who would I be?" Knowing what my family became, seeing all my cousins living around the world, working as doctors and lawyers and successful professionals in every field imaginable, it's hard for me to reconcile that with the place we come from. Would my mother or father have been the ones who left? Or my sister? Or me? But for Jivan's decision to leave and take his younger siblings with him, I could have been one of those kids on the street selling stuff to strangers on the road. And of course, even that isn't true, because if they hadn't left my parents wouldn't have met and I never would have been born at all.

But beyond the navel-gazing about "What would have happened to me," the bigger question I'd always had about the diaspora was why families like mine had left in the first place: Why does anybody leave anywhere? That's the universal question, and the trip did give me a much clearer understanding on that count. In the nineteenth century, India was *owned* by the East India Company. People lived lives of servitude, trapped in a caste-driven, sectarian, religiously segregated society. Between colonialism and the Indian system, you had no hope. You had no agency. So my great-grandfather and his brothers decided to go out and meet death wherever they found it rather than sit and wait for death to come to them. That is the only why, which means the important question to ask, given the odds stacked against them, is "How did they even survive?"

2

On Gandhi's Shoulders

Standing on the deck of a steamship off the east coast of Africa, Velshi Keshavjee, my paternal great-grandfather, could see where he needed to go. Out on the horizon, across the waters of Delagoa Bay, was Lourenço Marques, the capital of Portuguese East Africa, what we now call Mozambique. After the arduous trek across the Indian Ocean, from Lourenço Marques it would only be a short train ride to his final destination of Pretoria in South Africa, where he would be reunited with his brothers and where, hopefully, together they would build a new and better life than the one they'd left behind in India.

There was only one problem. To get to Lourenço Marques, Velshi would first have to make it across Delagoa Bay, and Delagoa Bay was filled with sharks—lots and lots of sharks. He couldn't see them, but he knew they were there: tiger sharks, hammerhead sharks, bull sharks, ragged-tooth sharks, white-tip reef sharks, oceanic black-tip sharks, you name it. Of course, most people on most trips would simply stay on the boat through the shark-infested waters and go right up to the dock and walk ashore. But for Velshi Keshavjee, on this trip, that was not an option.

The year was 1901. It had been seven years since his brother Jivan had left Chotila for the promise of opportunity in Africa. Velshi had already followed Jivan to Pretoria once before, in 1897, settling in the Indian ghetto of Pretoria known as Marabastad, where they worked as merchants selling goods in their small shop. They had only just begun to establish themselves when their efforts were interrupted by the outbreak of the Anglo-Boer War in 1899. As the British and the Dutch fought over who would control the colony, the Indians occupied the fault line between them. Not wanting to be caught up in the conflict or herded off to concentration camps, those who could afford to leave fled the country in order to wait out the war in some place where they were less likely to be killed. Many went north to Portuguese East Africa or British Somaliland. Others, like Velshi, returned to India for a spell. Then, in 1901, hearing reports that a British victory was in sight, he decided to return. But after the five-week journey from Bombay to South Africa, he arrived at the docks, most likely in Durban, and found he was unable to go ashore.

In those days, there were no passports. The captain of your ship simply carried a manifest with the passengers' names. As you disembarked, he checked off your name and down the gangplank you went. But when Velshi announced his name to the captain, the captain told him that he was already listed as having disembarked, meaning that someone had taken his name and, for whatever reason, used it to slip into South Africa under a false identity. This unforeseen circumstance left Velshi without many good options. As the ship continued on, chugging its way up the coast of Africa, he could try his luck at different ports of call, hoping the ship's captain or the local immigration officials might relent and wave him through, but if that didn't happen, he'd be stuck on the ship making the return passage to India, heading away from his life of prosperity and possibility in the New World. His first, best, and possibly only chance of making it to Pretoria was to dive in and swim for it. So that's what he did. He climbed up on the rail of the ship, said a prayer, leapt into the choppy, shark-infested waters below, and swam for dear life.

On February 11, 1990, a very cold and snowy day in Kingston, Ontario, a bunch of friends and I were all piled onto the sofa in the living room of my apartment at Queen's University, hot cups of coffee in our hands, glued to the television. That morning was the culmination of a drama that had been playing out in newspapers and television broadcasts for over a quarter century. Unjustly imprisoned in 1965 for leading the struggle against South Africa's Apartheid regime, Mandela had been locked away for twenty-seven years, during which time the brutal oppression of the country's nonwhite population had brought the nation to a breaking point. The campaign for Mandela's release had become a cause célèbre around the world. It had also become the symbol that embodied the fate of the nation as a whole: South Africa would only be free when Mandela was free. And now, he was free.

It wasn't just my South African heritage that had us tuning in. We all followed international news closely. We'd watched the Berlin Wall come down three months earlier, and we'd seen inspiring leaders like Lech Walesa and Václav Havel take over as the Iron Curtain fell. But I don't think I've ever been in awe of anybody the way I was in awe of Mandela. The first shock was what he looked like. The pictures I'd seen of him had been from the time before he'd been detained twenty-seven years earlier. The Mandela I knew was a big and maybe even chubby man, a boxer as well as a freedom fighter. But the man on TV was elderly and thin as a rail, with sharp features and, oddly enough, a smile on his face. The smile mystified me. I would be furious if I'd been wrongly imprisoned for twenty-seven *hours*, let alone twenty-seven years. How could he be this smiling, forgiving person after years of torture, confinement, and separation from the people he loved? It was the first time in my life that I witnessed that kind of grace.

It was also the first time I began to connect my family's story with the historic one playing out on the world stage. When I was a kid, there were endless conversations around our dinner table about South Africa. India played virtually no role in our lives. The fact that we were Indians was culturally apparent; it was the food we ate, the clothes my grandmother wore. But India wasn't nearly as dominant in our thinking as South Africa. Growing up under Apartheid was still the most prominent memory in my parents' mind. India was the background app, and South Africa was the foreground app.

But whatever you grow up with feels normal. No matter how exceptional or remarkable it may be, to you it's just everyday life, and as a kid growing up in Toronto, that's how it was with all the stories I'd hear about South Africa. I didn't grasp the magnitude or the danger of what my family went through living under Apartheid. The fact that my parents grew up not being allowed to eat in restaurants or use public restrooms wasn't extraordinary. It was life. It didn't register for me just what those experiences meant. To me, my relatives were a bunch of old and middle-aged Indian people who sat around reading the newspaper. The only photos we had of my great-grandparents were those old, sepia-toned pictures that every family has, with people standing and sitting in rows, posing like statues. In my mind, they weren't the sort of people you'd find on death-defying quests into the unknown, so the tale of my great-grandfather's leap into the Indian Ocean was not quite as impressive to me then as it is now. I think my primary reaction to that story was, "How did he even do that? Nobody in our family knows how to swim."

It was only when I went off to university and out into the world that my perspective started to change. Economic sanctions were bringing the Apartheid regime to its knees, and South Africa was front-page news every day. Then Mandela walked free, and I began to connect my family's story with the historic one playing out on the world stage. Mandela's incredible life was only one or two degrees away from my family's seemingly mundane life. My relatives knew people who'd fought and been imprisoned alongside him. My family had aided and abetted Mandela's struggle because it had been their struggle as well. In the early days of the freedom campaign in the 1950s, my dad's brother, Rehmtulla, had even been in secret meetings with Mandela and other revolutionaries, activities that got him thrown in jail as a political prisoner. Putting the pieces together, I started to think, "Wow, this crowd is more adventurous than these old-fashioned pictures of them would suggest. These people were really going out there and doing these daring things." I put on my journalist cap with my parents and started asking them to fill me in on the bigger picture.

The bigger picture starts in November 1860 aboard the SS

Truro, which carried South Africa's first consignment of Indian laborers from the port of Bombay to what was then the British colony of Natal. The Indians who arrived in Africa found themselves in the same position that they occupy to this day: stuck in the middle, the Brits on one side fighting the Boers on the other. In the long and contentious history for who would control the southern tip of Africa, the Dutch East India Company had established the first permanent European settlement in Cape Town in 1652 as a way station to resupply ships sailing for the Far East, only to have the British then wrest control of the territory from it during the Napoleonic Wars 150 years later. Chafing under British rule, the Dutch settlers trekked inland from the cape, severing their cultural and linguistic ties to Europe and becoming, in effect, a new nation of people: the white tribe of Africa, alternately called Afrikaners or simply the Boers, after the Dutch word for "farmer." By the time Indian immigration ramped up in the mid-nineteenth century, the antagonism between the British and the Boers had settled into something of an equilibrium, with the British asserting control of the coastal territories of the cape and Natal, and the Boers asserting control over two inland territories known as the Orange Free State and the Transvaal.

As they conquered and carved up the region for their massive farms, ranches, and mining operations, both the Dutch and the British faced a perennial problem: labor. Enslaved people had been imported from Malaya and other colonies, but never in sufficient numbers to make the colony grow. Then the British outlawed the slave trade in 1807, and while that practice never fully went away, it couldn't be used to drive the whole economy the way that it was with King Cotton in America's antebellum South. Meanwhile, the native tribes—the KhoiSan, the Zulu, the Xhosa, and others—had not yet been fully subjugated by their would-be colonial masters. Waging a centuries-long war of border skirmishes and incursions against the white settlers, the Africans fought fiercely to stop the invasion of their territory. Many were captured and put to work, but just as many escaped and returned to fight another day. And so, unable to impose a form of domestic slavery that they could exploit, the British were compelled to reinvent it in the form of indentured labor from India.

On the passage from India, indentured Indian laborers were crammed in among the livestock, and the resulting filth and disease made for a truly sickening mortality rate. Many thousands died en route. Once they arrived in Africa, having been contracted to work for five years, they were paid subsistence wages, fed minimal rations, housed in hovels, flogged and beaten, and given no medical care. It soon became clear that the "contract" they'd signed was merely a legal fiction created to justify their exploitation.

For the British, Indian laborers proved to be the key to unlocking the wealth of the continent. Soon after the first wave arrived, to cite one indicator, sugar exports from Natal nearly quadrupled. In the years that followed, mining operations began to tap into the continent's rich mineral deposits. For the empire's rapacious industrialists, men like Cecil Rhodes, no amount of economic expansion was sufficient, and the colonial appetite for Indian labor grew and grew.

For the Indian laborers themselves, the bottom line was that no matter how bad things were in South Africa, life was more prosperous than it had been in India. Like people all over the world, they were writing home and sending back whatever money they could, which made it seem to the people back home that things must be going well. South Africa had the demand, India had the supply, and the migration kept on flowing. The Indian population of Natal soon numbered in the tens of thousands. Its largest city, Durban, quickly became home to the largest community of Indians outside of India anywhere in the world, creating a market that demanded goods and services that the British saw no reason to provide, thus providing the catalyst for subsequent waves of passenger Indians, like my family, who set up the shops to provide those goods and services. Riding a wave of explosive economic growth, these passenger Indians who'd come to set up shop and run businesses soon found themselves relatively prosperous. In terms of profits, their businesses began to rival, and in some cases surpass, those of the British merchant class, threatening the latter's status and position.

And that's when the trouble began.

By 1890, the total Indian population of Natal was eighty thousand—sixty thousand indentured, ten thousand formerly indentured, and ten thousand passenger. The indigenous Zulu population was over four hundred thousand. Meanwhile, the white European population was a mere forty thousand. Driven by the fear that they would soon be overwhelmed, the British authorities in Natal petitioned the government back in London to, in essence, void the laborers' contracts. The workers had been brought over with the stipulation that once their indentures were over they could remain. Now, Natal was insisting that Indians either be forced to return to India or be compelled to reindenture. "You don't belong here," they were told. "We don't need you. You can go back now."

Initially, the Crown declined to grant this petition. Voiding the contracts and compelling the Indians to reindenture themselves would have exposed the legal masquerade, revealing that this was just slavery by a different name. Instead, in 1893, the British simply changed the legal status of Natal itself, demoting it from a "colony" to a self-governing "dominion." This new status allowed the territory to remain a part of the empire while granting it autonomous self-government, thereby absolving the Crown of complicity in the decisions that local politicians made regarding the Indian laborers and the natives. Natal soon undertook a campaign to put Indians back in their place. They did this by immiserating the lives of anyone who overstayed their indenture, at first by levying a poll tax of three pounds—about six months' wages—on every nonindentured Indian resident. Since the tax was levied per each individual family member, some families could end up owing twelve to fifteen pounds a year, an absurdly onerous sum for the time. Soon other laws were passed: disenfranchising all Indians who were not already registered to vote, limiting immigration to those who could pass a European language test, restricting the ability of Indian merchants to trade without a license. And on and on and on.

Still, as dire as conditions were in the British territories, the Indians there were at least technically subjects of the Crown, legally recognized as residents with certain limited rights to petition the courts for various grievances. As far as the Boer republics of Transvaal and the Orange Free State were concerned, they didn't want these brown people at all. Indians were an infestation, nothing more. There was a law in the Orange Free State that if an Indian stayed there beyond five o'clock in the evening, they'd be locked up. Although over eighty thousand Indians were right next door in Natal, at one point the total number of Indians in the Orange Free State was about ten, and nine of them were probably waiters at a hotel. The Boers' attitude toward Indians was clear: "Don't come here. You've got nothing to do with us. We don't want you."

Then, in 1884, gold was discovered in the Transvaal. Money came pouring out of the ground, and it changed the whole equation. With tremendous wealth now at their disposal, the Boers and the British finally succeeded in breaking the back of the native resistance. Thousands of prospectors flooded into the region. African laborers were dragged into the mines to work and forced into mining settlements around the boom towns of Pretoria and Johannesburg in an area that would become known to the natives as Gauteng, its name in the Sotho-Tswana language, meaning the "place of gold." The demand for shopkeepers and tradesmen exploded alongside the population. Indian traders were needed to open shops and so—officially welcome or not—they swept into the hinterland, hung out their shingles, and went to work.

Following the same blueprint as the British in Natal, the Afrikaner regime in the Transvaal immediately sought to curtail the rights and privileges of Indians while relying on them to perform a vital role in their new economy. Onerous taxes were levied on Indian businesses. They were denied the right to own land and limited to leasing within certain restricted ghettos. In Pretoria, that was a place called Marabastad, a tiny warren of four or five back streets running about twelve blocks, no more than a quarter of a square mile in total, one side of it abutting the sewage dump about half a mile from the center of town. If you ever needed to film a movie about South Africa set in the late 1800s or 1900s, you could do it in Marabastad because still to this day it's basically Pretoria frozen in time. It was its own self-contained village, two- and three-story buildings crammed together side by side, shops on the first floor and families living up above narrow streets with heavy traffic. Amazingly, despite its small size, over time more and more families kept moving in, Muslims and Hindus, everybody else all crowded in and living on top of one another.

By the 1890s, in both Natal and the Transvaal, the economic interests of the British and the Dutch had become wholly dependent on indentured Indians and the Indian merchant class. Take them away, and the entire colonial economy would collapse. The same was true of the brutal exploitation of African labor, but the key difference between the Africans and the Indians was that no one could say the Africans didn't belong there. The Europeans saw the Zulu and Xhosa tribesmen as inferior and uncivilized, but no one could tell them, "Go back to where you came from," which was the prevailing sentiment regarding the Indians.

The colonists thought they could use Indians as a resource, like copper or fertilizer or any other economic input that gets fed into a system. But labor is not merely an input. Importing that labor means importing human beings, and with human beings comes the human need for recognition and participation in society. Still, despite their dependence on Indian labor, neither the British nor the Dutch were prepared to treat Indians as human beings. But you can only dehumanize a people for so long before they stand up and demand that their humanity be recognized.

On May 23, 1893, a young Gujarati lawyer arrived in Natal. The law tried to put him in his place, and he was not content to stay there. Long before he became a world-renowned icon, Mohandas Karamchand Gandhi came to South Africa as a nobody. He had traveled there at the behest of Dada Abdulla, a Gujarati trader in Durban who was suing his cousin for failing to pay a debt. Abdulla already had a team of white South African lawyers representing his interests, but he wanted an Indian attorney on his team as well, to act as a liaison between the two worlds. When Gandhi arrived by steamer in Durban, he was woefully naive about what he was about to face in South Africa. He'd grown up in Gujarat, not far from where my family lived in Chotila. But unlike my great-grandfathers and their utter lack of prospects, Gandhi's family had managed to gain a foothold in the colonial government. His father served as the *dewan*, or first minister, of what was then the princely kingdom of Rajkot. His family paid for him to attend the University of Bombay. Then they sent him to law school in London, which Gandhi at the time believed was "the very centre of civilization." Though Hindu in his beliefs and his identity, Gandhi emerged from his time in London every inch the well-trained English barrister, dressed in patent leather shoes, a starched white shirt, a black jacket, and an Inns of Court tie. His only goal was to use his position as an attorney to seek justice for Indians within the colonial system in his home country. He was not yet the man who would stand up and say that the colonial system itself was unjust.

To meet with Abdulla's other lawyers, Gandhi had to travel, first by train and then by coach, from Durban to Pretoria, where the case had been filed. Nonwhites were not allowed to ride in first class on trains, but Gandhi had purchased a first-class ticket by mail from London. He had been ignorant of the railroad's policy, and the railroad officials had been equally ignorant of the color of his skin. As Gandhi boarded and settled into his seat in first class, he was wholly unaware that he had set in motion a chain of events that would change the trajectory of his life, collapse the British Empire, and revolutionize the world.

As the journey got under way, a fellow passenger complained to the railway conductor about having to share the compartment with a dark-skinned man. And so in the dead of night, at the station for Pietermaritzburg, the capital of Natal, Gandhi was ordered off the train and forced to sleep in the station for the rest of the night while his train traveled on to Pretoria without him. "Being at a high altitude, the cold was extremely bitter," he later wrote. "My overcoat was in my luggage, but I did not dare to ask for it lest I should be insulted again, so I sat and shivered. I began to think of my duty. The hardship to which I was subjected was superficial, only a symptom of the deep disease of colour prejudice." When his journey resumed the next day by stagecoach, Gandhi was made to sit on a dirty sack cloth on the footboard outside the coach's main cabin to make more room for the European passengers inside. When he asked to be seated inside the coach, he was beaten by the coach driver.

This was not Gandhi's first experience of exclusion and condescension at the hands of the British; he'd lived in London for three years, after all. But for whatever reason, this was the moment that finally opened his eyes to the brutality and the dehumanization at the dark heart of the colonial system. It was the moment he decided he wouldn't accept the insults and injustice anymore. He would stand up and defend not only his own dignity but that of all his countrymen. "I was born in India," Gandhi would later declare, "but was made in South Africa."

Despite the discrimination and hardships that Indians faced in South Africa, for families like mine it still beckoned. Arriving one year after Gandhi, in 1894, my great-grandfathers' older brother Jivan landed among thousands of other passenger Indians in Natal's Port Elizabeth. He was loaned a few shillings by the more established of his countrymen, who also taught him how to run a small street vending business, known as a ferry business. Despite his minimal broken English, Jivan took a pushcart filled with eggplants, okra, green chilies, and mangoes and went selling door to door in white neighborhoods. The friendlier people among the whites would buy his wares with a smile, casually calling him a coolie to his face— "Honey, the coolie is here. Do we want to buy anything?"—and not thinking twice about it. The unfriendly whites would sic their dogs on him.

Still, he pressed on, eventually saving enough money to pay for his onward passage to Pretoria, where the gold rush was in full swing and aspiring Indian merchants continued to cluster in the cramped, filthy streets of Marabastad. There was an unwritten code in the ghetto that anyone of Indian origin could live among them for three months at no cost, after which the newcomer was given a gift of five pounds to start a business, which served as both a leg up to success and a bond to hold the community together. In 1896, Jivan took a lease on a small shop at 112 Prinsloo Street and opened his own retail business, which he called KJ Keshavjee & Co. One year later, he sent for Velshi, who made the journey over, and together they opened a small grocery store. Then, right as they were beginning to gain a foothold and prosper in the New World, their lives were plunged into the chaos of war.

The agreement that the British and the Boers had worked out to divide their territory had been tenuous from the start. It held for as long as it did only because the far more powerful British were content to control the lush, beautiful farmland of the coastal areas, leaving the Boers to scrape out a living in the hardscrabble, mountainous terrain of the interior. But with the discovery of the world's richest gold, diamond, and mineral reserves in that interior, it soon became clear that the Boers had accidentally gotten the better end of the deal. The British, being British, felt they should control it all.

Once the war broke out, over five hundred thousand British regular troops were called up to bring the Afrikaners to heel, which would prove to be a far more difficult and nasty affair than the British anticipated. The Boers were hopelessly outnumbered. They had only eighty-seven thousand in their ranks, few of whom were professional soldiers; most were simply farmers taking up arms to defend themselves. But they managed to hold on by waging a successful guerrilla campaign, aided by their familiarity with the territory and fueled by their sincere belief that the British were the hostile invaders in the equation. The Boers, in their minds, were no longer unwelcome European settlers. They saw themselves as the natives. This was *their* land, no matter that the Xhosa and the Zulu and the Tswana might have felt differently.

To defeat the unexpectedly resilient Afrikaner forces, the British adopted a scorched-earth policy, destroying villages and towns and placing civilians in concentration camps. Over twenty-five thousand Afrikaner women and children died of disease and malnutrition in the camps, leaving a deep scar of bitterness and resentment among the Afrikaners that has never gone away. As subjects of the British Crown living in Boer-controlled territory, Jivan, Velshi, and their fellow Indians rightly feared reprisals. If the Boers emerged as the victors in the conflict, the already diminished status of the Indian population of the Transvaal would likely grow even worse. Fearing this outcome, many of them left, including the Keshavjee brothers. Then, when the British finally emerged as the victors, they were eager to return and get back in business, which is how my paternal great-grandfather Velshi Keshavjee came to find himself standing on the deck of a steamer ship in 1901, staring out across the shark-infested waters of Delagoa Bay, desperate to reach the shores of Portuguese East Africa. After leaping from the side of the boat and, luckily, making it safely to shore, Velshi then had to traverse miles through the jungle on foot before finally arriving at the capital of Lourenço Marques and catching a train south to Pretoria.

In the years that followed the war, the Keshavjee brothers grew their little empire of shops in Marabastad. Soon they were ready to bring over not only their wives and children but their other brothers as well. First came their brother Manjee, my maternal great-grandfather, and then, a few years later, their fourth brother, Naran, who migrated with his wife and twin sons in 1912.

In a close-knit community of only five hundred or so people, the Keshavjee family quickly emerged as one of the largest and most prominent. And despite the fact that Jivan was the oldest and had been the pioneer, Velshi, with a commanding presence and a big, booming voice, soon emerged as the natural leader of the clan. He was shrewd and savvy in business as well. Jivan had established the first jamat-khana in Marabastad, but it was Velshi who raised the funds to build the mosque's permanent home. It was Velshi, too, who headed the community association, handled the family accounts, and diversified the family businesses. At our family gatherings and reunions today, everyone acknowledges Jivan as the pioneer, but most discussion centers on Velshi. He was the main character, and he would be the one to befriend a young Gujarati lawyer named Mohandas Karamchand Gandhi.

After being thrown off the train at Pietermaritzburg in 1893, Gandhi had decided to remain in South Africa and take up the cause of the exploited Indian workers in Natal. He would begin fighting on behalf of the Indians of Pretoria only after British victory in the Anglo-Boer War extended British control into the South African interior; so long as the Transvaal was under the control of the Boers, Gandhi had no recourse against the system there. In Natal, however, he was well positioned to help. The British Crown had engineered the subjugation of Indians not through brute force but through a bureaucratic tangle of contracts and ordinances and license restrictions. As a licensed British barrister, Gandhi was able to work that system to the hilt, filing endless appeals and memorandums on the Indians' behalf.

In 1894, in an effort to thwart a new bill that would deprive Indians of the right to vote, he organized the Natal Indian Congress, which inundated the colonial administration with petitions signed by thousands of his fellow Indians. While Gandhi failed to prevent the passage of the bill, his efforts did succeed in creating a movement. He forged a new solidarity within the Indian community, encouraging Hindus and Muslims to set aside their religious differences and unite in a common cause. He was also remarkably effective at drawing the world's attention to South Africa, getting stories about the Indians' plight written up in major London newspapers to create a groundswell of support for their efforts.

What Gandhi was doing in South Africa was both incremental and insufficient and yet entirely radical at the same time. His argument was not fundamentally anticolonial. His argument was not that British occupation of South Africa and India was entirely illegitimate. Instead, he was saying, "We *are* British citizens and should be treated as such. The Indians of India and South Africa are subjects of the Crown, ruled by the same monarch as white citizens and therefore deserving of the same rights as white citizens." Indeed, when the Anglo-Boer War broke out, Gandhi argued that the Indians, as a part of making their case for the full rights of citizenship in the empire, ought to be loyal to that empire, and were therefore duty bound to defend it. He even set up an ambulance corps to support the British troops. It had over a thousand volunteers drawn from both the Indian merchant class and the indentured laborers.

Some contemporary scholars, citing Gandhi's early incrementalist approach, argue that he wasn't a radical or revolutionary figure at all but was essentially a brownnoser and appeaser of the British, a "yes man." So the question at hand is, Was Gandhi being naive, not understanding that under the colonial mentality a brown citizen could never be equal to a white one? Or was he being politically astute by saying, "Let's work within the structure to try and claim the rights that the structure allows"?

In my view, Gandhi was certainly not the sainted prophet that history made him out to be. Before the enlightenment that came in his later years, Gandhi fully bought into the racist ideology that underpinned the whole imperial project, the idea that the dark continent needed to be brought to heel and civilized by its betters. He believed that Black people were inferior to both Indians and whites. He called Black people "savages" who passed their days in "indolence and nakedness." He called them "kaffirs," which was the offensive slur for Black people, the equivalent of "coolie" for Indians. Indeed, when Gandhi began, his activism was driven by the concern that the Indian was "being dragged down to the position of a raw Kaffir." Both the English and the Indians, he wrote, "spring from a common stock." So Gandhi didn't reject the idea of a racist hierarchy; he just wanted Indians to be in what he considered their rightful place, way up closer to the whites.

Deplorable as those utterances certainly are, they don't represent the full picture of the man Gandhi later became. And even if he wasn't yet ready to reject the entire racist ideology behind the empire, he was still a revolutionary figure by any measure. Simply to say that the Indians were equal to the English was a radical notion for its time. Sadly, it remains a radical notion for many people to this day, and Gandhi was perhaps smarter than most in making that radical claim. You have to ask for unreasonable, outsized things to spark the world's imagination, to make people question whether a better world is even possible. Then, once people's expectations have been raised, you can set about the practical task of making whatever real-world gains you can manage. If Gandhi was naive about anything, it was his faith in the British system, thinking he could navigate its courts and its legislature to effect real change rather than understanding that the courts and the legislature had been explicitly designed to prevent any real change from taking place, at least in matters regarding its racist colonial project.

Whatever faith Gandhi put in the British, it was not reciprocated. After the war, the British and the Afrikaners made peace and set about consolidating their territories into what would later become, in 1910, the Union of South Africa, a dominion with the same semiautonomous, self-governing status as Australia and Canada. Bending the knee to the Crown was a bitter pill for the Afrikaner people to swallow. They hated the Brits, despised them. The leading Afrikaner politicians, however, saw the bigger picture. Men like Louis Botha and Jan Smuts, who would go on to become powerful prime ministers of the whites-only government, looked out at the vast sea of nonwhites who outnumbered them and knew that the tiny minority of Afrikaners and British would have to unite. Whatever their differences, they were all white. They both wanted to get the Black man in his place and the brown man out of the country, and the only way they could do that was to put their mutual enmity aside and close ranks.

With the political and economic epicenter of the country shifting north, Gandhi relocated his home and his law practice from Durban to Johannesburg. From there, he made frequent visits to Pretoria to meet and negotiate with Jan Smuts, who was now the government's designated official for handling Indian affairs. That is where Gandhi's history intersected with my own. Gandhi and my great-grandfather Velshi, both being Gujarati, shared the same Gujarati accountant. At some point following the war, this mutual acquaintance introduced them. Johannesburg and Pretoria being forty-five miles apart, at least a day's journey back then, whenever Gandhi was in Pretoria to deal with Smuts or some issue with the Transvaal government, he would stay the night at Velshi's house. There the two men passed many hours together and became friends.

In the years that followed, as the government crackdown on Indians worsened, Gandhi found himself in Pretoria quite often. Then in 1906 came a breaking point: a bill called the Asiatic Law Amendment Ordinance was submitted to Parliament for a vote. If passed into law, it would have forced every Indian over the age of eight to get fingerprinted for registration documents they would be required to carry on their person at all times. It would also permit the police to enter the home of any Indian at any time and demand to see these documents, and any Indian who failed to produce their documents could be fined, imprisoned, or deported.

Being forced to carry a pass in public was the sort of humiliation to which Indians and Africans had long been accustomed, but for the police to assert a right to enter an Indian's home, to force Indian women to be alone and intimidated in the presence of men who were not their husbands, was a bridge too far. It was dehumanizing on an entirely different level, and it provoked an immediate backlash. In September of that year, over three thousand Indians gathered at the Empire Theater in Johannesburg to protest the law. Under Gandhi's leadership, they took a pledge to defy the ordinance if it became law and to suffer all the penalties resulting from their defiance. A few hours after their meeting, the Empire Theater was burned to the ground; the cause of the fire was never solved.

Over the course of the following year, as the Asiatic Law Amendment Ordinance made its way through the legislative process, which included securing approval from London, Gandhi led a resistance campaign against it. Because the Afrikaners considered Indians to be foreigners, their initial attitude toward the protest was one of confusion. "What do these Indians want? If they think South Africa is treating them so badly, why don't they go back to India?" The irony is that the answer to that question lay in the identity of the Afrikaners themselves. Despite the white color of their skin, having been in South Africa for so many generations, they didn't recognize Europe as a place to go back to anymore. This was now the only home they knew. With each passing year, the same was increasingly true of South Africa's Indians, some of whom were coming up on half a century away from "home." They had children and grandchildren who knew nothing of the India they'd left behind. With the Johannesburg gold rush bringing people from all over the world, this would soon become true for thousands of immigrants from Germany, Switzerland, Italy, China, Portugal, Nigeria, the Congo, Rwanda, and every other point on the map. Like America in the late nineteenth and early twentieth centuries, and like western Europe, Canada, and Australia today, no matter what this land had been before the Dutch arrived three hundred years before, by 1906 the newly forming Union of South Africa was a multiethnic, multiracial, multisectarian, multilingual experiment. Gandhi understood then what he hadn't understood in 1894, which was that there was only one way to make such a society work: equal rights, representation, and recognition for everyone.

It was during the backlash to the proposed 1906 law that Gandhi became the figure we recognize today. Though trained in the law, Gandhi had begun to abandon his narrow legalistic defense of Indian rights under the British government. In its place grew a moral vision that spoke to the need for dignity and self-determination for all of humanity. He made himself a student of religion. He read the Quran, the Bible, the Torah. He delved deep into the Hindu scriptures of his own faith. It was through the comparative study of religion and talks with scholars that he came to the conclusion that all religions contained elements of truth worthy of consideration. He embraced the Hindu concept of *aparigraha*, or "nonpossession," the imperative to jettison the burdens of money and property that weigh life down. He embraced the idea of *samabhava*, or "equability," a stoicism that allows people to remain calm, controlled, and self-assured both in victory and in defeat, to persevere regardless of the odds of success or failure. He also embraced the African concept of *ubuntu*, being assured enough in yourself that you are open and available to others while also knowing that the suffering and humiliation of others will only bring suffering and humiliation on you. He celebrated the Jewish concept of *tikkun olam*, that we have a responsibility to live our lives in a way that repairs the fabric of the world.

He began to see how all social ills are interconnected, how every action we take—everything from choosing who we vote for all the way down to deciding how our food is grown and how our clothes are made—has an impact on every other decision we make and how all of those decisions must be made in the pursuit of healing the world and making it whole. Gandhi even began to see his legal work from a more spiritual mindset. The true function of a lawyer, he said, was not to sue for damages and remedies but rather "to unite parties riven asunder."

When it came to unifying his new ideas into a practical, strategic real-world campaign against injustice, Gandhi was profoundly influenced by the writings of three major thinkers. First was Henry David Thoreau, the American transcendentalist known for writing *Walden* and the essay "Civil Disobedience." Second was the English writer John Ruskin, whose essay "Unto This Last" inspired Gandhi to promote equality regardless of race or nationality. Third, and perhaps most important, was the Russian novelist Leo Tolstoy, who in 1902 was nominated for both the Nobel Prize in Literature and the Nobel Peace Prize. Tolstoy had written extensively on the idea of using a nonviolent approach to fighting oppression. Tolstoy himself referred to this approach as *nonresistance*. Gandhi would take the concept and make it his own, using the term *passive resistance*.

As the Asiatic Law Amendment Ordinance became law, Gandhi and his followers formed what was initially called the Passive Resistance Association. They refused to comply with the registration and fingerprinting. They burned their registration certificates at a protest outside the Hamidia Mosque in Johannesburg. As a result of the campaign, fewer than 5 percent of Indians complied with the law. Thousands went to prison for their refusal to cooperate, including

Gandhi, who was sentenced to two months' jail time. In that moment, a new spiritual and political philosophy was born. Even when faced with the most brutal forms of oppression, the oppressed and disenfranchised had refused to take up arms or rise up in violent rebellion. They simply refused to cooperate or participate. They would not fight back against the evil brutality but would rather invite it, thereby giving their oppressors the opportunity to demonstrate the full extent of their depravity for all the world to see. Feeling that the phrase *passive resistance* did not fully encompass the meaning of what the struggle was about, Gandhi eventually settled on the term *satyagraha*, from the Hindi word *satya*, meaning "love and truth," and *graha*, meaning "firmness." Satyagraha, then, is the power and resolve that is born of truth, love, and nonviolence, or "truth force."

The philosophy behind satyagraha would go on to reshape the world. It would bring independence to India in 1947, more than a decade before the rest of the British Empire finally collapsed under its own weight. It would later inspire the architects of the nonviolent civil rights campaign in post–World War II America. But in its initial trial, satyagraha was not an unmitigated success. After a few compromises and concessions to the resisters, the new Indian registration policies remained the law of the land. Once the Union of South Africa was formally incorporated in 1910, that bill would soon be followed by others, such as one limiting immigration to those who could speak a European language. Gandhi made deal after deal with General Secretary Jan Smuts to try to create a fair and just system for nonwhites in South Africa, only to have Smuts renege on his word time and time again. Indians who backed Gandhi's campaign faced deportation, jail time, beatings, confiscation of their property, forced relocation, and other harassment. Satyagraha required superhuman levels of patience, and many Indians soon grew impatient. Most were weary. Others were simply angry, feeling that all Gandhi had done was kick the hornets' nest and stir things up, making their lives worse while achieving nothing in the bargain. Gandhi even took a beating from an Indian man who accused him of failing the Indian cause.

A large number of Indians simply stayed out of it. They had families to care for and relatives back in India to support. Political unrest was bad for business, and they wanted to be left alone to make their money. And in 1910, that number would have included my family. Velshi Keshavjee was not a political man. He was civic-minded within his community, supporting the mosque and wanting children to have the best schools, but he was not someone looking to fight the system for better treatment for the Indians, and he certainly wasn't rocking the boat on behalf of the Africans or anyone else. The Keshavjees were business folk who had come to South Africa for survival. Gandhi was a friend and nothing more. Nowhere in our family history or in any of the surviving documentation do you see any of us involved in the political mobilization of that time.

Then, Gandhi asked Velshi for a favor.

———————

By 1910, the satyagraha movement was flagging, with barely a hundred true believers willing to march with Gandhi and risk arrest. To Gandhi, the fact that so many had abandoned the cause was evidence that they had not been properly trained or given the necessary resolve. That resolve, that inner strength, could only come from understanding the absolute truth about yourself and the world. The power that came from understanding that truth, "truth force" or "soul force," might be described as the potential for good that resides in all of us. And that power, Gandhi felt, could be cultivated. The "prolonged training of the individual soul," he wrote, was necessary for a person to become a strong adult *satyagrahi*, as they were called, and that training might be most fruitfully undertaken in the education of young children. In order to revive itself, what the movement needed was a school, and in order to support a school, Gandhi would need to build an ashram, a community.

To create what he envisioned, Gandhi relied on the aid of two men. The first was R. J. Tata, an Indian industrialist and philanthropist who offered Gandhi a gift of twenty-five thousand rupees to fund his efforts, the equivalent of more than two million dollars today. The second was Herman Kallenbach, a prominent Jewish architect who had become both Gandhi's partner as well as his benefactor. Since Indians were not allowed to own land, Kallenbach purchased a plot of more than ten thousand acres in Roodeport, about twenty miles outside Johannesburg, and gave Gandhi use of it to build his ashram. At Kallenbach's suggestion, Gandhi chose to name it Tolstoy Farm, after the Russian author whose writings on nonviolent resistance had inspired Gandhi so deeply.

As Tolstoy Farm was being built, Gandhi reached out to his friend Velshi, asking him to send his son, Rajabali, then only seven years old, to the school. From what I know of my great-grandfather, I can only imagine that he saw Gandhi's request as a strange one. Yes, the men were friendly. As Gujaratis, they shared a language and heritage. But Gandhi was deeply political while Velshi was not political at all. More importantly, Gandhi was Hindu while Velshi was Muslim. In some ways, it doesn't make a whole lot of sense for a prominent merchant and businessman to send his son to a boarding school based on renouncing the influence of money and material possessions. And yet, Velshi agreed. He sent Rajabali to Tolstoy Farm to be educated by Gandhi in the ways of satyagraha. But he did so on one very unusual condition: Gandhi would have to educate Rajabali in the prayers and traditions of our Ismaili Muslim faith. Gandhi agreed to do so. In the end, I think Velshi did it for no other reason than he liked Gandhi and trusted him.

When my grandfather arrived at Tolstoy Farm, he was the youngest of around twenty children and fifty adults, mostly men and a handful of women. The farm itself was a seemingly endless stretch of grassland with red clay dirt and an orchard of about a thousand trees bearing peaches, apricots, figs, almonds, and walnuts. At first, there was no more than a shed and a dilapidated stone house, but the adults and children alike were put to work cultivating the land, rehabilitating the existing structures and building new ones. Soon they had three large buildings housing a laundry, a kitchen, offices, and classrooms.

Gandhi called his experiment a "cooperative commonwealth," a place where individual self-interest was put in check for the good of the whole. In order to work, the whole enterprise had to be self-sustaining and self-reliant. Everyone worked together, and together they made nearly everything they needed. They made their own clothes. The men shaved each other and cut each other's hair. They cultivated, harvested, and cooked their own food, which, per Gandhi's teaching, had to be strictly vegetarian. Not only was the food itself vegetarian, but neither insects nor snakes could be killed in cultivating or harvesting it.

The lifestyle was spartan to say the least. There wasn't much in the way of furniture. Each resident was given two blankets, one to place on the ground and one with which to cover themselves. Every morning at 6:00 a.m. was breakfast, which consisted of bread and wheaten coffee, which isn't actually coffee at all. It's hot water strained through charred wheat. Lunch was rice and vegetables. Supper was typically wheat porridge and milk. Everyone ate with the same simple bowl and wooden spoon that they'd made themselves at the farm, and after each meal they'd team up to do dishes. In the evenings, the students would assemble for Gandhi to review the day's events and offer spiritual instruction. Then the meetings would usually end with readings from books on religion and the singing of hymns.

Whenever my dad talked about Rajabali's time at Tolstoy Farm, or about his father in general, he talked about how disciplined the man was and how that was such an admirable quality. Self-discipline and self-reliance were the cornerstone of life in the satyagraha movement. The whole point of nonviolent resistance is to expose your oppressor's cruelty by giving them the opportunity to be cruel. Kneel in prayer in the public square and let the cops come after you with billy clubs. Then turn the other cheek when they hit you. Don't fight back when they beat you. Let them arrest you and take you to jail. Then get out of jail and go right back and do it again. To do that takes enormous reserves of discipline. Self-reliance is the other key principle, simply because if you don't need anything, there's nothing people can threaten to take away from you. The average person is kept in line by the fear of losing their job. "I'd better not rock the boat. How will I pay for my house, my car, my clothes?" But if you grow your own food, make your own clothes, and are willing to walk twenty miles to go grocery shopping, the rest of the world has very little leverage over you. You're free from the material bonds that turn most of us into cowards.

Tolstoy Farm trained and equipped my grandfather in the same way a paramilitary camp might train a young revolutionary soldier, only it trained him for an entirely different kind of war, arming him with self-discipline and self-reliance instead of hand grenades and a rifle. Gandhi's aim, in his words, was to teach young minds "to conquer hate by love, untruth by truth, violence by self-sacrifice." More than giving students this set of skills, Tolstoy Farm also instilled a moral code by which to live. "The best way to find yourself," Gandhi wrote, "is to lose yourself in the service of others," a lesson Rajabali took to heart.

I can hardly imagine myself, as an adult, being able to handle the hardship my grandfather endured on that farm. How he managed it as a seven-year-old child, I have no idea. I never knew Rajabali (who by this time went by Rajabali Velshi instead of Rajabali Keshavjee, having taken his father's name as his new last name, a common Indian custom). He died eight years before I was born. I also know from conversations with my father and my aunts and uncles that Rajabali didn't talk about his time with Gandhi all that often. But like the tale of Velshi jumping into the shark-infested waters of Delagoa Bay, there is one story from Rajabali's time at Tolstoy Farm that's become a venerated piece of family lore.

It's the story of the walk to Johannesburg. Gandhi would sometimes take the students to get provisions at a store on the outskirts of the city, about a seven-mile walk each way since he forbade them from taking the train. The group would leave before sunrise and walk for several hours to reach the city in time for the shops to open so they could buy what they needed and walk back home. On those early-morning treks, my grandfather, being the youngest, was often too tired to continue, so Gandhi would hoist him onto his shoulders and carry him the rest of the way.

Today, whenever the subject of Gandhi and my grandfather

comes up, that's the image that comes to mind, the tired young boy being carried on the great teacher's shoulders. And though Rajabali rarely spoke of it, it's easy to see the profound effect that experience had on him because it was manifest in every moment of the life he lived from that day forward.

3

The Yeast of Our Problems

On July 19, 1914, the day Gandhi sailed for India from Cape Town, he left South Africa believing that he'd failed, and by many measures, he had. His efforts at Tolstoy Farm did briefly succeed in giving the flagging satyagraha movement a second wind, and for a brief window in 1913, South Africa's Indians united once again in a brave and inspiring moment that showed the world the potential of what Gandhi's ideas could accomplish.

In March of that year, a South African judge ruled that only Christian marriages would be recognized by the state. Like the 1906 ordinance that gave police officers the right to enter Indian homes, the refusal to recognize Hindu, Muslim, and other non-Christian marriages was dehumanizing on a deeply personal level and destabilizing to the whole idea of forming healthy families. Adding insult to injury, General Secretary Jan Smuts also reneged on an earlier promise to end the annual three-pound poll tax levied on the Indian population. In protest, some three thousand Indians went on strike in Natal. Gandhi led over two thousand men, women, and children on a thirty-six-mile march from the town of New Castle in Natal across the border into the Transvaal, a protest over the fact Indians were not allowed to move freely between the two provinces.

Typically, women served important support roles in these protests, as food preparation and ambulance corps volunteers. But they were not included in activities that might lead to physical violence or imprisonment. This time, the women were adamant. Several of them, including Gandhi's wife and partner in the movement, Kasturba, marched from New Castle alongside the men. Many of them were arrested and thrown in jail in Pietermaritzburg. Today, the jail that housed them is a museum, and there you can find a picture of Valiamina Moodaly, a sixteen-year-old girl from Tolstoy Farm who died of tuberculosis while in detention for taking part in the march. As there were only seventy people on the farm, and she was only a few years older than my grandfather, I have to imagine that they were friends. And if my grandfather, then eleven years old, had been a year or two older, he might have participated in that march, which meant that he could have been imprisoned and died in jail as well.

For his role in the march Gandhi was sentenced to nine months' imprisonment in a labor camp. Hundreds of others were arrested and sentenced to work in the mines. When they refused to go, they were savagely beaten and, in some cases, killed by the police, which only drove thousands more Indians to go out on strike. The situation spiraled so far out of hand that it became an embarrassment for the new South African regime. International pressure soon forced the government to the negotiating table. Gandhi, given leave from his prison sentence, journeyed once more to Pretoria to sit with Jan Smuts and resolve the issue. During his visit, as usual, Gandhi stayed with my great-grandfather Velshi. Velshi was one of the few Indians who owned his own dray, what they called a horse-drawn cart, and Velshi gave Gandhi the use of it to travel back and forth to meet with Smuts each day. In the end, the government made good on its initial promise to rescind the poll tax, all Indian tax arrears were wiped out, and an agreement was reached to recognize all marriages regardless of religion.

The following year, Gandhi made the decision to end his work in South Africa and return to India. His decision was motivated in large part by a desire to go home and fight for independence there. But it was also a recognition of the fact that he had failed. Despite the hard-won concessions that the satyagraha movement produced in 1913, a whole host of other racist laws remained in effect. Indeed, in the years ahead, conditions for Indians and Africans alike would only get worse.

What was important was not what Gandhi did for South Africa but what South Africa did for Gandhi and for the world. South Africa had provided both the catalyst and the proving ground for a movement that would soon liberate nearly 350 million inhabitants of the Indian subcontinent from colonial rule, that would provide the strategy and the tactics for the civil rights struggle in the American South, and that, ultimately, would lay the groundwork for what Nelson Mandela and the African National Congress (ANC) finally achieved in South Africa eighty years down the line. Seen from the long view, the journey that Gandhi began in the shivering cold of the train station in Pietermaritzburg can only be considered a resounding success. For me, however, the impact of Gandhi's teachings and methods was as much personal as it was political. I didn't need to go looking for it in the history books. I could see it right in front of me, inside my own home, on Saturday mornings.

———————

Growing up in Toronto in the seventies and eighties, I was a husky kid who ate a lot of donuts. After my school week was over, after I'd endured what felt to me like nothing but endless droning on Friday night at the jamatkhana, I would roll out of bed the next day and would only want to veg out and watch Saturday-morning cartoons. My father frowned on this activity. When he saw me sprawled out on the couch doing nothing in front of the television he would ask me if I wanted some chores to do. There was nothing I wanted to do less. My father, in a marked contrast, loved chores. I always knew my father to be an extremely disciplined, hard-driving guy. He needed to be occupied, productive. But his productivity wasn't about money. He was never materialistic or acquisitive. He lived sparingly, frugally, without excess. He went to work and worked hard. Then he'd come home from work and work some more, doing chores, spending time on his various civic engagements with the jamatkhana or in the community. But to him that wasn't "work." It wasn't drudgery. It was what he did to fill his hours with purpose and meaning.

As a kid, I never understood it. If I'm being honest, being his son sometimes bordered on the unpleasant. We didn't have any leisure activities. It was always work, politics, volunteering, that sort of thing. I grew up thinking that life is not fun, although that is not to say our lives were miserable. On the contrary, our lives were engaging, fulfilling, intellectually stimulating. But "fun" wasn't really a thing we did. We didn't go skiing and rarely skated, in stark contrast to most of my friends. Once in a great while, we would go to a restaurant and have pizza for a special occasion, like somebody's birthday.

What I didn't understand, living in the affluence of the West, was that my father's discipline is what had allowed him to move, survive, and thrive in so many different cultures. Over the course of his life, he'd moved from South Africa to Kenya to Canada. In his world, as opposed to mine, you couldn't make it if you weren't disciplined. And discipline is not something that one comes by naturally. It's a trait, a skill, that has to be learned, and my father had learned it from one man, his father, Rajabali.

If you want to know what Rajabali looked like, all you have to do is turn on MSNBC or glance at the front cover of this book. The man was the spitting image of the grandson he would never meet. My father says he had my speaking manner as well, a similarly booming voice. In those days, when you made a long-distance call, the quality was so awful you couldn't hear anything anyone was saying, so people would call Rajabali to come to their house to make these calls for them; he would speak on their behalf to their relatives or business associates because he could be heard.

It's an unfortunate turn of fate that South Africa's satyagraha campaign stumbled and dissipated just as my grandfather came of age, because from every story I'm told, I have to believe he would have made an excellent foot soldier on the front lines. But by the 1920s, Gandhi had departed, and the Union of South Africa, through the exploitation of its native peoples and its natural resources, had grown powerful enough to silence and repress virtually any and all dissent. There was no freedom movement of any significance of which to be a part. However, the training and education my grandfather received at Tolstoy Farm would not go to waste. He took those lessons and he lived them through his choices and his actions in business and in everyday life, altering the course of our family's history forever.

With the death of his older brother Jivan from the Spanish flu in 1918, Velshi had become the family patriarch. Savvy in business, he was soon expanding the family's operations from a few retail stores and wholesale shops to include a number of new businesses, such as a bakery and a Caltex petrol station, which would be the only Indian-owned auto garage in all of Pretoria for decades. Velshi's brother and my maternal great-grandfather Manjee jumped into the exploding business of talkies coming out of Hollywood, opening the Royal Kinema, which most of us would know today as a movie theater but which was known in South Africa at the time as a bioscope. Unable to attend the white cinemas downtown, Indian film lovers now had a movie palace of their own.

As long as they stayed inside the small world that white South Africans had allocated for them, the Keshavjees were allowed to prosper, and they did. They put their good fortune to good use. Like most Ismaili Muslims, the Keshavjees of Marabastad were community oriented and civic-minded. Velshi was a highly religious man who went to the mosque twice a day, every day, at four in the morning and again at seven in the evening. His faith was central to everything he did, just as it had been for his father, KeshavjeeBapa, back in Chotila. The Keshavjees used their money to build and support the local jamatkhana. They were also generous patrons of the neighborhood schools, the health clinics, and everything else you could name. In 1923, Velshi even journeyed back to Chotila to settle his father's unpaid debts, paying every one of his creditors in full and making sure that no one went without the monies they were owed. But the family's strict moral codes and civic-mindedness did not extend farther than the borders of Marabastad. Their devotion to community focused on *their* community. That changed when Rajabali entered the family business, bringing with him the values he had learned at Tolstoy Farm.

Among the many enterprises the family acquired in the 1920s, the one that would come to define their journey was the purchase of a commercial bakery from a Chinese businessman who was liquidating his assets. Renaming it the African Baking Company—or, as it would become known, ABC Bakery—Velshi promptly handed the reins over to Rajabali, then scarcely twenty years old. Rajabali managed the bakery's overall daily operations while his brother Cassim assumed the responsibilities of master baker in the kitchen and his other brother, Habib, took charge of the sales and delivery. The bread making started every night around eight o'clock, with the hot loaves ready by about three or four in the morning. Then the salesmen arrived at 6:00 a.m. to pick up their orders and take them out to their customers. In addition to wholesaling bread, during the day ABC Bakery was a confectionary selling cakes, buns, and sweets.

Under Rajabali's stewardship, over the course of the next thirty years, what started out as a small village bakery delivering bread by horse and buggy would grow into the eleventh-largest industrial bakery in South Africa, with a fleet of delivery trucks; a modern, state-of-the-art kitchen; over a hundred employees working day and night; and thousands of loaves of bread coming out of its massive ovens every hour. But my grandfather's real contribution to the family business wasn't something that can be measured on a balance sheet. Rajabali took the strong business ethic that Velshi had imparted to him, married it to the moral code that Gandhi had imparted to him, and ran the business the way any true satyagrahi would.

Despite being Indian-owned, ABC Bakery didn't sell bread to Indians, because Indians don't traditionally eat leavened bread; our diet is based more on rice and flatbreads, like chapati. While Apartheid and its Byzantine laws didn't actually forbid an Indian-owned bakery from selling to white people, whites simply wouldn't knowingly buy bread from *koolies*. Which meant that almost all of the company's customers were Black. During World War II, when there were food shortages and the government started rationing bread, profiteers would make their fortunes gouging customers in the underground economy. Rajabali refused to do the same. Indeed, he went the other way, supplying bread to African schools on a daily basis without charge. At the time, South African law stipulated that a two-pound loaf of bread had to be sold as a complete two-pound loaf. You couldn't sell half a loaf or by the slice. But Rajabali, even though it was technically illegal, would set a table of half loaves of bread outside the bakery office right across the street from the Black location—*location* being a South African term for any group's designated ghetto or township. The African families would line up there and buy half a loaf at a time, which was often all they could afford, and that way more people would have bread for the day.

When Rajabali wasn't running the bakery, he taught the Ismaili equivalent of a Sunday school at the jamatkhana. He seemed to be an informal teacher of everyone, a community sage, a dispenser of wisdom. Everyone I meet from that time seems in some way to have been a pupil of my grandfather. My father, who was born in 1935, used to tell me stories about accompanying his father on trips to a nearby leper colony and also a local mental asylum. Not only were these institutions places where Rajabali volunteered to work and to which he donated money, but like the African schools, they were also institutions that received daily deliveries of bread from ABC Bakery free of charge. Rajabali also hired ex-convicts who otherwise couldn't get work. For Black South Africans, being swept up and arrested by the police state was simply a matter of everyday life, not an indication that you were actually a criminal in any way, and Rajabali felt strongly about extending opportunities to those people when no one else would.

Living by your ideals sounds great in theory. But acting on them can be hard—and costly. Not every successful Indian businessman lived by the same principles as my grandfather. Many pursued a life that American rappers sometimes describe as "ghetto rich." Denied access to the real status symbols of South African society—positions in government, mansions in the suburbs, white skin—they compensated by overspending on flash and spectacle, fancy clothes and expensive cars. Because of his education on Tolstoy Farm, my grandfather simply wasn't interested in that sort of display. The way my father explained it to me, Rajabali could have made ten times the money he did if profit-seeking had been his only goal. But he'd taken to heart Gandhi's lessons: that the best way to find one's self is in the service of others, that all social and political maladies were intertwined, and that we all have a duty to repair the fabric of the world in whatever small ways we can. And that was a necessary mindset to have in a country where the ruling powers were bound and determined to tear that fabric apart.

By 1945, the cataclysm of World War II had completely upended the balance of power around the globe. A world that had been defined by the relationship between the colonizing North and the exploited South was now defined by a stalemate between the communist, authoritarian East and the capitalist, democratic West. The aging empires of Europe, weary from their fight against Hitler's Germany, were losing both the power and the appetite to continue their imperial adventures abroad. Meanwhile, the righteous crusade that liberated the death camps at Auschwitz and Dachau was forcing the liberators to examine the prejudice, bigotry, and injustice that plagued their own countries.

Perhaps most importantly, just as there were thousands of Black American soldiers who returned from the war ready to fight for the same freedoms at home that they'd fought for overseas, there were millions of young soldiers from Asia, the Middle East, and Africa who'd gone off to war on behalf of the same European powers who oppressed them at home. They, too, returned from the war with a newfound resolve, ready to fight for the dignity, respect, and independence their people deserved.

For the white colonists of Africa, from Algeria and Ghana in the north to Rhodesia and Tanzania in the sub-Saharan south, the writing was on the wall. It would be another fifteen to twenty years before independence finally swept across the continent, but it was increasingly clear that the days of white rule in Africa were drawing to a close. For the whites of South Africa, particularly the Afrikaners, that future posed an existential threat. Unlike the French, British, and Portuguese, the white tribe of Africa had become so disconnected from its European heritage that its people had nowhere to run back to, and they couldn't conceive of a world in which they would submit to a democratic, majority-Black rule. For many, preserving South Africa's status as "a white man's country" became viewed as the ultimate imperative.

Some white South Africans tried to take a moderate approach. As the elections of 1948 approached, faced with the uncertainty of a majority-Black future, Gandhi's old sparring partner Jan Smuts, who was by then the prime minister of South Africa, campaigned on a pragmatic approach, arguing that racial integration was inevitable and the government should gradually be reformed so that Black South Africans could exercise some measure of power—in a system that would, naturally, still favor whites.

Smut's United Party was running primarily against the National Party, which campaigned on a platform of naked racism and white nationalism, promising to protect the jobs of white workers while keeping white families safe from Black violence and crime. One party slogan in particular—*Die kaffer op die plek. Die koelies uit die land* (The kaffir in his place. The coolies out of the country)—tells you everything you need to know. To achieve their goals, they pledged to impose strict racial segregation in all spheres of life under a new system they called Apartheid.

On May 26, 1948—one year after Gandhi's satyagraha movement had won complete independence for India—South Africa's National Party rose to power on a plurality of the vote. They took what was already an unjust, unequal, and thoroughly racist society and said, "Now how can we make this even worse?" And they did. Over the decade that followed, through the passage of sweeping legislation, they constructed a wholly segregated society exhibiting the purest form of legal and institutional racism the world has ever seen. They passed the Population Registration Act, which forced everyone to register as a member of a racial group or an ethnic tribe. They passed the Group Areas Act, which forcibly uprooted over 3.5 million people and sorted them into segregated townships. They passed the Mixed Marriages

Act, which banned interracial marriage, and even the Immorality Amendment Act, a complete prohibition on interracial sex.

Having silenced all domestic dissent, drunk on absolute power and seemingly unlimited wealth, South Africa's new ruling party went a bit insane. They grew so powerful so quickly that somebody would suggest something in Parliament and—no matter how far-fetched or absurd—there would be full consent, and the next thing you knew, it would become law. Under the Population Registration Act, for example, in order to determine which people should be categorized according to which group, a racially ambiguous person who didn't easily fit into a category would be subjected to the pencil test, where a pencil was inserted into their hair to determine how curly it was. Since Black people generally have tighter, curlier hair than white people or Indians, if the pencil fell out, you were white. If the pencil stayed in, you were screwed.

There was also the Bantu Education Act, an education system designed to make Black people uneducated. This act was akin to the antiliteracy laws in the US antebellum South, which made it illegal for enslaved people to learn to read. The government even produced a dumbed-down dictionary for Black people to mold them into being subservient to everyone else. Instead of English, it taught only Afrikaans, a language that was not used anywhere else in the world, and all it contained was the minimal vocabulary a Black person would need to perform menial labor like picking fruit or digging in the mines. If Black people ever looked themselves up in this dictionary, they'd understand why, because they'd see themselves defined as manual laborers.

If Gandhi's goal had been to teach his followers to repair the fabric of society, the goal of Apartheid was to rend it to pieces. The literal definition of the word is "apartness" or "separation," and it was accomplished by dividing and conquering the people of South Africa, by alienating them from one another and sowing hatred for each other. The Indians looked down on the Africans for fear of being treated as poorly as the Africans were, the Africans resented the Indians for being treated slightly better than themselves, and the Colored people—as South Africa's mixed-race population was known—were stuck somewhere in between. And in a system supposedly built for the *benefit* of white people, the net effect was to create a world where white people were forced to cower in fear of 90 percent of their neighbors.

Apartheid was, by its nature, the opposite of a healthy, functioning society. As the National Party's new regulations took effect, the country's legal landscape began to reshape the physical one. In Pretoria, the metropolitan heart of Afrikaner nationalism, as the city center was cleared to make way for new whites-only neighborhoods, Black people found themselves uprooted from the crowded, ramshackle ghettos of the colonial past and pushed out to new locations on the outskirts of town, places like Bantuli, Vlakfontein, Mamelodi, Atteridgeville, and Lady Selborne, which was home to the convent where my sister would later be born.

Life in Marabastad, the Indian ghetto, which had always been difficult, grew even more so. Even though Indians were often left alone to run their businesses, because they were not allowed to own land neither their businesses nor their homes were secure. Properties could only be rented on a twenty-one-year lease, which the government could choose not to renew. Now, with a new government policy committed to pushing people out into faraway lands where they were born, the existence of Marabastad itself was in jeopardy.

Over the course of the 1940s, '50s, and '60s, more and more leases were being rescinded all the time as the government moved residents out of Marabastad to a new Indian location called Laudium, twenty miles away, and there was no legal recourse available for residents to protest. Before, under British rule, Indians were at least offered something like citizenship and a modicum of legal standing in the system. You could petition the courts for a claim and, though the odds were against you, you might actually get a hearing and some relief. Apartheid laws were far more stringent, far stricter, and far clearer. If you went to a lawyer, he would simply tell you, "Sorry, there's nothing you can do." The racist laws had been passed by the South African Parliament and upheld by the courts. It was a perfect example of a case where something can be 100 percent legal and yet 100 percent unjust.

Like their African and Colored countrymen, Indians were left to survive by the skin of their teeth. My father was thirteen years old when the National Party seized power. My mother was only five. The architecture of Apartheid would shape and define their lives. Marabastad sat less than a mile away from the administrative capital of South Africa, the equivalent of living right off The Mall in Washington, DC. Yet if they ever needed to set foot outside their own neighborhood, their parents would tell them, "Go to the washroom now, because you're not going to find a toilet until we get back." In Marabastad, the sole dentist available to Indians opened the office one day a week—on Tuesdays. So if you woke up with a toothache on Wednesday, good luck.

Tuesday afternoons were also the only time Indians could go to the zoo. If you went any other day, you'd get beaten by the white kids. And forget about food. If you went downtown and wanted to buy a hamburger or a hot dog, restaurants would serve you, but only through a side takeout window; you couldn't go inside or stay and eat anywhere on the premises. If there was a white person at the window, they would get served first. All the white people were served first, and then once all the white people were gone, the restaurant staff would come to you. Generally you'd bring your own sandwich with you, although it could still then be difficult to find a place to eat because if you sat down in the wrong public place, you would get beaten by the white kids.

Socially and culturally, my parents lived in a small community—maybe 3,500 people—one large extended family of "Indians." Outside of that, their associations and interactions with others were minimal. There was a Black neighborhood on one side of Marabastad and a Colored neighborhood on the other, so there were always minimal interactions in that respect. But all the children went to segregated schools, and there weren't any meaningful social relationships of any kind across the color line.

As far as white people went, there were some who would come to the area to do Christian charity for the poor. Largely, they were there to proselytize. If you were a Hindu or a Muslim who became Christian, they would bring you some clothing and give you food. There were also some white nurses and doctors, largely Jewish, who would come to the jamatkhana for a health clinic once a week. Those doctors, being the kinds of white people who would volunteer to go to the Indian location, were generally kind. But to speak to any white person under any other circumstance? Why would anyone do that? What would they speak about? You'd only exchange words with a white person if you met them on a street where you weren't supposed to be, in which case they'd kick you and shout, "Coolie, fuck off! You don't belong here." That was the life. You were stuck in your tiny ghetto with no swimming pools, no parks, no libraries. My father didn't even know what a public library was until he left the country for the first time. Everything was closed to you. You were brought up to understand that you didn't belong, that you had no rights. And nobody talked about it. It was simply accepted. My parents didn't consciously think about it. It was their way of life.

And it was, in the end, a life. Growing up in a free country, I'm not quite sure how anybody made it out of there without being angry all the time. But they did. Even under something as brutal and as cruel as Apartheid, life is not only struggle and misery and humiliation all the time. You live your life and enjoy what you can in spite of whatever constraints are imposed on you. People found their ways to have fun and experience joy. Marabastad was a place of culture, music, art, celebration. They had jazz. They had dancing. Having a movie theater in the family helped. Despite the fact that every film shown in South Africa had to be heavily censored, they still got to see many classic Hollywood movies with all the big stars, like Ava Gardner and Elizabeth Taylor, Charlton Heston and Tyrone Power. The censors couldn't hide the fact that America was a land of openness and excitement and freedom, and the movies gave my family a window into another life to which they could aspire. The Royal Kinema wasn't only a place for showing movies. Students had their concerts there. Political meetings were held there. Evangelists would preach there. They hosted variety shows from time to time. If you ask my parents about their childhoods, my mother will tell you that life was tough, and my father will tell you that life was good; neither of them are referring to Apartheid. For my mother, life was tough because her family was poor. For my father, life was good because his family was prosperous.

My father's family was not an exception in this regard. Many Indians of the time were prosperous, and in the thirty-plus years since Gandhi's satyagraha campaign, they had become an increasingly conservative bunch, and even in spite of the daily degradations of Apartheid, they were determined to preserve their gains and not upset the system that made those gains possible. At the time, the major organizational arm for South Africa's Indians was the South African Indian Congress (SAIC). It had grown out of Gandhi's movement and its ranking members all made a big deal out of their connections to those legendary marches and campaigns. It was considered quite a prestigious thing to be a member. It meant you were a respected individual, but it wasn't a vehicle for social activism in the way it had been in the past. They staged a few nonviolent protests here and there, but for the most part, they were not as interested in politics as they were in securing their trade licenses and not losing their property.

As my parents and cousins came of age, they were told by the older generation, "We've come here and we want to survive. Be law-abiding. Do your business. Don't get worked up over the fact that you can't go into a white cinema. Just go to the brown cinema. Don't get too clever." It's not that they were apolitical. They were politically conscious, but they were also politically pragmatic. They had come from Gujarat. They had lived through famines. They had lived through drought. Their attitude was, "We're living in Africa now and we're getting our three meals and making money. Do we want to stand up and fight and get sent back to India?" Which made sense to them in terms of where they'd come from, and it's not an uncommon attitude in small minority and immigrant communities. But for many of their children, it would not be enough.

Apartheid's brutality made a mockery of the idea that South

Africa's Indians could be free or in any way fulfilled under oppression, no matter how prosperous they were. A whole generation of Indian children, many of them from wealthy families, defied the old order, men like Yusuf Dadoo and Monty Naicker, Ahmed Kathrada and Ismail Cachalia, women like Zainab Asvat and Amina Cachalia. Many of them had gone to London for school. They'd seen firsthand what real freedom and opportunity looked like. No longer content to live inside a gilded cage, they seized the reins of leadership at the SAIC and began agitating for real change in the country.

Just as the SAIC was being energized by its Young Turks, the African National Congress was undergoing a rebirth as well, emerging from a long dormant period thanks to the energizing efforts of men like Walter Sisulu, Oliver Tambo, and of course Nelson Mandela. When Mandela and the others first began building their movement, it was pro-African to the exclusion of others. They didn't want Indians or anybody else in their organization. Then they came to the realization that the Indians had all the money. What Gandhi had always lacked was the numbers; there were never enough satyagrahis on the ground to make life truly inconvenient for the white majority. But the Africans had the people and the Indians had the money, and by combining those forces, they were finally able to mount a serious challenge to the Apartheid regime.

After years of smaller-scale protests and resistance, that united effort first came together on a national scale in the Defiance Campaign of 1952. Starting in July of that year, for nearly ten months, nonwhite South Africans openly violated the rules of Apartheid through various forms of nonviolent protest. Black people burned their pass books, boycotted segregated buses, and entered "whites-only" areas—all of which was then against the law. Many were shot and killed. Thousands were imprisoned, filling the jails in an effort to overwhelm and break the system.

The same year that the Defiance Campaign was bringing a new generation of activists onto the South African political scene, the Keshavjee family underwent a generational shift of its own. Half a century after leaping from a steamship and swimming through the sharks of Delagoa Bay to live an improbably successful life in Marabastad, Velshi Keshavjee met an untimely end. As a part of his daily ritual, every evening he spent an hour walking the neighborhood, stopping by friends' and relatives' houses to check in and say hello. He would then walk across Boom Street to the mosque when it was time for evening prayers. Marabastad's main thoroughfare, Boom Street, was always busy, and on this particular day, Velshi crossed at the bus stop, where a bus had stopped to pick up its passengers. Velshi went to cross in front of the stopped bus, but in the adjacent lane, another bus was speeding past to overtake the one that was parked. Not seeing the oncoming vehicle, he stepped out in front of it and was struck and killed, instantly. My mother, who was nine years old, happened to be standing across the street at the time and witnessed it firsthand.

With Velshi's death, Rajabali now assumed the role of the family patriarch. More of the day-to-day business operations then fell on the next generation, including my father, Murad, and his older brother, Rehmtulla. When it came to running ABC Bakery, my father was every inch his father's son. At seventeen, he was already self-disciplined and dutiful. He got up early every day, worked hard, carried on with Rajabali's efforts to provide bread for those in need, hiring and helping out employees who'd had problems with the law. Rehmtulla was a different character. He was a maverick of sorts, enormously charismatic and a committed activist. But Rehmtulla did not see things the way his father had. The ideal satyagrahi was a paragon of patience and self-discipline, but Rehmtulla was a bit too hotheaded for that. He was determined to resist Apartheid not by providing free bread to Africans but by storming the barricades. In keeping with his spirited temperament, Rehmtulla also smoked and drank and caroused into the late hours of the night, which was not entirely compatible with the hours required to run a bakery. That left the actual operation of the business to my father, which, since the two of them were technically equal partners, caused a few problems.

Six years earlier, in 1946, Rehmtulla had gone to England to study, though how much studying he did remains unclear. His plan had been to enroll at the London School of Economics; however, the soldiers returning from World War II had been given priority for admission, so he failed to secure a spot. Instead, he lived the good life, partying his way around London and eventually falling in with the socialist intellectuals and communist agitators who were then congregating at youth conferences across Europe. He traveled to East Germany and Poland and Romania and Czechoslovakia, becoming very much the self-styled revolutionary. By the time he returned home and the Defiance Campaign was gathering steam, he was ready to join the fight.

During the Defiance Campaign he'd been on the front lines, going to secret meetings with leaders in the struggle and joining in protests. He marched through the "whites-only" entrance of the Pretoria Railway station only to be arrested on the other side. Black leaders like Walter Sisulu would come by the bakery and Rehmtulla would slip them money for ANC operations. After the government banned all meetings of more than ten people, Rehmtulla joined a large group of non-Blacks who entered the African township of Germiston without a permit. He was arrested, again, and jailed along with thousands of others.

Rehmtulla even looked the part of a revolutionary, complete with a Che Guevara goatee. At the time, my father often felt his brother was simply playing the part as well. He wasn't a serious revolutionary, merely a dreamy idealist tilting at windmills, too unmotivated to be involved with actually running the business when he could be running off to Prague and meeting with communists—which, if you were the one getting up every morning at 4:00 a.m. to run a bakery, is how you might feel, too. Rehmtulla got to have all the fun and all the fame. In my research, whenever I spoke to Indians who were deeply involved in the struggle, they don't know my father; they know my uncle. He's the name. They'll say, "Oh, yes. I knew Rehmtulla. I was in Budapest with him." Or "We were at a training camp together." Meanwhile, the efforts my father and his father were making, quietly going to work and seeing that the students at African schools got their daily bread for free, would never make the history books.

Hindsight, reporting, and research have helped my dad understand Rehmtulla's activism quite differently. South Africa's prisons were no place for dilettantes. Ahmed Kathrada, one of the key movement leaders who would be imprisoned alongside Mandela on Robben Island, knew Rehmtulla and worked alongside him. There was no doubt within the SAIC and the ANC that my uncle's commitment was genuine.

But if Rehmtulla's revolutionary spirit was real, so too were its consequences for the family. Even as the international order condemned the most brutal of Apartheid's practices, South Africa was able to go right on with its abuses, for two reasons. The first was the vast mineral wealth and natural resources that the country possessed and that the industrial West relied on; America and Europe needed South Africa more than South Africa needed America and Europe. The second was the ever-creeping threat of communism. From Ghana to Egypt, as colonial governments began to fall, each new African nation went up for grabs. Would it align itself with the West or become a client of the Soviet East? As the last "white man's country" on the continent, South Africa sold itself to the West as the only bulwark against communism in Africa, thus justifying any and all actions its government took to keep "communism" at bay.

The Suppression of Communism Act, passed in 1950, did more than simply ban the Communist Party. It gave the state expansive powers to find and root out communist influence wherever it was found and however the state defined it. Indeed, the act defined *communism* so broadly that defendants often found themselves convicted of "statutory communism," whatever that is. Basically, all the government had to do was label you a communist—and everyone who was antigovernment or anti-Apartheid was automatically labeled a communist—and at that point, it was legally justified in taking virtually any action against you that it wished.

The Suppression of Communism Act became the blunt-force instrument that the government used to silence any and all dissent against the regime, and it was brutally effective in the hands of the men who wielded it. The Security Branch of the South African Police, known as the Special Branch, was the elite force within the government tasked with keeping order, stifling dissent, and enforcing all the Byzantine laws that kept Apartheid in place. In terms of spying on, torturing, and killing people, it was maybe the most sophisticated security apparatus anywhere in the world, matched only by the Soviet KGB or Israel's Mossad.

If my family had just run a small retail shop serving Indians in Marabastad, they might have flown under the government's radar more easily. But by the early 1950s, ABC Bakery was making four thousand loaves of bread an hour, putting them onto trucks, and delivering them to the Black locations across Pretoria. The bakery employed dozens of Black workers as well. There were licenses and permits and regulations for everything, which meant they had to interact with the government far more than the average citizen, not to mention the fact that the family's entire livelihood was built on land that could be taken away the moment their lease was up, which gave the government a great deal of leverage over how they did business. Once Rehmtulla went to jail, this humble family of Indian bakers somehow became viewed as a den of communist subversives, and the harassment began.

Among the many ridiculous rules and regulations of Apartheid was the government control of yeast, a common household item that was nonetheless treated as a controlled substance on the level of a prescription drug. If ABC Bakery had 320 one-pound packets of yeast at the close of business one day, and they used 25 packets the next day, that twenty-five-pound difference would have to be documented and the balance of 295 packets had to be accounted for. The cops could literally come and arrest you if it wasn't. The reason for that regulation was that Black people were not allowed to buy or own yeast, because in addition to making bread it could also be used for making beer, and Black people were not allowed to brew or distribute alcohol. Black people found ways to make alcohol anyway. Illegal bars known as *shebeens* were always popping up to sell booze in Black locations, which meant that they had to be getting the yeast from somewhere.

In Pretoria the suspicion of that fell on Rehmtulla and ABC Bakery. The Special Branch was bound and determined to catch them selling black-market yeast. Every few weeks, ten or fifteen armed agents of the state would surround the bakery, come rushing into the kitchen, bust into their room-sized refrigerator, and start counting the number of yeast packets to see if it matched their records. A SWAT team, basically. For yeast. And all to keep Black people from being able to enjoy a nice cold beer.

Even though the raids always came up empty, at some point my uncle was charged with selling yeast on the side. Apparently there was an informant involved. It was a whole thing. The record isn't entirely clear as to whether Rehmtulla was selling black-market yeast or not. And if he was, I don't know whether he was doing it for money or for legitimate political reasons, as a subversive act, a way of saying, "Black people are entitled to drink whatever they want." In the end, however, the actual facts of the case mattered not one bit. Once the family was under suspicion for engaging in antigovernment activities, their days in South Africa were numbered.

Shortly after the bakery raids began, in 1954, under the Suppression of Communism Act, the state took away the family's passports. The fear that the government could step in at any time and take everything had always been present, lingering in the back of their minds. After the confiscation of their passports, the Keshavjees could no longer ignore this possibility. Losing their passports made real the fear that they might lose everything. That's when the problem became, "When the time comes, will we be able to get out? And, if we are, will we be able to get our money out, too?"

At that point, Rajabali decided that my father, his sister, and one of their cousins needed to leave the country. Traveling internationally without papers was incredibly dangerous, but as in any police state, an underground railroad of sorts had sprung up to help people move through the system. The Jewish community played a major role in that effort, and a Jewish travel agent my family knew arranged for my dad, my aunt, and their cousin to get out on an El Al flight from Pretoria to Nairobi in Kenya.

"When you get to Immigration at Johannesburg Airport," the agent told them, "one of the officers will have a rose on his lapel. Go to him with a document, any document you've got, even if it's not a valid document, stand in his line, and he will stamp your papers and get you onto the plane."

At the time, nonwhites in South Africa had to have a Certificate of Identity, which was required to travel from one province to another. It wasn't valid for international travel, and even if it had been, the certificates that my dad and the others had were expired. Still, they took their invalid documents to the airport and brought them to the immigration officer with the rose on his lapel, who dutifully stamped them as if they were the real thing. Then they got onto the flight. When they landed in Nairobi, the other end of the underground railroad was there to intercept them and wave them through without documents.

My dad went to live and work with his uncle, Rajabali's brother, Habib, who'd immigrated to Nairobi a few years before and opened a dry cleaners. Even though Kenya was still under British rule, compared to South Africa it was a world of absolute freedom. Indians could go to cinemas and restaurants, walk in the streets, play in the parks, and use public restrooms. It was so unnervingly different that it took them a while to get used to it, and my father found he couldn't. He was homesick. South Africa, for all its oppression and unfreedom, was where his roots and his family were. Marabastad was his home, and after ten months in Kenya, he decided to go back.

Because he didn't have papers to fly back into Johannesburg, he took a coastal flight from Mombasa to Lourenço Marques in what was still Portuguese East Africa. From there, he took a train home to Pretoria. Like all trains at the time, it had two sections, the white section and the nonwhite section. When the trains stopped at the border, the officers would go to the nonwhite cars to check everyone's documents and visas; they never went to the white cars to check documents because that wasn't a concern. While my dad doesn't look as white as your average Norwegian or Swede, South Africa had a lot of whites from the Mediterranean who aren't that white to begin with; they're more olive-colored. So it didn't matter that he was a bit darker than some. He went in, found an empty seat, and went to asleep, avoiding detection by not talking to anyone.

When he arrived at Pretoria station at eight o'clock the next morning, Rehmtulla picked him up and drove him home. The whole trip had been planned and executed as secretly as my father could manage. Nobody was supposed to know about it. Still, not two hours after he returned, a Special Branch agent showed up, knocked on his door, and said, "Welcome home," which was just to let my dad know that the police knew exactly where he was, when he was coming home, and what he'd been doing the whole time.

When you stop to think that the South African Police were putting that much effort into tracking the movements of a nineteen-year-old kid whose dad ran a bakery, it gives you a clear sense of the regime's reach and power as well as its paranoia. As the decade progressed, independence movements across the continent continued to gain momentum. Black political leaders were coming out of prison. Once released, they were no longer enemies of the state but rather the leaders of major political parties. In 1957, Ghana became the first African colony to declare its complete independence from the British Crown. It's newly elected president, the prosocialist Pan-Africanist Kwame Nkrumah, was everything white South Africans had been taught to fear. In February 1960, British prime minister Harold MacMillan visited Cape Town and gave what would become a historic speech. "The wind of change is blowing through the continent," he said, and the rise of Black national consciousness was a fact to be reckoned with "whether we like it or not."

As if preparing for war, South Africa responded to the changing climate by plunging the country into its darkest days yet. The National Party's new prime minister, Hendrik Verwoerd, banned all other political parties. The armed forces of the Special Branch cracked down that much harder. A month and a half after MacMillan's speech, in what would become known as the Sharpeville Massacre, the police responded to a nonviolent citizen protest by indiscriminately firing into a crowd of some five thousand people, killing dozens. In response, Nelson Mandela and the ANC began to pivot away from peaceful, nonviolent resistance. Founding a new paramilitary wing known as uMkhonto we Sizwe, the "Spear of the Nation," they set themselves on a course that would result in armed insurrection and the eventual capture and imprisonment of Mandela and his fellow Black leaders.

It was a dark time. The raids on the bakery increased in frequency and brutality. ABC's Black workers had to have special permits to leave their locations and travel to the bakery. The police would show up and harass anyone if they didn't have their pass or even if there was some technicality wrong with the paperwork. The bakery's employees would routinely get beaten on the spot, arrested, and dragged off to prison. As Ghana's new Black president Kwame Nkrumah was visiting Buckingham Palace and attending political conferences in England, outside ABC Bakery policemen were ruthlessly throwing Black men to the ground and beating them to a pulp.

The sentence for not having the proper pass was one week in jail and a five-pound fine. If you couldn't pay the fine—and no Black workers could—you'd be sentenced to three months of hard labor on a farm, which was nothing more than a scheme to get free slave labor for the farmers. And the sentence was automatic, like a mandatory minimum. None of the accused ever had representation, and nobody ever challenged it. No one ever asked questions. The police arrested scores of Black people over the weekends, when the bakery was closed. So come Sunday night, my dad would get calls telling him which employees had been locked up and where to go to get them out. On Monday morning, he would go to the court with fifteen or twenty pounds, depending on how many of his workers had been arrested, and he'd pay the fines and get them home to save them from being taken to the farms. By the end of the 1950s, my father was spending every Monday morning in the courts trying to get these guys out. It was not a pleasant or sustainable situation, and then came the final nail in the coffin.

Under British rule, Black people had been forced to live in their own areas, segregated from whites and everyone else, but the bakery vans could go into those areas and deliver bread unmolested. Now, under Apartheid, not only had all the Black people been relocated to new townships north of Pretoria, but also the townships were surrounded by fences and barbed wire. There was only one road in and out, and the government controlled who went in and who could leave. Any business that wanted to enter a Black location to sell bread or anything else had to obtain a special permit at the entry of each individual location.

By the late 1950s, having failed to catch the bakery selling illegal yeast or committing any other infraction, the government began to systematically reduce the term of ABC Bakery's permit to enter the Black locations. At the start, my father had to renew the bakery's papers once a year. Then that was reduced to six months. Then it was knocked down to monthly, and then weekly. Finally, the government reduced it to a daily permit. Literally every single morning, after baking thousands of loaves of bread, my father would have to go to the municipal office at the gate of each Black location and apply for permission to enter. Only the office didn't open until 9:00 a.m., and the bread had to be delivered at 6:00 a.m., which was when the white bakeries were permitted to enter. So for three hours the white bakers got to monopolize the market and by the time my father's vans got permission to go in, everyone had already had their breakfast and gone off to work. ABC's drivers started coming back to the bakery with trucks full of unsold bread.

ABC Bakery was, at the time, a member in good standing of the Pretoria Master Bakers Association, an organization whose purpose, in theory, was to support and lobby on behalf of the welfare of its members. Since Rajabali had recently suffered a heart attack, my father was the one attending the meetings, and he knew if he couldn't get the association to take up his cause he would soon have to close his doors.

"I'm having a problem," he told the group, explaining the issue with the permits at one of their meetings.

"There is nothing we can do," the other members said. "This is government policy."

"It may be government policy, but you're benefiting from my loss of business. You're selling the bread that I was supposed to sell. You've got all my customers."

He then told them that if they weren't going to help him, they could at least buy him out. He even gave them a price, which they declined. "No, no, no," they said. "We don't need to buy you out. You'll just close down one of these days."

They knew they had him up against the wall. The permitting laws were being deliberately applied in a draconian way to drive ABC Bakery out of business, in part as a retaliation for Rehmtulla's political activity but also to prevent them from expanding and growing, or even surviving, because they were in competition with white-owned bakeries. The white police and the white courts and the white city officials did not exist to uphold the law. They existed to abuse and manipulate the law to protect and promote the interests of whites. All those other bakers had to do was wait my father out. So my father did what any reasonable baker would do. He started a bread war.

At that time, there was a gentlemen's agreement between the bakers of Pretoria and Johannesburg that they would not sell bread in each other's territory. But with no way to sell bread in Pretoria, my dad decided to start delivering bread to Johannesburg. There he not only sold it but sold it at a discount, offering thirteen loaves to a dozen. The Johannesburg bakers were furious. They told Pretoria's bakers, "You're breaking our agreement, so we're going to break it, too." The Johannesburg bakers then went up to Pretoria and started selling bread at a discount there. Soon, bread prices were plummeting, and all the bakers in both cities were losing money.

The Pretoria bakers called up my dad and asked him to stop, to which my father replied, "No, I'm not going to stop. You can stop it any time you want. Allow my vans to go into our own area to sell bread. Then I'll have no problem. But as long as you're blocking me from going into my own area, I have to go to another area. I don't have a choice. Either I continue, or you buy me out."

They refused to buy him out, so the bread war dragged on and on and on. It went a full six months before the Pretoria bakers finally called my father up and said, "OK. We'll buy you out." They initially tried to pay him his original asking price, but that wasn't going to work anymore because my father had lost so much money in the war. He quoted them a higher price, and they finally caved and gave it to him.

When my father's family was bought out of the bakery, they got no money for the land, which was only leased from the city because Indians weren't allowed to own property. They got no money for the buildings, either, because the appraiser said the buildings were so old they didn't have any value. So the only thing my dad actually sold was the business itself. Once the sale was complete, the city announced their plans to level the building.

At that point, in July 1960, my father, mother, and grandparents decided to leave. After considerable wrangling and letter writing, including a great many written assurances that he was not a communist, my father convinced the government to agree to reissue their passports. My mother and father booked tickets for Nairobi. Rajabali and his wife, Jena, found a property in Mombasa, Kenya's seaside port, and made plans to retire there.

A week before my family's planned departure, the government began demolishing the bakery. The heart of any bakery is the oven, and to remove the coal-fired ovens, the government workers first had to break down the building's two old chimneys. My father and his father were standing across the street when it happened, watching the bricks rain down as the chimneys cracked and fell, watching everything they'd built over seventy years be reduced to nothing. It was the first time my dad ever saw his father cry.

A few days later, on the day he was scheduled to leave South Africa forever, Rajabali suffered a major heart attack. He died a few days later. He was fifty-eight years old.

When it was time for Rajabali to be buried, the hearse at the only Ismaili funeral parlor was in the shop; for whatever reason, it wasn't running properly. When no other hearse could be found in time, the family had to use the broken-down one anyway and pray for the best. Knowing that this car wasn't going to make it the two miles from the jamatkhana to the cemetery, my father put his car in the procession in front of the hearse. When it broke down, as everyone knew it would, my dad got out, tied a rope from the front of the hearse to the back of his car, and towed his father's body to the cemetery.

To this day, my dad believes that his father died of a broken heart.

4

A Splinter Up Your Ass

In the late 1970s, if you'd broken into my parents' house in Toronto, you'd have thought you were in a Kenyan home or, at least, the home of someone who loved to visit Kenya and go on safari and bring home a bunch of Kenyan stuff. Because that's pretty much all you'd have found. Carved masks, zebra-skin rugs, curios, and so forth.

There was a good reason for this. Since my family left India with nothing, we didn't have any Indian stuff. Other than my grandmother's saris, the only Indian culture my parents brought to Canada was what they carried inside them, the Gujarati language and recipes for Gujarati food. Nothing physical came from India. Or from South Africa, for that matter. My parents had never embraced South African art and culture because they'd been told, under threat of force, that it wasn't theirs. Whether it was the culture of the Anglo or Afrikaner ruling class or the language of the Xhosa or the Zulu, my parents were never allowed to participate in it, enjoy it, or have any ownership of it. So while they formed an attachment to the country, to the place, they never formed a strong attachment to any culture outside of their own.

Kenya was different. In Kenya, my parents were able, for the first time in their lives, to live where and how they pleased. They were free to engage with any person or art or cultural institution they found interesting or compelling. So when it came time to acquire all the things that go into making a house a home, what they had access to, and what they appreciated and admired, was all Kenyan. We went back to Kenya, too, nearly every year. My father is one of five siblings. Four of them immigrated to Canada, one to Edmonton and the other three to Toronto, but one of my aunts remained in Kenya, as did a few other cousins and distant relatives. That aunt was the one to whom I was the closest, though, and I loved going back. Nairobi is an amazing and eclectic city, and we would go on safari, which is awesome if you're a kid. To this day, I still love being among wild animals.

But going on safaris and collecting curios for home decor was as far as it went. Other than that, we weren't Kenyan by any stretch. There was nothing about the country that informed my identity in any deeply meaningful way, despite the fact that I was born there. Even though South Africa was farther in the rearview mirror of my family's history, the politics and the crucible of that country were far more front-of-mind in our conception of ourselves. South Africa dominated our dinner-table discussions; Kenya was a nice place to visit.

When I was growing up in the South Asian community of Toronto, our ties to South Africa made us the outliers, a minority within a minority. There were a few thousand Ismailis in the city at the time, and when we would go to the jamatkhana, we were the only family of South African origin. The overwhelming majority were from East Africa, mostly Tanzanians, some Kenyans, and eventually a large number of Ugandans. You'd show up at jamatkhana, and they would all be speaking Swahili to each other. I don't know why, because they all spoke English, but Swahili was their lingua franca for whatever reason. Since we didn't speak Swahili, we didn't interact with them as much. I always thought it was weird that I felt like an outsider in a community of brown people who all shared my faith. But that's how it was. They were East African, and we were still very much South African. But for the annual safari and the carved masks on the walls, it was almost as if the decade my parents spent in East Africa never even happened. We turned the page on that chapter and rarely looked back, and with good reason. Because for my parents, Kenya was the dream that failed.

———————

In the late nineteenth century, having largely conquered and colonized the Far East and the Americas, the nations of Europe turned their gaze to Africa. Up to that point, Europe's primary commercial interest in the continent had been the purchase of enslaved Africans for the plantations of the New World, which confined their plundering largely to the coasts. All that was about to change. The Industrial Revolution was generating a rapacious appetite for the raw materials and resources that Africa had in abundance, everything from rubber and precious metals to cotton and coffee and cocoa. Europe's explorers and adventurers, having mapped out most every other corner of the globe, were racing to map the continent's vast interior, to find the sources of the Nile, the Niger, and the Congo. Meanwhile, thousands of Europe's Christian missionaries were racing in right behind them, eagerly in search of the greatest treasure of all: tens of millions of pagan African souls, just waiting to be harvested for the Lord.

What followed was the aptly named "Scramble for Africa." Starting in 1885, the nations of Europe convened at conferences in Berlin, Paris, London, and Brussels, where they pored over maps of Africa, carving out chunks for their own needs and arguing over who would get what. All of this was done with zero regard for the African people. Drawing arbitrary lines on inaccurate maps, the European powers took traditional kingdoms, tribes, and language groups that had existed for hundreds of years and randomly sliced them up or smashed them together, often on nothing more than the whim of some European monarch who'd never even set foot south of the French Riviera. Quite famously, Queen Victoria of England "gave" Mount Kilimanjaro to Kaiser Wilhelm of Germany as a birthday present, transferring a massive chunk of land from the control of one nation to another without the slightest thought for how it might affect the people who actually lived there.

By the time the Scramble for Africa was done, the French, British, Germans, Spanish, Portuguese, Italians, and Belgians had taken some ten thousand different and distinct ethnic groups, each with its own culture and traditions; divvied them up; and sorted them into forty brand-new colonies, dominions, mandates, and protectorates. As in Natal, all of these designations were different legal mechanisms dreamed up to justify the brute-force annexation of property. Or to put it more simply: a way to keep the natives in their place in order to plunder their goods and rape their women. More than anything, these various colonial structures were a means of exerting control without having to assume accountability, meaning Africans could be counted as "subjects" without being accorded the rights of "citizens." Indeed, decades later when several Kenyans tried to sue the United Kingdom for human rights abuses, the British defense was "We were not in charge. We were not the government. The whites in Kenya were the colonial government, and the responsibility lies with them."

Different parts of Africa had different relationships to their European overseers. Nigeria and Uganda were controlled through what was known as a system of indirect rule, with African kings and chieftains left in place to run the colony on behalf of the Crown, reporting to only a handful of colonial administrators and magistrates. Both the Portuguese in Mozambique and the French in Algeria took a far more controlling attitude toward their new subjects, declaring their new African nations to be, not colonies per se but noncontiguous territories of the mother country itself—*le plus grande France*, as the French put it. And then you had the Congo Free State, which was initially not a colony of Belgium but rather the personal property of Belgian king Leopold II. Selling himself as a humanitarian who would end slavery and bring religion to the Congolese people, Leopold was in fact a brutal despot with his own private army, the Force Publique, a band of African soldiers led by European officers. They kidnapped and murdered the families of Congolese men who took up arms against the king, and they were notorious for cutting off the hands of the natives, including children, if they refused to build Leopold's railroads and harvest his rubber trees.

Kenya was different, and what made it different, in part, was its relationship to India. For most of its early years, it was administered via India, largely because it made sense from a logistical point of view. Though the British East Africa Company was chartered in

London in 1888, the initial currency used to run the colony was not the British Pound, but the Indian Rupee, and the colony's legal system was built on Indian Civil Procedure, not English Common Law. Most of the company's clerical and administrative staff, its clerks and accountants, all hailed from India as well. After a few years, the East Africa Company relocated its headquarters to Mombasa, a port city on Africa's coast, and those Indian clerks and accountants followed. So did more than 30,000 indentured Indian laborers who were recruited to build the Uganda Railway in 1895. After construction began, the rail soon climbed over six hundred miles up from the African coast, through the Western Highlands, all the way to the lush, fertile farmlands surrounding Lake Victoria. In the eight years it took to complete the project, over 2,500 of the Indian laborers died. Of those who didn't perish, many chose to stay and settle, largely in Mombasa or in the area of Nairobi, which had been founded in 1899 as a beachhead for the construction of the railway.

As the Indian workers cleared and settled the land, following behind them to own and occupy it were the European farmers. British East Africa, like Rhodesia to the south, became a white settler colony. While precious few whites were rushing to set up summer homes in the malarial rainforests of the Congo, Kenya's incredible beauty and rich, bountiful farmland enticed a large white minority to venture south and make it their home. It became a society of "spares," the flotsam and jetsam of the aristocracy, the second-born sons and the disappointments and the washouts. They all made their way to Kenya as expatriates, aiming to make the life there that they'd never be allowed to make back home. The Western Highlands, full of rich, volcanic soil, offered some of the best ranching and farming land anywhere on the whole continent. The spares arrived and cheated the Africans into selling large areas of land for a pittance. The native tribes who had occupied the territory for centuries, primarily the Kikuyu, were barred from owning the land on which they'd been born. They were pushed off into reservations and consigned to menial labor on the farms, which is how the Western Highlands became the "White Highlands."

Halfway up the ladder, sitting between the whites and the Africans as always, were the Indians. In addition to the initial population of colonial clerks and indentured laborers, a second wave of traders, merchants, and teachers was now streaming over from Gujarat and Punjab and elsewhere. They were Sikhs, Muslims, Hindus, all eager to capitalize on the prosperity and possibilities of the Kenyan frontier. Like the African natives, Indians were also barred from owning or cultivating agricultural land. However, they were permitted to own property in certain nonwhite areas in Nairobi. By the mid-1960s, many Indians owned nice properties in the heart of Nairobi. Immigrants who started out as street vendors soon grew to become retailers, wholesalers, manufacturers, and professionals. While the Africans owned nothing and the white settlers owned the farms and the large multinational concerns moving Kenya's exports around the globe, the Indians soon developed a near monopoly on small business trade. In Nairobi and Mombasa, if you bought something at a local retail store, odds were you were buying it from an Indian. By the time Nairobi established itself as one of the most economically vital cities in the region in the early 1900s, fully one-third of its population was Indian, and by and large, they prospered.

However, as my parents would learn all too well from the fate of ABC Bakery, economic prosperity without political power or the rights of citizenship made for a precarious existence at best. Without full participation in the legal and legislative processes of the colony, the Indian merchants would remain second-class citizens in the society that their labor had helped build.

In the wake of World War I, as the British East Africa Protectorate evolved into what would become the colony of Kenya, Indians who had amassed sufficient economic power to speak out began to do so. Absent the fear of brutal repression that existed in South Africa, they founded independent newspapers and started working through institutions like the East African Indian National Congress to agitate for political equality. As a result, in 1927, Indians won the right to five seats on the seventeen-seat colonial legislative council. Those seats, however, were appointed rather than elected. By whites. So one could hardly call their participation anything more than an appeasement measure.

Kenya's African subjects, meanwhile, continued to have no representation at all, and that clear difference in status was deliberately engineered by the British as part of a brutally effective divide-and-conquer strategy. So long as the Indians were given some measure of rights and status they would remain loyal to the Crown and not want to jeopardize that status by allying themselves with the indigenous Africans—the Kikuyu and the Luo and the other native tribes who were even more marginalized, exploited, and oppressed. Those indigenous Africans, for their part, would look on the Indians with antipathy and resentment for enjoying rights and privileges that had been denied to them, leaving the nonwhite majority unable to unite against the rather small white minority.

It was a complicated situation. In the words of scholar Mahmood Mamdani, Indians were "neither settler nor native." They were not the oppressors, nor were they the oppressed. Or, looked at from a different point of view, they were both the oppressors *and* the oppressed, at the same time, which sowed a great deal of confusion about where their loyalties and their aspirations should lie.

In any society, most people look up rather than down. We aspire to what we see above us, not what we are told is beneath us. The Indians living under British rule were no different. They wanted to go one step higher rather than one rung lower, and the wealth, power, and dominance of the British Empire put "Britishness" one step higher, which is why many Indians accepted the narratives of Black inferiority and cozied up to and emulated their colonial overseers, even as those overseers denigrated and exploited them in return. But whatever affection Indians had developed for the British, it was never reciprocated. Indians were expected to assimilate, speak the King's English, and study at British schools, but even as they did those things, none of it ever made them fully equal, politically, socially, or culturally. On the other hand, Indians in Africa could never be fully African, either. Even if they were stripped of the paltry political and economic rights accorded them by the British, they would still remain outsiders in a place that didn't necessarily want them.

More than anything, Indians were pragmatic. They couldn't afford idealism, and no one Indian was any one thing. On Monday, you were an Anglophile because you wanted your kids to go off and study at university in London. On Tuesday, you were a committed Indian nationalist because you went to an East African Indian National Congress meeting and marinated in the grievances and complaints of your countrymen. On Wednesday, you became a strident Pan-Africanist because you couldn't run a business when your Black employees and customers were getting arrested, beaten, and shot. Then on Thursday, you'd need to get a trade license approved to keep your business open to feed your family, so you'd put on your best English and go and curry favor with the British once again. You were forever going back and forth, caught in between, trying to survive, which in turn opened you up to accusations of playing both sides, of being untrustworthy and unprincipled.

As the struggle for independence began to break out across Africa in the wake of World War II, more and more Indians found themselves uncomfortable staying in the middle. And once the fight for Kenya's independence began in earnest, at some point you had to pick a side. As my father always told me, "In politics, if you sit on the fence, you get a splinter up your ass."

Before the war had even ended, the British tried to head off the independence movement by offering Africans token representation on the legislative council, starting with one seat in 1944 and expanding to eight by 1951. But these seats were appointed by the governor from a list of approved names. They offered no actual democratic input into the process, did little to pacify demands for equal treatment, and did nothing to address the one burning issue that was on everyone's mind: land. Land is sacred to Africans. The biodiversity of the environment and the role it plays in their folklore and ancestral traditions are vitally important, and when that land was taken from them, they had no recourse to get it back. This was true all over Africa, but with Kenya being a settler colony where whites moved in and pushed the natives out, the resentment and anger there was especially keen. Nowhere was this truer than in the White Highlands, which became the symbol of everything that colonialism had stolen.

The freedom struggle in Kenya did not start out as a struggle for Kenya's freedom. It began as a movement by the Kikuyus to get back their land in the White Highlands, a movement that would come to be known as the Mau Mau, a name that came from the Swahili phrase *Mzungo Aende Ulaya, Mwafrika Apate Uhuru*, which means "Foreigners go back to your land. Let the African be free." Mau Mau rebels began arming themselves and calling for violent resistance against the British. They launched attacks against colonial authorities and settlers as well as against fellow Kikuyu who were loyal to the British.

The response from the colonial government was brutal and swift. In October 1952, it declared a state of emergency that would last for the next eight years. African political parties were outlawed, and nearly eighty thousand men, mostly Kikuyu, were captured and re-located to "reeducation camps," the ostensible purpose of which was to rehabilitate them into good, submissive Africans. In reality they were forced labor camps where men were beaten and put to work building roads and airports and any other infrastructure the British required. In the process of being "reeducated," thousands of Africans died.

The brutality of Britain's crackdown, naturally, had the opposite of its intended effect. It did not quash the rebellion. It inflamed it, and what began as a regional fight over land reclamation quickly morphed into part of the global freedom struggle for African independence. Having just fought a war against Germany to liberate Jewish people from concentration camps, the British now found themselves having to make a moral case for concentration camps of their own, and the stated rationale for England's imperial adventure—that it had been the white man's burden to civilize his little brown brothers for whom Christ also died—began to collapse under the weight of its own hypocrisy.

When any civil rights movement or freedom struggle begins to take shape, one individual inevitably seems to find their way to the fore. They come to embody the movement's struggles while simultaneously serving as its moral compass, mouthpiece, ideologue, and lightning rod. In South Africa that person was Nelson Mandela, and in Kenya that person was Jomo Kenyatta. Born Kamau Wa Muigai, the Kikuyu tribesman adopted the name Jomo, meaning "burning spear," and Kenyatta, after the beaded Maasai belt he commonly wore. Kenyatta spent most of the 1920s and '30s between Nairobi and London, advocating for his tribe's interests from within the system, writing newspaper op-eds and testifying before the House of Commons. Stifled at every turn, he increasingly began to agitate outside the system as well, briefly joining the Communist Party and strategizing with the leading Black nationalist thinkers of the day, men like W. E. B. Du Bois of the United States and Kwame Nkrumah, the future leader of Ghana, with whom he organized the fifth Pan-African Congress in Manchester, England, in 1945.

In the wake of World War II, Kenyatta returned to Kenya, became the president of the newly formed political party the Kenya African Union, and quickly emerged as one of the major icons for the Africans' struggle to get their land back. Kenyatta advocated for a peaceful transition to independence; he was never formally affiliated with the Mau Mau rebellion, whose members found his nonviolent approach far too accommodating. But that fact didn't stop the British from conflating the two. In 1952, Kenyatta and several others were charged with leading the Mau Mau movement, put on trial, and sentenced to seven years in prison.

With Kenyatta and the Mau Maus leading the charge and making the necessary sacrifices, more and more of Kenya's Indians felt impelled to come down off the fence and join the fight. Again, this was likely due to a mix of pragmatism and idealism. Siding with the Africans against the British was clearly the right thing to do. It was also increasingly the prudent thing to do, since all across Africa it was becoming clear to everyone that colonial rule was going to exhaust itself sooner rather than later, and when the natives eventually rose to power, you didn't want to be seen as being on the side of the oppressors.

When Kenyatta was put on trial, of the seven people in his legal defense team, four were Indians, all of whom worked on the case pro bono. As in South Africa, many younger, more militant Indians joined the struggle in substantial ways. Makhan Singh, a Sikh, spearheaded an interracial trade union movement that included both Indians and Africans and was later incarcerated for selling arms and ammunition to the Mau Mau rebels. He went to jail with Kenyatta and was also sentenced to a seven-year term.

The era of the Mau Mau uprising was when Kenya's history intersected with my own. My great-uncle Habib—Rajabali's brother, with whom my father had lived during his first brief stay in the colony—immigrated to Kenya in 1951 and opened a dry-cleaning business, which soon brought him both financial success and a place of some prominence in Kenya's Indian community. Having lived through the political depredations of South Africa, Habib was determined to play a role in the Kenyan freedom struggle. His home was a meeting house and a way station for South African refugees and African dissidents and nationalists. He came to know Kenyatta, sent him provisions while he was in a detention camp, and helped the rebel leader's family by giving his daughter a job. He did the same for the children and families of several other freedom fighters. With the men confined to the camps, Habib set about getting their children into schools and finding them scholarships, all of which brought him under considerable scrutiny from the colonial authorities. Luckily, managing to avoid any serious trouble himself, by the end of the 1950s, Habib had successfully integrated himself into the social and political worlds of Nairobi, establishing the beachhead that would allow many other family members to join him in the years to come, including my parents.

From the time they fled South Africa for Kenya in 1961 and then left Kenya once again for Toronto nine years later, my parents' existence sat halfway between that of immigrants and that of refugees. Technically speaking, they were immigrants. They were never forced out of anywhere. They always left willingly and were always free to return; indeed, only a few months after the move to Kenya, my pregnant mother returned to Pretoria so she could give birth to my sister, Ishrath, there, which she did in order to be near her family and because my parents did not yet hold Kenyan citizenship. At the same time, on both occasions my parents' "voluntary" departures were made with deep senses of foreboding. Like the Jews who looked around Germany in 1933 and thought "This isn't going to end well," my parents packed their bags with the belief that it was better to leave as an immigrant while they still could than risk being forced out as a refugee later.

They moved in with my dad's sister, who had a home in Parklands, a formerly whites-only residential area that was becoming increasingly mixed. (Technically, the law still prohibited nonwhites from owning property in the area, but with independence growing more likely by the day, no prosecutors were bringing those cases to trial anymore. By that point Indian families could live anywhere they could afford. Black people still lived mostly in informal settlements around the city.)

From the vantage point of two people who'd grown up in Mar-abastad, Nairobi, despite the underlying tension, felt like the Promised Land. But that didn't mean life was easy. While in Pretoria, they had been prosperous but unfree; now they were free but not prosperous. When my parents made the move to Kenya, their money wasn't allowed to leave South Africa with them. The pittance that the government had paid for the ABC Bakery had to stay in South African banks because of currency controls, and it was only with a great deal of legal wrangling that the South African government agreed to transfer a sum of £250 a month to my father in Kenya. Based on the expectation of that income, my father decided to go back into the baking business. Borrowing heavily, he bought a new property, invested in some secondhand industrial dough mixers and ovens, and opened his doors for business. He even kept the same name, ABC Bakery, hoping to salvage at least the memory of what his family had built and lost in South Africa.

It was a small operation at the beginning, and it never got bigger. Almost as soon as he'd launched, the South African government stopped sending him his money. My father was stuck with no funds and a lot of debt, and the new bakery went under in less than a year. My parents lost everything. They had to move out of the place they'd found and into a guest house behind some other family's home. My dad's sister was paying the rent and covering their bills. My sister remembers she had to share a bed with my parents, and it was one of those deals where you had to crawl across the bed to get to the doorway because the bed took up the whole room.

To keep them afloat, my mother found work, first at a perfume shop and then as a reservations and ticketing agent for KLM airlines. Meanwhile, my father turned to the Help Wanted ads in the paper and found a listing for a job at Erskine and Price, a commercial food manufacturer that that had been one of the vendors for his bakery. They were looking for a factory manager. My father owed this company a considerable amount of money, but he went in to apply and said, "You know me. I owe you money. But that's lost, and I want the job." And they gave him the job, which, luckily, was a job that came with not only a good salary but also a house and a car.

From that point on, my parents started building their lives back. My mother stayed in the travel business. My father eventually left Erskine and Price and started his own real estate company, VelCo Properties Limited. He brokered rentals and sales for residential properties. Once he was a bit more established, he started buying older homes, living in them while fixing them up, then selling them and moving on to the next one. They were never quite as well off as they'd been in South Africa, but that was OK because every morning they could wake up and console themselves with the fact that life was better than if they had stayed.

During the years my parents spent struggling in Kenya, life under Apartheid only grew worse. In the wake of the Sharpeville Massacre, Nelson Mandela and the ANC had abandoned the use of nonviolent resistance. With the formation of the group's military wing, uMkhonto we Sizwe, they launched a campaign of sabotage against the regime, detonating bombs in government buildings around the country. Then, in August 1962, shortly after returning from secret paramilitary training in Algeria, Nelson Mandela was arrested, put on trial, and imprisoned. My uncle Rehmtulla managed to avoid a similar fate, but only by being coerced by the government into, essentially, taking a plea bargain. Like thousands of other South Africans, he formally disavowed his activist youth and pledged to keep his head down and trouble the regime no more. It was a bitter pill to swallow, but he did it in order to protect his family from further persecution and to keep his children safe.

Outside of South Africa, freedom was on the march, but it often came at a hefty price. Algeria won its independence from France in 1962, but only after a bloody insurgency that dragged on for eight years. When Belgium pulled out of the Congo in 1960, no preparations were made for an orderly transfer of power. Civil war broke out among the rival tribal factions, plunging the nation into five years of chaos that would result in the death of over one hundred thousand Congolese, including Prime Minister Patrice Lumumba, who was assassinated.

Even in colonies where the transfer of power was relatively uneventful, there remained the open question about what would happen next. Which of the tribal factions would dominate? Would they maintain a healthy multiparty democracy or succumb to single-party cronyism and corruption? Would the new government align itself with the capitalist democracies of the West or the communist and socialist dictatorships of the East? Would they work with the existing European banks and multinationals or toss everyone out and nationalize their economies?

In Kenya, the British had initially planned on a gradual turnover. They would give Black people token, symbolic participation in the government, then take ten, maybe fifteen, maybe twenty years to train up a class of technocrats capable of operating the levers of government. In other words, they would leave "once the Black people were ready." That didn't happen. Regardless of the chaos happening in Congo and elsewhere, once Black Kenyans realized they had the UK back on its heels, they refused to wait. They told the British,

"Don't worry if we're not ready. That's not your business. Give us our independence. We will mismanage ourselves the way we feel. It's our right to mismanage ourselves rather than have you mismanage us. We want independence now. We're tired of waiting. This is our right."

In the streets of Nairobi, as my parents walked to work or ran their daily errands, they could feel the tension. Black workers were marching through the streets waving flags, while Black politicians rode around in open cars giving speeches about their right to be free. Nearly all of the white people were hightailing it out of the country, filling up the boats and planes headed back to Europe, but the whites who remained—mostly the farmers, the landowners with a lifetime's investment to protect—would come into town in Jeeps wearing fatigues and a side belt with a gun. Overseeing these opposing factions were the British colonial soldiers, young guys, some of them barely eighteen years old, roaming the city with rifles. And moving in and among all of them were the Indians, the outsiders who were asking themselves, "What about our businesses? What about the corner shops we started? Will the children that we educated overseas be able to come back and practice medicine and law? What's going to happen to us?"

Given everything that might have gone wrong, in the end, luckily, Kenya was the powder keg that didn't go off. In May 1963, Kenyatta was elected president under a constitution that gave Kenya autonomous self-government. With that milestone achieved, a date was set for Kenya to become fully independent on December 12. The British, with many ongoing economic concerns in East Africa to protect, had a vested interest in a smooth transition. They didn't cut and run. Right up until the moment of departure, they were still repairing the roads. For those first elections, they sent in experts to train the local poll workers and vote counters. They sent in independent monitors to ensure that the election would be legitimate and free from ballot stuffing and other forms of fraud. When the reins of power were handed over, Kenyatta had assembled a cabinet of ministers educated at some of the best universities in the world. Njoroge Mungai, the health minister, had gone to Stanford. Kenyatta himself had attended the London School of Economics, and, separately, had studied anthropology. On that level, Kenya was well prepared. More importantly, in his campaign appearances and public speeches, Kenyatta said and did all the right things. He didn't drum up antiwhite or anti-Indian fears to consolidate power. He made overtures to brotherhood and peace, using slogans like *harambee*, meaning "let us pull together," and *uhuru na umoja*, "freedom with unity."

The weeks leading up to the official handover were like one big party. My parents and their friends were ecstatic, celebrating day and night because they had never seen independence happen before firsthand. Given everything they had lived through, the transfer of power from a colonial government to the local people was an earthshaking event. When the appointed day finally arrived, dignitaries and diplomats flew in from all over the world, and as the clock struck midnight, ringing in the early morning of December 12, 1963, the new Kenyan flag was raised for the first time at Nairobi's Independence Stadium. The people of Kenya were free. What that would mean was anyone's guess. With most of the white people long gone, the Africans and the Indians would have to figure it out.

On the morning of December 12, 1963, when the sun rose on an independent Kenya for the first time, there were over three hundred thousand Indians living in this new country that was—and in many ways was not—their home. They knew, however, that they would have to make it a home one way or another, for there was no turning around. Jawaharlal Nehru, India's first prime minister after independence, had enough challenges to manage, and in his speeches he explicitly told members of the Indian diaspora in Africa, "You don't belong in India. You are not Indians. You've gone off to Africa, and now you are Africans. Fight for Africans. Live with them. Make Africa your home."

So they did, and my parents did as well. They applied for citizenship and were granted it. But citizenship, as I would learn during my time in Minneapolis, is many things. First and foremost, it's a legal status that allows—and I would say *obliges*—you to participate in the civic life of a nation. Second, but equally important, it is also a sense of belonging, a kinship with your fellow countrymen. It's easy to have one without the other. You can enjoy the legal status of citizenship and still not feel any sense of belonging, as was the case of the young Black man I met in Minneapolis. Conversely, you may lack the legal status of citizenship, yet still feel passionately that a place is your home, as was the case with the "Dreamers," the young people brought illegally into America as children; despite the Dreamers' lack of legal residency, America was nonetheless the only home they'd ever known.

In South Africa, my parents had been citizens, albeit second-class ones, on paper. But they were allowed no sense of belonging in the country. Now, Kenya had offered them true citizenship, the right to vote, the right to do business, the right to participate in the electoral process. But would it offer them a sense of belonging? How would these Gujarati Indian Muslims *become* African? Every group within the Indian diaspora—the Hindus, the Bengalis, the Punjabis, the

Sikhs—would answer that question differently. Some had no desire to become African at all; they were content to stay in their ethnic enclaves, make their little money, and do their own thing. My parents, having previously been confined as prisoners inside their own ethnic enclave, were determined to do the opposite.

Ismaili Muslims are not the Muslims most Westerners think of when they think of Muslims. We are a subsect, a minority of a minority. The vast majority of Muslims, around 85 percent, are Sunni Muslims. The remaining 15 percent are Shia, and within Shias, the overwhelming majority are non-Ismailis. So out of around 1.6 billion Muslims worldwide, Ismailis number only about 12 million souls. During my parents' time in Kenya, the total population of Ismailis was probably around eight thousand to ten thousand, so they were not a big community. But Ismailis, for reasons this story will soon illustrate, have always had an impact much greater than their numbers alone would suggest.

On issues of theology and religious doctrine, there are a number of distinctions that separate Ismailis from other Shias and from Sunnis, but for our purposes here, what matters most about the Ismaili sect are two important characteristics: (1) its institutional hierarchy, and (2) its attitude toward the modern, secular world. Like the Roman Catholics, Ismailis are a top-down organization, with one important person calling the shots for millions of adherents around the globe. The spiritual head, or imam, of the Ismaili Muslims is known as the Aga Khan. Aga Khan is a bestowed title. Not all imams have been Aga Khans; in fact, there have only been four of them throughout history. The Aga Khan is of direct, lineal descent from the Prophet Mohammed. He is not only a spiritual leader but a secular one as well, guiding the community in how to live their lives in the material world, adhering to certain principles in order to have the proper balance between faith and life. Throughout history, the Aga Khans have traditionally been very modern and worldly in identifying the degree to which their communities need to resettle and move and engage with other cultures. Ismailis might be thought of as the polar opposites of Islamic fundamentalists like the Taliban. Instead of being so rooted in tradition that you literally have to make war with modernity, Ismailis are concerned with how you take the core principles of your faith and apply them to the modern world so that you will continue to thrive.

The Ismailis of my parents' generation were fortunate to have as their leader a man who was young, upbeat, and especially forward-thinking. Karim al-Husayn Shah was only twenty-one years old, a student at Harvard, when he was chosen to succeed his grandfather as the fourth Aga Khan in 1958. As this young man stepped onto the world stage, the fate of the Ismaili diaspora in the upheaval of Africa was at or near the top of his list of concerns. As he saw it, the idea of Indians becoming Africans was perfectly natural. He had a pragmatic view toward what it would take for Ismaili Muslims to thrive as a part of this far-flung diaspora around the world, and his message was that the best way to preserve the nucleus of what was important in Ismaili culture was to be willing to adapt and change at the margins of that culture. He believed that a person's Ismaili-ness was rooted in their spiritual identity and religious faith, but when it came to living in this world, Ismailis owed their loyalty and their cultural identity to the country responsible for their well-being. To live in any other way was to succumb to reactionary nostalgia. His attitude toward the British was sober and forward-thinking. The British colonization of India and East Africa was a great and terrible crime, no doubt. But it happened. There is no undoing the past. There is only the chance to build a better future. We live in the world as it is now, and in the world as it is now, English is the dominant language. It's the international language of business. So: learn English. Kenya was now a European-style parliamentary democracy. So: embrace European democratic norms. Don't close yourself off from the cultures and the people that surround you. Work with them. Be compassionate to them. Educate your children to understand them and integrate with them. If you participate in civil society where you are on the best terms that are available to you at the moment, that will allow you to prosper and your spiritual life as an Ismaili will prosper right along with you.

The primary tool that Ismailis used to put this philosophy in practice was, and still is, the institution. It's almost impossible to be an Ismaili all by yourself. I mean, I suppose you *can*, but you don't get nearly all the benefits. Ismailis are born community organizers. The myth of the American dream is that of the self-made man, the idea that individuals can and should lift themselves up by their own bootstraps. Ismailis, like Mormons and Jews and Catholics, know that bootstrapping only really works as a community effort, with the strong lifting up the weak, the experienced reaching out to the new, and everyone rowing together in the same direction. We put a tremendous amount of stock in resilience and self-reliance but primarily as a group, which is why you can drop in on any Ismaili community anywhere in the world, from Pakistan to Tajikistan to Dallas, Texas, and you will immediately find a jamatkhana and a school and a health service. You'll find blood drives and school boards and job fairs and marriage counseling and vaccination clinics. In certain parts of the developing world, you might also find something like a bank or a credit union, giving out microfinance loans to entrepreneurs who can't get credit through more mainstream institutions. There are always civil-service structures designed to serve the local population. Being a community of organizers, the Ismaili community itself is naturally very organized, very structured, very hierarchical. From the Aga Khan at the top all the way down to the local Sunday school teacher, there's a clear chain of command and an open channel of communication, which means this tiny group is able to raise money and allocate and deploy its resources at a level far above what its size would suggest.

In the separate and unequal world of South Africa, these qualities served the Ismaili community well. Self-reliance suited the Apartheid system. You took care of yourself because you had to take care of yourself. The state was not only failing to provide you with basic services but also was actively denying them to you. In Kenya, the Aga Khan believed that the best way to help this segregated, postcolonial society knit itself together would be to take the services Ismaili institutions had to offer and extend them to the broader population, lifting the whole country up as one. Guided by this principle, Ismaili Kenyans rapidly began to expand their institutional footprint well beyond the boundaries of their own community.

Recruiting the best teachers available and paying handsome salaries, the Aga Khan opened schools in Kenya, Tanzania, and Uganda at the primary, secondary, and postsecondary levels. They were all quickly recognized as top schools, and from the start, they were open to all races because the Aga Khan firmly believed that if Mohammed and Jonathan and Njoroge can take school certificate together and play football together, chances are that they would get to know and understand each other far better than their parents were able to. He understood that building the foundation of any functional society was to raise a new generation that understood and empathized with each other and saw eye to eye on the future of the country.

Kenyan Ismailis also oversaw the building of the first multiracial hospital in all of East Africa. Located near where my parents lived in Parklands, it housed the region's first-ever nursing program for non-European women, bringing in Indian and African students from Zambia and Malawi and Rhodesia and Tanzania to study and become nurses. It was also the hospital where I would be born, in 1969.

With help from Canada's *Globe and Mail* and a few other institutions, the Aga Khan also started the first truly independent press in East Africa, *The Nation*, a newspaper run by Africans, for Africans. It was not an Ismaili venture, but the Aga Khan was sophisticated enough to recognize that making Kenya work for Africans was a prerequisite to making Kenya work for Ismailis and everyone else.

And the list goes on. Under an umbrella organization known as the Aga Khan Development Network, Ismailis built up a whole range of businesses and philanthropies. Banks, insurance companies, you name it, most of which are still operating successfully in Africa and around the developed world to this day. All of this is to say that Ismaili Muslims were all-in on the postcolonial Kenyan project.

My parents were excited by all of it. They were never what you would call "well off" in Nairobi, but they were back on their feet and getting by OK, and with their careers going reasonably well, they were as actively involved as they could be, in both Ismaili institutions and in any aspect of civil society where they thought they could make a difference. At the time of independence, Kenya had three separate trade organizations, one for Blacks, one for Asians, and one for whites. My father joined all three, working with a special task force to bring them together to work as one, which they did, forming an umbrella organization called the Kenya Committee Business Association. My mother, working at a local travel agency, joined the Black women's organization, Maendeleo Ya Wanawake, an advocacy group working to provide education for women, job training for women, and infrastructure for women to run for Parliament, which many women did.

My parents also got into politics in a major way. They became members of Kenyatta's party, the Kenya African National Union, and began volunteering for campaigns, helping drive people to the polling stations, and doing everything they could to make democracy thrive. Eventually, my aunt's husband, my dad's brother-in-law, a man named Amir Jamal became a member of parliament representing Kisumu, a city on Lake Victoria in western Kenya.

Above and beyond their institutional and political work, my parents were thrilled to be free from the prison of segregation. They hosted big dinner parties at their home, inviting everyone they knew from the worlds of business and politics, including members of parliament and local ministers. They wanted to be part of the informal social fabric that would hold this new society together.

In doing this, unfortunately, my parents and their fellow Ismailis were a distinct minority. As far as the other Indian communities were concerned, many of them said, "If they throw us out, we'll go. Until they throw us out, we'll remain. We don't want to mix with Black people. We don't want our sons to marry Black women. We don't want our daughters to marry Black men. We have our shop. We're making money. We're happy." Theirs was an insular, even bigoted viewpoint. And unfortunately for those Indians, too many Africans felt the same way about them.

———————

Kenya did well economically after independence. The place never stopped growing. If you bought property in Nairobi in the 1960s, you became rich. The problem was that Kenya's success wasn't well distributed. Many Africans on the lower end of the economic scale were left out, and when those Africans came into the city from the native villages to look for jobs, the people they saw who had all those jobs were Indian.

All through the 1950s and '60s, depending on what part of Nairobi you were in, whenever you walked into any small shop or retail establishment, the person you saw behind the cash register was Indian. The real economic exploiters of Kenya were the British and the other European spares who'd tagged along on their colonial adventure. They owned the hundred-acre farms and the big multinationals. Even after independence, they controlled the extractive industries that siphoned millions of dollars a year out of the Kenyan economy and sent it off to London. But the young African guy coming into the big city didn't see that. What he saw was the Indian guy and his wife running a shop, and that made him angry.

It's hard to envy or be resentful of something you cannot see. When people get pissed off, it's rarely because they're looking ten rungs up the ladder, pissed off at the guy who's way up there hogging everything to himself. They're looking one rung up the ladder and thinking, "This guy's in my way." And that's what you had in Kenya. The disenfranchised and the dispossessed who'd been left out of the country's success didn't aspire to run a big auto manufacturer like Mercedes-Benz or an agricultural machinery conglomerate like Caterpillar. They aspired to run a small shop or work as a clerk somewhere, and from what they could see with their own two eyes, it was obvious to them that the Indians were occupying that rung and standing in their way.

Where Kenya succeeded politically and economically during the 1960s, it failed socially and culturally. For all of Kenyatta's lofty talk of harambee and uhuru na umoja, Kenyans themselves failed to do the hard work of building an integrated, pluralistic society where people of different ethnic and religious backgrounds respected and understood each other. Other than the small handful of people like my parents, most of Kenya's groups wanted to remain isolated from one another, which was bound to cause problems. Black people needed independence, land, and businesses, but there was little co-operative social infrastructure to work together to make that happen.

There are two different narratives you can use when describing the history of the Indian diaspora in Africa. The first is that the Indians, forced into indentured slavery after their own native land was plundered and decimated by the British, were exploited right alongside the Africans. Dying by the thousands to build the British railroads and work the Afrikaners' gold mines, Indians were nonetheless instrumental to the African freedom struggle, using the money from their subsistence economy to build the movement and help develop the political consciousness to get to independence. And if Indians enjoyed some small measure of elevated status over the native tribes, that status was only accorded to them as part of a divide-and-conquer strategy designed by the British to keep all the Black and brown people apart, which was all the more reason for those Black and brown people to see themselves as political allies once the British were gone.

The other narrative, the purely Pan-African narrative, goes something like this: "You Indians were colonizers and exploiters, too. You're parasites. You only came over here to make money. You were never fighting for Black people. You were only fighting for yourselves. You were living in better areas and you drove better cars and your children went to better schools and at the end of the day you were nothing more than the bootlickers and lackeys of the British. The African freedom struggle was won by Africans and Africans alone, so why don't all you brown people go back to where you came from?"

Depending on which set of facts you use and how you want to frame them, either of those narratives can seem entirely plausible. And then, underneath both of those narratives lies the far more complicated truth, which is that day to day most Indians were simply trying to survive—and, unfortunately, just as happened under Apartheid, when you're trying to survive inside an unjust and immoral system, very often your actions have the effect of bolstering and perpetuating that system, no matter what your intentions may be.

When someone doesn't know you, it's easy for them to believe the worst about you, and the fact that Kenya remained so socially segregated and stratified allowed politicians to play on people's resentments and fears. Kenyatta didn't, but the right-wing reactionaries who wanted to challenge him did. As the honeymoon of independence wore off, by the mid- to late 1960s, "Africa for Africans" became the battle cry of the indigenous militants. If you were an Indian, you'd have to listen to third-rate politicians talking shit about you on the radio from morning to night. It was in the newspapers and on television, too.

"We've got shortages in the economy," these demagogues would say. "And it's because the Indians are hoarding. The Indians have got all the money. All they want is to take all your money." Everything that had gone wrong since independence was the Indians' fault because they were controlling the economy. Indians were the stepchildren of the empire, the colonial hangover, the bad aftertaste of the British. "Let's get rid of them," the demagogues would say, "and take over their shops."

When I talk to my father or my aunts and uncles or any other Indians I meet who lived through that time, they truly did believe that Kenya was going to end up better than it did. When they saw the Aga Khan opening these Ismaili institutions, they felt proud. They believed in his vision of a society where Black, white, and brown kids could all go to school together and learn to build a better future than the one they'd inherited. The tragedy is that the better future they envisioned was entirely possible. But as history has shown, time and again, racist words have racist consequences.

For my parents, the first unsettling signs came out of Zanzibar, off the coast of Tanzania. The sultan and his government, which was principally made up of the island's Arab population, were overthrown by Black insurgents who overran the cities, looting Arab- and Indian-owned homes and businesses and murdering Arab and Indian civilians. Once they took control, the rebels, who were now the senior government officials, started kidnapping young Indian girls, saying they were taking them for their wives.

Not long after, in 1967, Tanzania president Julius Nyerere implemented what was known as the Arusha Declaration, a sweeping socialist nationalization of the country's industry, intended to wipe away the stain of colonialism and Africanize the economy. It collectivized the country's farmland and said the state should have exclusive control of all property. Many Indians had their homes and other properties stripped away from them. A year later in Uganda, where anti-Indian sentiment would soon reach its fever pitch, the government passed a draconian "Africanisation in Commerce and Industry" law, which introduced onerous work-permit and trade-license requirements on Indian-owned businesses, endangering the ability of Indians to continue to make a living there.

No one could blame the Africans for wanting to take ownership of their countries after decades of exploitation, and in truth, many of these drastic actions were taken because England reneged on its promises to provide the necessary aid to facilitate a smooth transition to independence. Still, none of that mattered much to the Indian families staying awake at night wondering if their properties—or worse, their daughters—were going to be taken from them in the morning.

By 1968, after the events in Zanzibar, and then Tanzania and Uganda, East Africa's Indians found themselves in the same quandary faced by every marginalized ethnic group being demonized and vilified by the powers that be. How bad is it going to get? Do we hope for the best or assume the worst? Should we stay, or should we go? One by one, a slow drip of Indian families started lining up to try to get out of East Africa. But they had limited options. Most no longer had full Indian citizenship, and in his speeches, Prime Minister Nehru had made it abundantly clear that India didn't want them back.

The logical destination for those looking to get out was the United Kingdom. Kenya, as a former British colony, was now a part of what had become known as the British Commonwealth, the family of independent nations that had once been ruled as pieces of the empire. As subjects of the Commonwealth, Kenya's Indians had the right, in theory, to immigrate to the UK. But the English, seeing the wave of Indians preparing to come their way, suddenly got very busy closing their doors. Under the leadership of conservative minister Enoch Powell, a racist fearmonger for the ages, an anti-Indian immigration campaign started up and spread across the UK. In his infamous "Rivers of Blood" speech, Powell declared that if all these brown people were allowed in, England would lose its identity and become a "colored country," a degenerate, mongrelized nation, with the whole of the Indian Ocean washed up on its shores.

Powell's campaign for tighter immigration controls led to the passing of the Commonwealth Immigration Act of 1968, which limited immigration to those who had a parent or grandparent who was born in or was a citizen of the UK. The bill sailed through Parliament in three days, supported by the leadership of both the Labour and Conservative Parties. In other words, the general attitude of the British government was, "Yes, you have the right to come back here, sort of, but not yet. When we're ready, we'll call you." Even Indians who held valid British passports were denied entry. The passport numbers that these Indians had been issued were all coded as "GBD," and for years nobody knew why or what it meant. As they soon learned, it was a "British Overseas Territories Citizen" passport, a marker of lower status. Everybody with a GBD passport would not be allowed to come into England.

When I've asked my parents to describe their life in Kenya in the 1960s, they've described it as idyllic. They had their family. They'd rebuilt their lives. They had the true freedom and citizenship they'd been denied in South Africa. Kenya had welcomed them and they'd made it their home. They had no desire to leave and saw no reason to leave. Then they started to see the writing on the wall.

The first warning came not long after the events in Zanzibar. Two senior members of the Kenyan cabinet with whom they were friendly, Joseph Nyagah and Lawrence Sagini, often came to my parents' house for tea or dinner. One evening they simply said, "You should consider another place to go." It wasn't a threat; it was concern. It was "We like you, and we don't want anything bad to happen to you."

My parents had another friend whose warning was even more dire. Through my father's real estate business, he had started brokering properties for several of the foreign embassies and consulates, and one of his clients was the Canadian High Commission. He became close friends with the people there, especially one of the midlevel bureaucrats, a Lebanese Canadian guy named Albert Nasarallah who often came to our house. One day at dinner, Nasarallah told my parents point-blank, "You need to get out of this country."

"But we're happy here," my parents replied. "We don't have a problem."

"You do have a problem," he said. "You just don't know it. We talk to the Black politicians, and the things we hear in private are troubling."

He encouraged my parents to apply for landed immigrant status in Canada, "landed status" being a residency permit that was only one step shy of full citizenship and that led very quickly to full citizenship; it would provide my parents with the right to stay in Canada, the right to work, and even the right to vote. Nasarallah was adamant about it and kept pressing my parents, almost to the point of twisting their arms, dragging them into his office on a Sunday to fill out the forms and put them in the mail so that they would at least have the option if they needed it.

Over the months that followed, as the paperwork was being processed, my parents started seriously considering whether they should leave. By that point, my mother was pregnant with me, so they now had my future to consider as well. Many Indian people never considered leaving at all. They were happy to stay in their own enclaves and make their money and do their thing. If that had been my parents' attitude, they might have stayed on in Kenya for the rest of their lives, which many Indian people did. But my parents wanted more than that. They wanted to participate fully in society. They wanted a place to belong. They had grown up with racial nationalism and ethnic chauvinism and had no stomach for it. They wanted to know that they lived in a place where their daughter—and, soon enough, their son—would truly be free.

Everything about their lives in Kenya up to that point would have indicated that they'd have a great life there. Economically they were doing fine. They didn't fear for their livelihoods or their personal safety. They weren't holed up in some domestic compound behind gated walls. They had lots of friends, played tennis, got invited to the club for tea. Their day-to-day experiences were quite positive, but seeing what was happening to Indians in the surrounding countries, my parents had a creeping, nebulous fear that the good times weren't going to last, that it all might go horribly wrong.

In terms of allaying those fears, Kenyatta proved to be a disappointment. He was a good politician and a popular figure, always happy to talk about harambee and uhuru na umoja. He would stand smiling next to the Aga Khan at the ribbon-cutting ceremony for a new hospital or a new school. But he was never committed to the vision of a thriving pluralistic society. Kenyatta never exploited racial divisions. He never incited violence from one group against another. But he was still a Pan-Africanist and a populist. No Indian ever became a minster in his cabinet. Not one. And when demagogues like Uganda's Idi Amin started stirring up hatred against the Indians, Kenyatta didn't stand up and say, "This is wrong. Don't do it." He just sat quiet.

More and more, the government was "Africanizing" and "Kenyanizing" different jobs and business sectors, which really meant de-Indianizing those jobs and business sectors. To my parents it soon became clear: "We are not going to realize our potential here," they said. "And given how much we've already given up because we weren't going to realize our potential in South Africa, why don't we try to find somewhere to go where we can realize our potential."

While all this was percolating, my father took a trip with his brother-in-law to Uganda, and as the border guard checked their papers, he said something to the effect of "You know this is our country, right? You don't belong here." And that's when they knew for sure. After that trip, they said, "It's time to leave."

At that point, for a young Ismaili Muslim couple who'd known nothing but Africa their whole lives, Canada might as well have been the far side of the moon. They'd never seen a professional hockey game, and I doubt they could have told you how to spell *Saskatchewan*. But while they waited for the paperwork to go through and for me to be born, they took my sister for a visit. Even though it was the dead of the Canadian winter, they found the country welcoming and beautiful, and they said, "Let's give it a try." My father's mother, Jena, despite having other children who weren't yet ready to leave, decided she'd join my parents in Canada when the time came. I was born a few months later, in October 1969. That made five of us. We received our landed immigrant papers shortly thereafter.

In the meantime, my parents got ready. My father started making preparations to leave. He sold his business to his brother-in-law, Ameer Keshavjee. My father even started taking French classes at the Alliance Française in Nairobi, while my sister, who was then in fourth grade, started taking after-school French lessons as well.

By August 1970, we were all packed up and ready to go. Then, a week before we left for Canada, Rehmtulla had a heart attack, and we went back to South Africa to see him. It was the only trip I would take to South Africa before Mandela finally walked free. We stayed in Rehmtulla's house. He had actually done reasonably well, all things considered. Because he hadn't left the country, he'd been able to keep the money he got when ABC Bakery closed, and he was running a small café. But his health was failing and he still couldn't get his passport to travel. My father appealed to the Canadian High Commission office in Pretoria, and they offered to welcome Rehmtulla to Canada as a political prisoner fleeing persecution. So that paperwork was put in motion, and he and his family would follow us to Canada a couple of years later. My parents said goodbye to South Africa one last time; then, we flew back to Nairobi, picked up my grandmother, and from there headed on to Toronto.

In the end, it would turn out that our timing was perfect. Just as my parents had left South Africa right before the crackdown that put Nelson Mandela in jail and broke the back of the resistance movement, we got out of Kenya not a moment too soon. The anti-Asian sentiment that had been simmering across East Africa finally exploded the following year, on Saturday, August 5, 1972. On that day, Ugandan strongman Idi Amin, who had seized power in a coup the year before, declared that God had commanded him to expel all Asians from the country. Uganda's eighty thousand Indians had ninety days to leave. Or else. He accused them of "sabotaging Uganda's economy and encouraging corruption" and declared that he was "giving Uganda back to ethnic Ugandans."

Amin's rule in Uganda had been a reign of terror for some time, with thousands of people imprisoned without trial and political opponents murdered or mysteriously disappeared. Despite the fact that Amin was an obvious madman, many native Ugandans held him up as a hero, the man who would avenge them after years of colonial exploitation and misrule. In what was called Operation Mafuta Mingi, Ugandan soldiers launched a campaign of theft, harassment, brutality, and rape against Asian residents, driving them from their homes and out of the country. Tens of thousands of people were uprooted overnight. They fled with nothing more than what they could carry on their backs and stuff into their pockets. They left their homes, their corner shops, their medical practices. The most successful among them, the ones who'd been the most reluctant to leave because they had the most to lose, walked away from multimillion-dollar factories and manufacturing concerns. Like my father and grandfather watching ABC Bakery being torn to the ground, they saw their whole lives brought to nothing in the blink of an eye.

Some fled to the airport, hoping to catch the first flights out of the country. Countless others flooded onto trains into Kenya, only to arrive at the train station in Nairobi and be escorted directly to the airport and told to leave. Kenyatta, in his final disappointment, declared that Kenya was not a dumping ground for Uganda's unwanted people, leaving Kenya's Indians feeling none too good about their position in that country. Thousands of Kenya's Indians started packing their suit-cases as well.

For the Indians lucky enough to escape Amin's soldiers, now came the real problem. Over fifty thousand of them still had British citizenship, but they held D passports, meaning the UK didn't want to let them in. Over twenty thousand of the refugees had taken up Ugandan citizenship, and once Uganda delegitimated their passports, they immediately became stateless. Stranded, they went from em-bassy to embassy, begging. They went to the African governments, the Indian and Pakistani governments, and the British government, and all the countries did was pass the buck to one another. Nobody wanted these people. They had no idea who or what they were, what they were supposed to do, or where they were supposed to go. Thanks to my parents' foresight, my sister and I were long gone and safe from all this chaos. Even better than that, the Velshis were already halfway around the world, standing on a train platform, ready to welcome these people with open arms.

5

42 Hoyle Avenue

─────────────

I grew up at 42 Hoyle Avenue in Toronto, Canada, and the first of every December my grandmother Jena would be out on the front porch of our bungalow hanging up our Christmas decorations. She had a wreath that she'd put on the front door, lights to decorate the front windows, an artificial tree that would go up in the living room—all in keeping with the neighborhood. Hoyle Avenue was a charming one-block-long street in North Toronto. Everybody lived in modest bungalows like ours, built on narrow lots with small front yards, all of them thrown up after the Second World War as subsidized housing for returning soldiers and their families, who were mostly working class and mostly Presbyterian. It was a WASPy street, so you never saw the big, garish displays with full-on, lit-up Santa and Rudolph out on the lawn, and the same was true of my grandmother's tastes, though our wreath was plastic and most of the other houses had real ones that looked much nicer. On a scale of one to ten, I'd say her Christmas display was a respectable four.

When I was growing up at 42 Hoyle, Jena was the unbroken chain to our Indian heritage and our culture and our past. She was my living link to my grandfather Rajabali, whom I never knew since he died before I was born. She wore a sari every day of her life. She was always in the kitchen, cooking up curries. She took me to Indian movies at Indian theaters where the concession stands had Indian snacks, which I enjoyed and would eat while I kept her company.

But she also loved Christmas. Some Christmases my grandmother wasn't around, because she would go stay with my aunt in Nairobi, and, if I recall correctly, in those years my parents would do the lights but not the tree. So they were sort of into it, but she was the driving force. I probably was, too, in the end. Because there were gifts and some sense that there was a Santa Claus, and what kid doesn't want presents from a jolly fat man in a red suit?

Sometimes this was a point of conversation when we would go to the jamatkhana. Other Muslims asked us why we participated in this non-Muslim holiday. But it was never a big deal. It might seem at first glance like an attempt at assimilation. But there was little evidence that my family was trying to hide who we were or pretend that we were something we were not out of fear of being different. And I don't ever remember my parents or grandmother urging me to do anything to "fit in."

Christmas decorations aside, 42 Hoyle Avenue was very much the home of newly arrived immigrants, by which I mean inside it was crowded. All of the bungalows on Hoyle Avenue were 1,250 square feet with an upstairs, a ground floor, two bathrooms, three bedrooms, and an unfinished basement that everybody at some point finished and used as a living area. But unlike the WASPy families with just one or maybe two kids, in our house my parents had one bedroom, my sister had another, and I shared a third with my grandmother. On top of which we always had at least one cousin or aunt or uncle, and sometimes three or four, coming through to stay for a week or a month or longer. Yet somehow we managed. The house was like an airplane. There was a storage space for everything. It never felt cluttered, and it never felt as crowded as it was.

Culturally speaking, inside the home we were Indian. On top of that, we had our Kenyan decor and our dinner table conversations about South Africa, which was erupting in new spasms of violence seemingly every day. But outside in the neighborhood, the Kenyan and the African stuff didn't matter. For the purposes of our neighbors, we were simply Indian. The fact that my parents spoke Gujarati and not Hindi, that we were Muslim and not Hindu, that we were technically from Africa and had never set foot on the actual subcontinent of India, none of those specifics registered with people. We were just "Indian."

In fact, from the time we first arrived, and for many years thereafter, Toronto was so white that the different gradations between all the different kinds of white people were the thing that mattered. People would introduce themselves by saying "I'm Irish," or "I'm English," or "We're Scottish." And they had the accents to prove it. The English people would gripe about the Scottish people and the Scottish people would gripe about the Irish people and the Irish Catholics would gripe about the Irish Protestants and the Irish Protestants would go back the other way, all of which was completely puzzling to me because they all just looked like white people, same as how we were "just Indian" to them.

Parts of Toronto had begun to change. There was a smattering of Chinese and Italians here and there, a sprinkling of Greeks and

Portuguese. If you wanted to find them, all you had to do was look for their restaurants, and that's where they'd be. There was a small Black Canadian population, many of whom were descended from formerly enslaved people who'd escaped to Canada via the Underground Railroad. There were also Jamaicans and other Caribbean folks coming on the same wave we rode, but not a ton; growing up, I didn't cross paths much with them.

Still, despite this small influx, there weren't yet enough nonwhite people to change the city's complexion, which was white and European by default. In terms of identity, the big divide, the one that mattered politically, culturally, and in every other regard, was the one between Catholics and Protestants. And it always flummoxed me, because how did you know who was what? Over the years, I learned the nuances, like how you could tell with names and where people lived and how they spoke and the schools they attended.

On Hoyle Avenue specifically, you had the Velshis at No. 42, and then two doors down from us was my best friend Mikey, who's still my best friend to this day. Mikey's family was half Sicilian, quarter Arab, and quarter French Canadian. To look at him, Mikey was as white as you can get, but in Canada, between the half Italian and the quarter Arab, to some of our neighbors he qualified as "ethnic," a fact that was made plain because the WASPs were always asking us if we were brothers even though we looked nothing alike. So we were the outsiders on the street, and I was conscious of that. Everyone was polite and would make small talk with my grandmother from their front porch, but it was simply apparent that they had their world and we had ours. They had their social circle from the Presbyterian church, we had ours at the jamatkhana, and the two didn't mix. It was one of those social norms that you follow because you can sense it even though nobody ever talks about it.

Of course, that was the parents. All the kids on Hoyle just played together and thought nothing of it. Back then, the only "extracurricular activity" was the neighborhood. We had several elderly couples on our street—at least they seemed elderly to me—and they would sit on their porches all the time, which made it safe. Everyone knew everyone else's comings and goings. We played a ton of street hockey—our street was good for it, you could go twenty minutes without seeing a car—and if we wanted to explore, we'd just hop on our bikes and go. The main rule was that we weren't allowed to cross the two major thoroughfares that bounded each end of the neighborhood. We'd go to the smoke shop, as they called it back in the day, and buy comics. Or we'd ride around on our bikes and skateboards and do tricks until it was time to come home, which usually meant going home to Mikey's.

When my parents got to Canada, they had to do something to earn a living, and they weren't going to try again with another bakery. Since my father had business operations skills and my mother had travel agent skills, they decided to open a travel agency. Building a business from the ground up meant they worked all the time. On top of which, they were already involved in so many civic and political activities. So with my parents, we never really knew what time they were coming home in the evening, but Mikey's mom and dad worked a regular nine-to-five, and once they were home, it was understood that they had total authority to act in loco parentis with me. Mikey's dad had this freakish ability to whistle so loud you could hear it several blocks away. I don't know how he did it—it was a very specific whistle—but in any event, the condition was whenever we heard that whistle we had to come home.

When we weren't out and about, we were at one or the other's house. It was like we had our own little cultural exchange program. We literally had a meal at each other's house every day because both of our grandmothers were always around, and both of our grandmothers liked to see us eat. Mikey's grandmother used to fill me up with pasta and different Italian foods, and my grandmother used to make us *rotlis*, the flatbread that we ate with curry, which is nothing more than wheat and water rolled with a pin and thrown on a flat griddle to cook. Mikey and I would sit there, grab them hot off the griddle, put butter and sugar on them, roll them up, and eat them faster than she could make them. What this meant was that we often had dinner with my grandmother at my house and then a second dinner with Mikey's grandmother at their house and then a third dinner when our parents got home late from work, with the inevitable result that Mikey and I grew quite fat.

Because Mikey's family was Catholic, at Christmastime they'd invite me to go with them to midnight mass. I loved it, because when you're a kid anything that lets you stay up until midnight is fun.

School was the one place I didn't go with Mikey, because he went to Catholic school along with every other Catholic kid in Toronto. The Catholic school kids lived in their own separate world from 8:00 a.m. to 3:00 p.m. each day; we didn't even compete with them in sports. But even though my school was public, it was assumed that everyone was Protestant, so all the other students and I would be excused from class to sing Christmas carols in the Christmas show out in the main hall. And I enjoyed it. I knew that Muslims didn't sing carols, and I knew that Jesus wasn't our guy. But I never felt stifled being surrounded by all these Anglicans and Presbyterians. I never felt put-upon because this WASPy culture wasn't my culture. In fact, I enjoyed that culture *because* it was someone else's culture, which was clearly something I inherited from my parents just through osmosis by virtue of the way they lived.

Before I was even born, when my father was still investigating Canada as a possible place to live, he'd visited Toronto in the middle of winter, flying from the lush, temperate beauty of Kenya to the snowy, frozen tundra of the Great North. For years I used to joke around with him, "Why didn't you just turn around and go back?"

His reply was always the same. "Because the snow was freedom to me," he'd say. "The snow was liberty. It was a new life."

To this day, you'll find many other Indian immigrants who say the same thing, that Canada, for all its bitter cold, gave people the warmth of acceptance by opening its doors. To this day, my dad still loves a snowstorm and a snowy picturesque landscape because it feels like it did when he first got to Canada and found his new world, our new world; in this new world, we still had our Muslim and Indian traditions, which we enjoyed, but we were also surrounded by people with different traditions, which we got to enjoy, too. We didn't see any contradictions in any of that. We embraced it and we treasured it, and every year my grandmother put up Christmas lights to show how much we treasured it. I don't think my grandmother ever once thought in terms of "assimilation" or "integration" as political concepts. I think she decorated the house because she thought it looked pretty. And it was pretty. Christmas lights in the window on a cold, snowy evening while you're enjoying a nice warm fire—what could be better? It's a lovely tradition to take part in. We celebrated Christmas because celebrating Christmas seemed less like a Christian tradition and more like a Canadian one, and that's who we were now: We were Canadian.

It was my family's good fortune that, at the end of the 1960s, under the prime ministership of Lester Pearson, Canada faced two serious, existential crises, either one of which had the potential to cripple the nation's growth and progress. Birthrates in the West had started to decline. Canada's leaders had realized, mathematically, that Canada wasn't giving birth to enough children, which meant the country was punching well below its weight economically among the other modern Western nations. This left two options. Option one was that Canada could shrink into some small country that did nothing but supply oil, timber, and hockey players to other still-growing, more prosperous nations. Option two was that Canada rapidly and radically increase its population through immigration. Since there wasn't a flood of immigrants fleeing northern and western Europe, as had been the case a hundred years earlier, that meant Canada would have to shift from a whites-only immigration policy to taking people from non-European areas, meaning brown people, immigrants and refugees, and evacuees from the far-flung corners of the world. Making the challenge even greater, Canada had to compete for these new immigrants against America, which had recently emerged from a nearly fifty-year period of shutting out immigrants almost completely. So Pearson's government began to make a point of aggressively recruiting people from places like Kenya, which was a good thing for us. But it was potentially a risky thing for Canada. Any large and rapid shift in a national culture risks a backlash, and it needs to be handled with care, especially in a place that's already suffering from an identity crisis of its own, which Canada certainly was.

By the mid- to late 1960s, the French-speaking Canadians of Quebec—the loudest ones, anyway—had been fighting for the separation of their province into its own country for some time. The way they saw it, taking Canada and the United States together, they were 10 million French speakers in a sea of about 200 million English speakers and they were going to get swallowed up. For the fringe Quebecois extremists, the solution was terrorism and violence. For the more moderate separatists, the solution was simply to pull up the drawbridge, dig a deep moat, and have as many children as possible to grow and preserve their own language and culture. But low birthrates were an issue in Quebec as well. The provincial government had resorted to giving out baby bonuses to pregnant couples, and the Catholic Church basically came out and told everyone, "Your job is to have babies." So Quebec was growing at a better clip than the rest of Canada, but it wasn't growing fast enough, and as far as solving the problem through immigration, Quebec only wanted to grow its population with French-speaking white people, except that there weren't any French-speaking white people interested in moving to Canada.

So, in the early 1970s, the Canadian government had to find a solution to both the problem of its aging population and, simultaneously, the problem of Quebec separatism. I don't want to be too dramatic about it. It's not like the country was teetering on the brink. It wasn't about to descend into a bloody reckoning of civil war and sectarian violence. I mean, it is *Canada*, after all. If neither of these problems had been addressed, the worst outcome probably would have been that Canada today would still be a nice place where tourists go and look at quaint buildings in Montreal, but it wouldn't have been a powerful or influential country on the world stage. It would have been like a very large Belgium, essentially. So if the country wanted to avoid that fate, if Canada wanted to be dynamic and grow and enjoy a place of pride in the upper tier of nations, something needed to be done.

Enter Pierre Elliott Trudeau.

Pierre Trudeau succeeded Lester Pearson as prime minister in 1968. He was in every sense a visionary, and his vision was global, back before that became a dirty word. He'd gone to school at Harvard, the London School of Economics, and the Sorbonne. In 1957, he'd attended Ghana's independence celebration, sitting and cheering with the ordinary folk in the stadium. He had swum the Bosphorus Strait. He'd been in Gujarat in India, sitting with the people, eating food with his hands. He was aware of what was happening with the disenfranchisement and expulsion of the Asian populations in East Africa. Trudeau was versatile and cosmopolitan, not to mention daring and dashing, and he was very much ahead of his time.

Being a Quebecer himself, Trudeau realized that addressing the fears of the separatists and welcoming large numbers of new, nonwhite immigrants could be accomplished in one sweeping measure. And so, addressing the House of Commons on October 8, 1971, he announced that "multiculturalism" would now be the official policy of the Canadian government. It was a new law that would make Canada the opposite of America's assimilationist "melting pot." Instead of compelling everyone to adopt the same Anglicized names and language and culture, the law would preserve the cultural freedom and autonomy of all individuals and recognize the contributions of diverse ethnic groups to Canadian society.

At first, no one had any idea what this policy of multiculturalism meant, and white people were wary of it; however, what it boiled down to, essentially, was language. The law included various provisions about assisting people with fighting discrimination and fostering intercultural exchange. But really it was a language-oriented matter.

Prior to 1970, Montreal was Canada's major metropolitan area. Toronto was the backwater. Montreal was where everything important was happening. It was bigger, more cosmopolitan, and more dynamic, and because of these qualities, it attracted a lot of immigrants, many of them Jewish merchants in the *shmatte*, or clothing, industry. But in a prejudice unique to Quebec, the issue with the Jews wasn't so much their Jewishness as the fact that they spoke English. So you had this Francophone city where you started to hear a lot more English in the streets. English signs were popping up outside restaurants and there was a fear that the city was becoming Anglicized. The Quebecers decided to fight for their culture, and they did it through language, because they believed that if you preserve the language, you preserve everything else, because the rest of the culture hangs on that.

Trudeau's new law recognized the right of Quebec to prioritize the use of French in business and education. If you go to Quebec today, French signs dominate everything. If there's any English on a sign, it's always in small print, underneath. It's all in French because it has to be, by law. It's the only place like that in the world. You probably won't even find as many French signs in Paris.

At the same time, the new policy of multiculturalism extended many of those same rights to every other ethnic group coming into the country. One of the most prominent aspects of the policy was that in any public school that had twenty-five students of any one language group, they had to provide language lessons for that group. If they had twenty-five Greek students, they could ask for Greek language lessons after school, free of charge. Twenty-five Indians, same thing. At the same time, it provided non-English-speaking immigrants with free English-language instruction, often before they entered the country, in order to help them acclimate, find jobs, and get a foothold when they arrived.

The policy never really affected us directly. We already spoke English so didn't need any assistance in that arena, and we never qualified for Gujarati lessons because back then you'd rarely find twenty-five

Gujarati-speaking kids under the same roof. But we knew it was going on around us, and we could feel the impact it was having because
with each passing year, more and more immigrants were coming into
Toronto, and the language policy was the vehicle that allowed them
to do so. It was an open hand that said, "You are welcome here. We
will not only give you the tools you need to get ahead in this new
culture, but we'll help you retain your own culture as well." You could
come to Canada and be a Canadian citizen while remaining as culturally Italian or Portuguese or Indian or Chinese or Ismaili as you
wanted. For us, that made all the difference. My parents had been citizens of South Africa and Kenya, but only on paper. Until we settled
in at 42 Hoyle, they had never been allowed to enjoy true citizenship
and everything it entailed all at the same time. They had never been
in a place that allowed them to fully belong.

For any country, absorbing immigrant families one by one is easy
enough. It's when they come in waves that you face real challenges,
both logistically and culturally, from those who fear what kinds of
change it will bring. And almost as soon as it was implemented, with
Idi Amin's expulsion of Uganda's Asians in 1972, Canada's new immigration system was put to the ultimate stress test. With thousands
of stateless refugees filling East Africa's rail stations and airport ter-
minals, Canada jumped into the fray and said, "We'll take as many
as we can." Canadian diplomats were on the ground in Kenya and
in Uganda, expediting the paperwork to allow all those refugees in,
literally shielding Indian refugees behind doors to protect them from
the Ugandan police until they could be taken out of the country.

In the end, Canada ended up taking about seven thousand people,
mostly Ismaili, all at once. (Under immense international pressure,
the UK finally relented and let in some twenty-seven thousand refu-

gees, about half the number who ought to have been legally entitled to immigrate, as they were already British citizens with valid passports. A few thousand went to India and the rest were soon scattered, a thousand here and a thousand there, in different countries around the globe.) For Canada, it was a brilliant move, and not just because it was the right thing to do. Most of the Ismailis expelled from Uganda spoke English. They'd run businesses and shops. They were precisely the kinds of hardworking people Canada needed to bolster and grow its own economy.

In a matter of weeks, in Toronto and other major cities, a massive institutional effort was organized to welcome these new Canadians. Some of it was done by the government. Other programs were set up through the Ismaili community itself. Both my parents were a part of it. For weeks, every morning my father was down at the train station meeting families as they arrived. Most of them flew from Kampala to Montreal, and there they separated to different provinces. My father and others would meet them and escort them to Government House in Toronto, where they were given clothes, shoes, boots, and other necessities. After that, my father kept in touch with the community members who were sent to different parts of Ontario.

The city's Ismaili community, some who had arrived only a few months before themselves, stepped up to offer structure and familiarity to these new citizens. You'd find Ismailis in some borrowed high school gymnasium, setting it up to give refugees a place to have evening prayers. Someone would be cleaning, someone else rolling out the carpets, another providing the coffee, tea, and donuts. Others would welcome the guests as they arrived. As had always been the case in Ismaili communities around the world, the foundation was built on solidarity: bringing people together, getting them organized, and helping them.

The Ugandan experience taught the Canadian government how to be creative about absorbing refugees and displaced persons into an existing society and economy, what the United Nations High Commissioner for Refugees calls "alternative pathways to resettlement." The Aga Khan National Council of Canada became a sponsoring entity to ensure that these newly arrived people did not become a drag on the economy, that they were taught English if they didn't already know it, that they were coached on how to get jobs. Other funds were established that helped people get into universities when they otherwise wouldn't have had the funds to enroll.

One of the things my father taught me, because his father had instilled it in him, is to help everyone, not just your own. You aid everyone in society, and that lifts up your community as well. Guided by that philosophy, my father became the chair of the Ismaili Settlement Committee for Ontario, which set up a system with the banks so that the Ugandans and other South Asian immigrants and refugees could get financing for mortgages and car loans. Everyone was eligible. In order to encourage the banks to take on what many felt were high-risk loans, the Aga Khan's network guaranteed, in the event of a default, half the amount the bank had lent, but the system was so efficient that there wasn't a single one—no defaults at all. This allowed many new immigrants to start their own companies. Eventually, these new immigrants proved to be such dependable and loyal customers that some of the local banks started setting up kiosks at the airports, aiming to sign up families the moment they hit Canadian soil.

Canada learned in 1972 what America still has not learned—that refugees are a good bet. The Ugandan refugee crisis proved to be a massive turning point for Africa, for Canada, and for displaced persons the world over. With one grand gesture, Canada had established itself as a new beacon of liberty and opportunity. All across Africa, in Kenya, Angola, and even in parts of Europe, the word among the Indian diaspora was "Go to Canada." The same was true across the Caribbean and other developing regions as well, and the nonwhite, foreign-born population of Canada soared, primarily in its major cities. I have a large extended family. If you include every descendant of the children of Keshavjee Ramji who left Chotila in the nineteenth century, there are roughly a thousand of us spread around the world. Of that thousand, maybe a hundred stayed in East Africa, endured the anti-Indian backlash, and came through to the other side. Another two hundred or so are scattered across different parts of Europe and Africa, and a few wound up in America. But the vast majority, about 70 percent of them, settled in Canada. They came from Mozambique and South Africa and Kenya, and they wound up everywhere from Vancouver to Calgary to Toronto to Edmonton. Today you can drive clear across North America, from British Colombia to Newfoundland, and odds are you're going to bump into some cousin of mine somewhere along the way.

All across the Western world, the issue of nonwhite and non-Christian immigration into the West has been one of the defining issues of the past half century. At the southern border of the United States, Mexicans and Central Americans have gathered seeking refuge and better economic opportunity. In rickety boats across the Mediterranean, displaced Africans and Arabs have risked life and limb trying to reach the southern shores of Europe. And on both sides of the Atlantic, populist demagogues have used the immigrant crisis to ignite fear and hatred for their own political gain. In England, the xenophobic seeds sown by Enoch Powell would grow into the economically disastrous Brexit movement, led by men like Nigel Farage. In France, Marine Le Pen's blood-and-soil faction, the National Front, has stoked baseless fears of Muslims and Jews as foreign interlopers. And in America, of course, it's been Donald Trump and his Muslim bans and "Build the Wall."

And because of this fearmongering, in all of these countries, vast swaths of the white majorities have ended up fearful and anxious about these foreign invaders supposedly coming to "destroy their culture." And on the other side of the coin, the hostility and marginalization faced by these groups has driven many of them to extremes of their own. In Europe especially, Muslim and African immigrants and refugees have often been shunted off and warehoused in massive, isolated apartment blocks, leaving them mired in poverty. With no way to integrate culturally or economically into mainstream society, some of those immigrant communities wound up becoming breeding grounds for ISIS and al Qaeda. You had all these bored, unemployed, unassimilated young men, which are the scourge of the world, sitting around on soccer pitches with nothing to do. So when these radical imams came along and said, "We'll give you $400 a week to go to Syria or Iraq and fight for Allah," they went along for the fight. Not because they were religious fundamentalists. They hardly knew anything about Islam. They were just angry and aimless and bored.

When one group is closed off and defensive and bigoted, the other group feels it has no choice but to be closed off and defensive and bigoted in return, and both sides lose. In Canada, however, instead of fighting all this nonwhite, non-Christian immigration, they actively welcomed it. They opened their arms to it, and the difference in the results could not be starker.

———

Because my parents had come from Kenya—a sister country, if you will, of Canada, as it was also part of the British Commonwealth—the legal part of our path to citizenship was quick and painless. We were granted landed status right away, which gave both of my parents the right to vote in local and national elections from the moment they arrived. Then, once we were here, they immediately applied for full citizenship, which we were granted in less than two years.

But then came the "sense of belonging and kinship" piece of it. That part is trickier. With its open embrace of refugees and its policy of multiculturalism, the Canadian government had done everything possible, from an official point of view, to make its new residents feel welcome. But the bonds that hold communities and countries together cannot be dictated by administrative fiat. They have to grow organically, from the bottom up. They also take time, and no matter how well you sell the idea, not everybody is going to buy it.

There was a famous incident in Toronto in the 1970s where a brown man was pushed in front of a subway train and killed, the racial epithets yelled by his assailant leaving no doubt as to the motivation for the crime. The blanket slur wielded against brown people in Canada in those days was *Paki,* the pejorative term used to describe someone from Pakistan. In the streets or on the subway, immigrants would hear "Paki go home" or "Smelly Paki." Things like that. This held true no matter what country the brown person in question hailed from, which was more than likely not Pakistan.

It was a searing incident, more so for my family and me by virtue of the fact that we used the subway every day. While my parents grew up with such fears, it was the first time I realized as a kid that bad things can happen to you simply because someone else fears and despises the color of your skin. There was a terror throughout the community that this would be an epidemic of attacks directed at people from South Asia, and I can still remember the conversation my parents had about it with my sister and me. "Don't stand near the tracks," they said. "Stand on the stairs." Interestingly, it was one of the few times we discussed racism and prejudice in our home. When it came to talking about society and politics, my parents were much more inclined to talk about positive changes they wanted to make, like raising funds for a new health care center, than they were to dwell on the negative aspects of challenges we faced. This tactic wasn't really about pretending the problems weren't there but more about keeping focused on the future and moving forward.

Naturally, there were less explicit but more pervasive forms of hostility to deal with as well, like the ways in which nonwhite immigrants were denied jobs. You would see job listings in the paper that said "Canadian experience needed," which was nonsense. You don't need experience polishing Canadian shoes to know how to polish shoes, and you don't need experience fixing Canadian toilets to know how to fix a toilet. My mom's best friend was Irish, and she remembered signs that read "No Irish Need Apply" back in the day. Same with Mikey's family and the "No Italians Wanted" signs. But you couldn't be that blunt anymore, so now it was "Canadian experience needed."

I still remember seeing those ads well into my teens, if not longer, so they hung around for a while. They never had much of an

impact on me because until I became a journalist most of the jobs
I was applying for, like parking valet, were jobs that went to immigrants anyway. Nowadays, everybody in Canada knows that we need
doctors and pharmacists, and almost no one cares where you got your
experience, only that you have it. So there was some of that and the
odd racial slur being thrown around and how much you experienced
it depended on where you lived and whether or not you were dealing
with the people who weren't buying what Pierre Trudeau was selling.

Canada is a vast country. It covers more than six percent of the
landmass on the planet, second only to Russia and bigger than China.
Yet while China manages to hold nearly 1.5 billion people, Canada
is home to fewer than 40 million, and almost all of them live within
one hundred miles of the American border, mostly concentrated in
major urban areas like Toronto and Vancouver. Those were the places
where nonwhite immigrants were settling; this large influx of people
was, in reality, only having an impact on a handful of areas. The rest
of Canada's vast, sprawling territory was, for the most part, empty.
Yet there was this fear among some native Canadians that immigrants were "taking over the country." It was the Canadian version
of the "Great Replacement Theory" that gets touted on right-wing
social media and FOX News in America today.

I can remember a political cartoon that ran in the paper when
we were growing up. My dad saved it and showed it to me. It was
of a man talking to his wife on the front porch of their farmhouse
somewhere out in Saskatchewan, deep in rural Canada. All around
them, there's nothing to see for miles and miles and miles. Below the
cartoon, the caption read, "Where will we put them all?"

And that was the joke. Fear of immigration in Canada didn't
make any sense because there was so much of Canada just lying

around, unused. "There's nothing in this country but land," he'd say. "They need people to work it, and yet they have these fears of immigrants." My father would chuckle about it. Both of my parents had a good sense of humor about these things, and they'd tend to focus on the absurdity of racism rather than the cruelty of it. It was the same with Apartheid and all the ridiculous laws about tracking yeast. You found a way to laugh about it as a way of dealing with it.

The whole "Where will we put them?" thing was humorous, to a point, but my parents didn't openly mock it because they also understood it. People worry about change. Any time people feel like culture is changing too fast and leaving them behind, they get anxious. It's not entirely about racism or xenophobia. What *is* racist is someone coming along and exploiting that anxiety for political or economic gain. It's someone saying, "These brown people are coming to take away what's yours." And that's what Canada had little of. The racists and the xenophobes were there, but they were never given the megaphone to rile up and spread baseless fears among everyone else. We didn't have xenophobic rabble-rousers like England's Enoch Powell or France's Marine Le Pen. Unlike in America, we didn't have paramilitary white-supremacist groups like the Ku Klux Klan. Nor did we have these right-wing demagogues like Father Coughlin fanning the flames of nativist fears on radio and television. Instead, we had cool, cosmopolitan Pierre Trudeau saying, "These people are welcome here, and basically this is all going to work out fine." Trudeau, and the Liberal Party as a whole, were thorough and meticulous and persuasive when it came to laying out the economic necessities for immigration. The argument was as simple as it was obvious: These brown people aren't here to take your piece of the economic pie. They're here to work and make the economic pie bigger for everyone. Given the country's negative birth rates, we don't have any other choice." For the most part, I think Canadians understood that.

There was only one real point of friction that I remember, and it came many years later, in the late 1980s, when the first generation of immigrants raised in Canada began trying to make inroads into many still very white avenues of employment. Baltej Singh Dhillon was a Sikh who had immigrated to British Columbia from Malaysia as a young man in the early 1980s. After a stint volunteering as a translator for Royal Canadian Mounted Police, the RCMP, which most Americans probably know from the Dudley Do-Right cartoons as "the Mounties," Dhillon decided to apply to become a Mountie himself. He met all the entrance requirements save two. The dress code forbade facial hair and required every Mountie to wear the RCMP's traditional hat or Stetson. Dhillon's religion required him to have a beard and wear a turban, not a hat.

The facts of the case were on Dhillon's side. The Sikhs have a long military history in India, fighting for the Commonwealth and the British army. They'd served the Crown quite loyally wearing whatever headwear they pleased, and it had never been an issue. (Indeed, much of Canada's Sikh population well predated the massive influx of nonwhite immigrants in the 1970s. While the nineteenth-century Ismaili diaspora had clustered mainly in Africa, Sikhs were one of the few groups that had come to North America at that time, helping to build the railroads in the Canadian and American West.) And it wasn't as if the RCMP uniform had never been changed before; in the early 1970s, skirts and women's heels had been introduced to accommodate female officers.

In 1990, the government officially changed the policy to allow beards and turbans for Sikh officers, enabling Dhillon to be able to serve, but that wasn't the end of it. People wouldn't let it go. Legal challenges were brought. It became a huge issue, one of the few flashpoints where the policy of multiculturalism rose to the level of dominating the national conversation. The whole thing dragged on in the courts forever. People talked about it all the time, how this was a bridge too far and it was changing our culture. If we let Sikh police officers wear turbans it would somehow be the end of Canadian culture as we know it. We're literally talking about years of drama playing out on the nightly news, all because of a hat. Of course, the fight about the hat wasn't a fight about the hat at all. It was a proxy battle over the browning of Canada as a whole. Since you couldn't have an argument about Sikh people without seeming openly racist, we all had to have a big row about a hat.

And I'll grant you, this wasn't any old hat. For many people, the Canadian Mountie, along with the maple leaf and Tim Horton's coffee, is one of those symbols that makes Canada Canadian. At the time, as an opinionated young man in his early twenties, my attitude was definitely "It's just a hat." I couldn't see why it was that big a deal. Besides, the Mounties only dressed up in those costume uniforms with the red coats and the jodhpurs and the big hats for events and parades and such. You never saw them wearing that in the streets on the job. As a kid I went to Disney's Epcot Center in Orlando, where we visited the Canada pavilion, and it was wilderness and moose and Mounties with the big hats; I remember thinking, "This is not my life. I've never seen anything like this in Toronto."

So it was obvious to me that the Sikh officer was right and all these Canadians needed to let go of the hat. However, with age and, hopefully, a bit of wisdom, I can empathize with the older Canadians on the other side of the fight. I get it. Symbols are important. Change is difficult. And if you want change to happen, the best way to get it is to go to those people and say, "Look, I understand why your hat is important to you. But maybe you can see that the reason your hat is important to you is the same reason why the turban is important to Officer Dhillon. His tradition means as much to him as yours does to you. And if we're all going to live here together, there has to be room for both."

In the end, that's pretty much what happened. Luckily, even when Canadians are fighting with each other, with the exception of the militant Quebecois extremists, it never gets that heated. We never had Sikhs and whites showing up at rallies to protest each other and wave guns at each other, which is what probably would have happened in America. The whole thing quietly made its way through the courts, and finally, in 1996, the Supreme Court upheld the government's new position allowing turbans and beards, and in true Canadian fashion, it all worked out; everybody went on with their lives. An effort was made to compromise with the cops as well, by designing a turban that fit with the existing look of the police uniforms. Today, you'll see Sikh policemen in Vancouver and Toronto, and they have beautiful turbans designed like a police hat with a badge, which looks excellent.

Growing up, I never encountered anything like what the Sikh policemen went through over their turbans. In fact, the number of times I experienced overt racism I could count on one hand, and it was typically a childish, low-level kind of racism, like name-calling. Some kid down at the Eaton Centre Mall in downtown Toronto called me a Paki once. I wasn't offended. I was confused, because I wasn't from Pakistan and didn't yet understand that this kid didn't actually care whether I was from Pakistan or not. So I yelled back,

"I'm not from Pakistan!" And then, quite confident that I'd got the better of him, I went home and told my parents what had happened, at which point they explained to me that my assailants weren't so concerned with the particulars of my geography lesson. I remember the conversation clearly. My dad was deadly serious about it. "It was actually meant as an insult to you," he said, "and it's interesting that you were able to brush it off in the way that you did. But remember that it wasn't about where you're from."

The thing about racism in Canada—and here I can only speak for myself—is that I never felt like I was in a "racist" country. I felt like I was in a country that had racists in it. I was in a largely white, largely Protestant society that was getting less white and less Protestant, and that process came with some growing pains. Knowing what I did about my parents' experience in South Africa, I knew that the distinction between a racist society and a society with racists was a critical one. Yes, there were certain people out there who felt a certain way about people like me—and there will always be certain people out there who feel that way about people like me—but I also knew that the majority of people in Canada and the powers that be in Canada, from the prime minister on down, were more or less on our side. Bad things did happen, but the good—at least from my point of view—significantly outweighed the bad.

This isn't to say that I never had any problems. As I grew up, I had to learn to deal with the nagging, persistent feeling of being different, of being an outsider. It's true that my parents and grandmother never felt any pressure to assimilate, but the same wasn't true for me or my sister, Ishrath. My family was at the leading edge of this wave of Muslim and Indian immigration. Ishrath, eight years older than me, was completely isolated during her entire teen years. She was the only brown student in her class, and she had a rough time of it. But even in my grade, I was more or less on my own. My schools were still predominantly white, and part of me always just wanted to fit in, which is much less a social and political issue and more just the nature of being a kid.

Realizing I was different, for me, started with taking food to school. All the white kids had ham and cheese sandwiches or peanut butter and jelly on white bread, while I had samosas and leftover chicken curry on brown bread. *Nobody* at school had brown bread except me. Today, people celebrate these things. They take their people's food to school, and they're proud of it. That was not the Toronto in which I grew up.

Then there was my name. I can still remember getting forms to fill out and the blank spaces were never labeled with "Last Name, First Name." They'd say "Surname, Christian Name." As if everyone was by default Christian. So that was odd. My sister, again, had it much worse than me. She has a beautiful Persian name, Ishrath. But what a pain-in-the-ass name that was in Canada. It's not that complicated, but people couldn't get their heads around it. Since Canada had already been on my parents' radar when I was born, they gave me a three-letter name. Ali was easier to spell and pronounce, but it didn't make me any less ethnic than "Ishrath." Most of the Chinese kids in my school had Anglicized names like "Ellen" and "Susan," and for a long time, I would have loved if I could have just been "Dave."

Another thing that I felt marked me as an outsider, ironically, was the fact that my parents were married. The seventies were the decade of divorce and liberation in the West, but not for Ismaili Muslims. Most of my classmates' parents were divorced, so at the time, because it made me feel different from the other kids, I hated the fact that my parents came to parents' night together, walking hand in hand down the hall, much in the same way they do to this day.

But the biggest thing was hockey. All the kids in Canada play hockey. I didn't. Hockey, at the time, was something kids played on Friday nights and Saturday mornings. But for me, Friday night was our big night at the jamatkhana, and then Saturday mornings were when I went to the Muslim equivalent of Sunday school. When all the other kids were out on the ice, I had to be at the mosque doing all this rote memorization work that I found at the time to be torturously boring.

The fact that I couldn't skate or play hockey wasn't a big deal until junior high. Like many Canadian middle schools, the junior high I attended had its own skating rink, which meant the rink was now the de facto school playground. At that point, my parents thought, "Well, we should get him some skates." So they went to a used skate exchange and got me some skates. Only, they were figure skates. You'll get a wedgie in Toronto showing up to a hockey rink with figure skates. Everyone else had hockey skates. I think I went out with them once and that was it. I didn't skate again the entire time I lived in Canada.

More than anything, I grew up with a sense that there was a whole world going on that I wasn't a part of. Even when I didn't feel like I was on the outside, I still knew I wasn't fully on the inside. With immigrant parents, I missed out on a lot of extracurricular activities, simply because we weren't even aware that they existed.

The risk for many kids in my situation is to come away bitter—resentful of their immigrant parents for not being able to do more to help them integrate and resentful of the white people who excluded them. They're so angry about having to go the extra mile to be involved that they refuse to go that extra mile, with the net result being that they're more alienated and marginalized than before. I could have grown up thinking that way. Fortunately for me, I didn't. Whether that was because of how my parents raised me or just the fact that I learned how to get along as a coping mechanism, I don't know. But whatever cultural and social barriers there were between me and the other kids, the result was only that I felt left out; I was not bullied or the recipient of overt malice. I just figured I'd have to do a bit of extra work to overcome those barriers. Eventually, I did, and, in the end, it turned out OK.

For a long time, though, I didn't want to be different. I didn't want to have multiple identities to juggle. I'd look at all my friends and they were just "Canadian" or "English" or "Irish." It all seemed so simple for them. But then I'd look at my family and think, "Well, are we *really* Canadian? Are we Indian? Are we Kenyan? Are we South African? What are we?" And it never sat right with me. It confused me, because what I didn't understand as a kid was that I didn't have to pick one of them. I could pick all of them.

———

As a fat kid who parked himself on the couch every weekend to watch cartoons and eat donuts, one of the best parts of my life was that those donuts got delivered right to our house. Every Saturday morning, two dozen hot and fresh donuts showed up on our doorstep. I thought that was the greatest thing of all time. I mean, what kid wouldn't? We had so many donuts we didn't know what to do with them. After we got to eat as many as we could, my mom would be giving them away up and down the block. Whatever was left we would freeze. (And if you didn't know that you can freeze donuts, now you do.)

What I didn't know until recently was that these donuts came from an Ismaili refugee from Uganda who'd shown up in Canada with nothing. He'd received a loan from the government to set up a bakery, and he'd decided to make donuts. My dad bought two dozen donuts every week as a way to help this guy out. As a result, because of the Canadian government's official assistance and the informal assistance of customers like my dad, this man was able to send all three of his children to college to become productive members of Canadian society.

We also had our groceries delivered. Nobody got their groceries delivered back then, but we did. Once a week, before sunrise, they'd arrive, and we'd wake up to find our groceries on our front porch. Similar to the donut man, this grocery delivery service was run by an Ismaili Ugandan refugee. He'd started a grocery delivery service, and my father subscribed as a way of helping him out. What my father didn't know, and didn't find out until years later, was that this guy didn't have a car. He was doing it all by public transportation. He would get your grocery list, buy everything the night before, store it at his apartment, then take the bus and the subway around in the predawn hours hauling bags and bags of groceries to people's homes. Later in life, after graduating from hand-delivering groceries to other successes in business, this man donated $100,000 to a local hospital.

There are thousands of similar stories. These refugees had all been craftsmen and businesspeople and manufacturers in Kenya and Uganda and Tanzania, and they all wound up in Canada in whatever odd niche businesses they could find. They brought their experience from Africa and put it to use wherever they could find the opportunity, or they learned some other new trade if they had to. One of my favorite stories is one I came across during my days as a Canadian journalist, about a man, an Ismaili Muslim, who ran a mechanized egg farming operation somewhere out west. This man had emigrated from Mombasa all the way to the farthest reaches of western Canada with his wife, two sons, and two daughters-in-law to end up in mechanized egg farming. His whole life up to that point he'd been in watch repair. He'd had a watch shop in Mombasa, and all he knew how to do was fix watches. I asked him how he got into mechanized egg farming from watches, and he said it was because that was the loan he got and the training that was available when he arrived. So now instead of fixing watches in a bustling port city in Africa, he and his family were up at five in the morning in subzero temperatures to get their farming equipment up and running.

They adapted, in other words. The donut guy and the grocery-delivery guy and the mechanized egg farmers, they integrated themselves into a new part of the world and became part of a new order. It worked because it was a two-way street. The Canadian government, along with various nonprofits, had given them the tools to adapt, and they had done the hard work of adapting and starting over, which is why Ismaili Muslims became pioneers on virtually every frontier in Canadian society. You pick any professional field in Canada—law, medicine, academia, politics, mechanized egg farming—and you'll more than likely find it was Ismailis who paved the way. And they did it because they've had active leadership encouraging them to adapt and integrate in every foreign port where they've landed for the last hundred years.

My parents wholeheartedly embraced the Aga Khan's philosophy of openness and adaptability. Their takeaway from Apartheid was that something had been stolen from them. They'd been denied the opportunity to participate in everything the other South African cultures had to offer. They understood the dangers of living in a segregated world, one in which you'll never realize your potential because there are so many places in society where you're not allowed to go. So when they came to Canada, they wanted that pluralism. They craved it.

There were some doors in Canadian culture that my parents didn't know to open for me. Sports was the big one. But every door they knew to open, or could think to open, they did. They didn't want to place any limits on who I could be or where I could go. We were not parochial in any sense. At 42 Hoyle, we had all sorts of people all the time. It was a way station, a first stop for immigrants and refugees newly arrived in the country. Most of the time that meant people we actually knew, cousins and friends and distant family members coming in from various parts of Africa. They would stay for a week or a month while they got settled. But often it was random people, a friend of a friend of a friend, a refugee who'd heard from someone at the mosque that my parents had a couch they could spare for a few days, or students coming from overseas to go to the University of Toronto. And there were no cell phones. People would just show up. They would take a taxi or get a ride from someone to our house and knock on the door and hold up a note or a phone number explaining who'd sent them and how they got my parents' address. I grew up thinking, "Wow, Mom and Dad have so many friends," because there were people in and out of that house all the time. Hindu, Muslim, African, Pakistani, Sikh—it didn't matter. They were all welcome.

To this day, I'll meet people and when they learn that I'm Murad and Mila Velshi's son, they'll say, "Hey, 42 Hoyle Avenue! I stayed there in 1972 when I first arrived from Uganda!" Or Nairobi. Or London. Wherever. It was all informal. Our house was a place where you could walk in at any time and go into the kitchen and my grandmother would say, "Have you eaten? Here, let me get you something." There were times I would come home and my friends would be hanging out with my grandmother before I got there. Sometimes, I think they knew my grandmother better than I did.

We would have parties all the time, too. My parents loved to entertain, and when the music was playing it looked like the cantina from *Star Wars*, upward of fifty people of all nationalities from different places and different religions circling and mingling in our tiny house. Probably about half the people we knew were somehow tied into the Ismaili community or the larger diaspora, with all the different religious sects and ethnicities it contained. But most of the friends my parents met through work and politics were white. All their employees were white. My mom's best friend Joan was Irish Protestant. And there was no sense of "Don't mix that crowd with this crowd." This multicultural atmosphere was something that my family, especially my paternal grandfather Rajabali, had wanted to nurture back in South Africa, but it simply wasn't possible because it wasn't legal.

My parents' circle of friends grew quickly. They often hosted gatherings that fell somewhere between a salon and a party. There'd be a wet bar for people to make drinks, and sometimes there would be music. I always had a great time. Sometimes there would be interesting, serious discussions about politics and history, too. That was the world in which I grew up, which very much resembles the world in which I exist today. You gather people around and ask them to tell their stories, and you learn something about the world you never would have learned talking to someone from the same universe as yourself.

Our kitchen table was a place of open debate. We kept the traditions that were important to us, Indian food and Indian movies with my grandmother and religious instruction at the jamatkhana, but outside of those things, my parents believed that good things come from exposing yourself to lots of different ideas. Never once did they think of these outside influences as diluting or diminishing who we were or what was important to us.

With the way we chose to live, my parents were clearly on one side of the conversation that was taking place in Canada in the wake of the mass immigration of the 1970s. The question was, "What does multiculturalism actually mean?" Will all these groups remain their own distinct societies, or not?" On the other side of the conversation were the extremists of Quebec, who wanted to do their own thing and never change. People like my parents claimed that it was possible to create an open and shared society where cultural differences could be celebrated, and shared respect for those differences could be the bond that held us together. My parents felt that was not only the far healthier option but also the only practical one.

The modern West is racially and religiously heterogeneous. It just is. In fact, we should probably table the argument about whether or not diversity is "better," because it's here whether you want it to be or not. The mass migrations and dislocations caused by war and the collapse of colonial rule aren't going to reverse themselves. The modern technologies that allow us to circle the globe in a day and spread thoughts and ideas in an instant, those technologies aren't going away. And technology is a helpful metaphor to understand what's happened. The transition from a world of homogenous, blood-

and-soil nation-states to a world of diverse and pluralistic countries is no different than the transition from typewriters to computers. I love typewriters. I have several. As I write this, there's actually a huge painting of an Underwood No. 5 hanging on the wall behind me. We can look back at typewriters with nostalgia and go on all day about how great and simple the typewriter was, and we can argue all day about the complicated problems that computers and the internet have injected into our lives. But the fact is that hyperconnected computers have replaced typewriters. You're free to stay home and use a typewriter if you want to, but as a society, we'd better learn how to use these new machines responsibly and teach our kids how to use these new machines responsibly—and, let's be honest, teach our parents how to use these new machines responsibly. And learning to use these machines responsibly means we have to develop good laws and social norms about how we let them shape our world.

The same thing is true for our newly multiracial, multiethnic landscape. It's here now. The question we face is simply this: Do we allow our newly diverse societies to become balkanized (i.e., places where our religious and cultural differences fragment us and drive us apart), or do we fight to make our societies pluralistic (i.e., places where different cultures live in harmony by cherishing and honoring their differences)? And what laws and social norms are we going to use to guide us?

The Francophone culture of Quebec is an interesting example, because it is simultaneously a majority within its own region and an extreme minority on a continent dominated by its Anglophone rivals, so it sometimes manifests the worst paranoias of both. The die-hard extremists of the separatist French-Only movement are no longer merely chauvinist. They're full-on racist. They say it's about language, but there are plenty of West Africans and Haitians and Lebanese who speak French, and Quebec doesn't want them, either. They'll take them, but only begrudgingly and only because all the white people who speak French are happy staying in France. The separatists aren't even separatists, really. They wanted to stay a part of Canada and still get all the money Canada has given them for nice roads, but they just don't want anyone but their kind to live there.

And I get it. It's racist, but I get it. They believe if they lose this battle, French will be gone in a generation, and they'll lose it forever. And that idea may be true. And if the Quebecers weren't white, we wouldn't call them racist at all. If they were an Indigenous brown people fighting to hold on to their language, the same people denouncing them would be rushing to celebrate and defend them. So there's that. I think all of us can empathize with the desire of any person or group of people to hold on to their identity and their language and their culture. The question is *how* you do it, and that's where my beliefs and the beliefs of people like my parents and the Aga Khan diverge from the Enoch Powells and the militant nationalists of the world.

I understand the nostalgia among those who'd rather live in more homogenous societies. It's probably less work to wake up and be a part of the culture that surrounds you by default. It's easy to imagine that world as being safer, easier, more comfortable. The MAGA Republicans want to go back to some Norman Rockwell Mayberry Street America where everybody went to church and everyone at church looked like them. That's not how I was raised, but I get the appeal. If my ancestral homeland in Chotila were more of a place to get nostalgic about, I might nurse those same feelings of grievance and loss myself. But ultimately, pulling up the drawbridge to try to isolate your culture and keep it pure from any kind of outside influence may allow you to preserve it for the briefest of moments, but in the long run, the isolation turns into stagnation. Eventually the milk goes bad. You start out with a nostalgia for something positive, like language or religious ritual, but then it curdles into something else.

As an economics guy, I like to look at Japan as another example. Japan is not a world power anymore because they mismanaged their economy. They also had no immigration, which was a big part of that mismanagement. They didn't want immigrants for the same reason some Quebecois don't want immigrants, for fear of diluting their culture. They don't have full participation of women in their workforce, either. So they ran out of people to grow their economy, as Pierre Trudeau feared would happen in Canada. Japan had the fasting-growing economy in the world, and then one day they stopped growing because they let a little bit of sexism and a lot of xenophobia guide their policy decisions.

Pulling up the drawbridge doesn't work, and it especially doesn't work today, now that we live in such a hyperconnected world. What my parents understood, what the Aga Khan taught, and what Pierre Trudeau believed is that the best way to ensure that your culture will thrive in a pluralistic society is to be as open as possible and to be as welcoming and curious about other cultures as you are open and generous with sharing your own. Indian culture doesn't thrive in Canada because parents like mine demanded that their kids only socialize with other Indians and only marry good Indian spouses and never eat pizza. It thrives because they invited Italians and Jews and WASPs over to our house and shared curry and samosas with them, and then those people embraced those things and went out and enjoyed them on their own.

It's share and share alike. Two of my roommates and best friends in college were Jewish. You can't have a Jewish service without ten Jewish people—it's called a minyan—and they could never get ten Jewish people at this homogenous white college we went to. So this one time when they needed an extra body, I went to their services with them, which was technically not kosher since I am not Jewish, but they let it slide. Maybe they knew something I didn't know: one day I'd be married to a Jewish woman and have two Jewish children. Anyway, it was lots of fun. I would go to midnight mass with Mikey, and that was fun, too. The backdrop for our jamat-khanas was usually a school gym, so I was always impressed by the grandeur of Catholic churches, with all of their incense and stained glass and high ceilings—they even gave everybody little wafers to eat. I've never understood people who see that kind of multicultur-alism as dilutive of one's own culture, even though so many people do. It never occurred to me that these things were dilutive of my Muslimness or my Indianness. They added new dimensions to who I am. They enriched the identities that I already had.

You have to be fluid with your identity because you yourself have to be fluid to exist in the world. Your identity, your sense of belong-ing, your commitment, they are all constantly changing depending on where you are and who you're with. As a kid, I struggled with my identity. Am I Indian? Am I African? Am I an immigrant? Am I a Canadian? It was all jumbled and mixed up. Now I understand that I'm all of those things, plus an American to boot. I'm comfortable being all of those things, and I enjoy being all of those things. My identity as a pluralist who belongs to all the categories is stronger than my identity as any one of the categories. My social-media bio used to say "Citizen of the World." Which sounds like some hippy-dippy bullshit, but it's true. I'm a card-carrying member of the world. I am able, thankfully, to grapple with my multiple identities without allowing one to impinge on another.

I see so many immigrants who hold on to their culture with a death grip that my parents never had. Am I going to suffer for the way they raised me? Are my kids going to suffer for it? I don't think so. No one has ever brought it up in my family; we don't think about that stuff. I'm sure someone out there might look at my situation and say, "Your poor kids. They don't know your language. They don't know your dress. They don't know your food." And maybe when I'm seventy-five and my kids can't make samosas, I'll regret it. I don't know. On the other hand, since my wife and kids are Jewish, I now know how to make—or at least reheat—a mean matzo ball soup.

What I do know is that I can look back at India and South Africa and see that in many ways I'm nothing like my grandfather or great-grandfather, but I can understand them and their motivations because there is a common link that ties us together, and that is our values. And that, ultimately, is the point. In Chotila, my great-great-grandfather KeshavjeeBapa used his success to help build a mosque and dig a well for the good of the community. In South Africa, my great-grandfather Velshi did the same for the tiny Indian ghetto of Marabastad. A generation later, my grandfather Rajabali worked to improve people's lives outside of Marabastad, in the larger South African society. In Kenya, my parents worked together with whites and Africans alike to build hospitals and run free elections. In Canada, they've done the same. None of this would have been possible if they had clung too fast to our culture. People have every right to do that, if they choose. But if we still spoke and dressed and behaved exactly like my great-great-grandfather did in Chotila, we would not fit into Canadian society in any meaningful way, and therefore, we would have no opportunity to share and live our values in a way that had any effect on Canadian society. We'd have struggled to make a living, and we wouldn't have advanced. We wouldn't be able to communicate with the local politicians who could offer us help and assistance, and we wouldn't be able to meaningfully contribute to the institutions that serve the Canadian people.

Conversely, what my family has done never would have been possible in a society that demanded complete and total assimilation. A system like that would have required us to jettison everything about our past lives, our culture, and our values and reinvent ourselves in the mold of the majorities where we were. But by traveling right up the middle, by holding on to our values and some key parts of our culture while being flexible and adaptable about the rest, we've managed to thrive. I can and do carry my family's history forward without having to eat samosas and wear saris, but I can eat samosas or any other snack in the world whenever I want to, simply because I enjoy it.

How does it all work? How do we decide which cultural practices survive and which ones don't? My view has always been that the free market sorts it out. Most people aren't deeply ideological. They're practical. If immigrant parents learn that people can't pronounce their kids' names and it's an impediment to their progress, they'll give their kids more pronounceable names. Or they might find that having a unique name helps their kids stand out in a way that helps them in a world that's more accepting of unusual names. If anything, the kid will pick up a nickname. Either way, it sorts itself out in the end. Canada's Chinese immigration is a good example. Chinese immigrants are one of the big reasons Canada has shot to prominence. Vancouver and Toronto attracted families from Hong Kong who brought in boatloads of money, but they demanded a certain type of living. They were multigenerational apartment dwellers more than they were single-family house dwellers, so they needed four- and five-bedroom apartments, which didn't exist in Canada. So they took these areas of Toronto that were sparsely populated and created these massive apartment cities, to the point where parts of Toronto look, from an architectural perspective, like Shanghai. In and around those areas they had all of these shopping centers where all of the signs were in Chinese. If you didn't speak Chinese, you wouldn't know what's where. The backlash was swift, with a lot of Canadians saying that these Chinese shops needed to put their signs in English. But the politicians were like, "What's the problem? If the Chinese stores aren't selling their goods, they'll go out of business. If they are selling their goods, they're paying rent and paying their taxes. Why are you concerned about it? Just go buy your groceries at the place with the English sign you can read and forget about the other ones." At that point, the backlash sort of fizzled before it even got started.

Of course, when I say that a free market sorts everything out, anybody who understands economics knows what I mean is a *well-regulated* free market, and that's precisely what Pierre Trudeau's multiculturalism policy was: a set of rules for how this cultural marketplace needed to operate. Prior to 1971, Canada was a very white, very provincial place. People had no idea how they would adapt to an increasingly brown and beige country. So you start out with a multicultural society, where everyone is being taught the rules about how to respect each other's cultures, and that then gives way to a truly pluralistic society, where the social norms of respecting and celebrating different cultures are simply woven into the social fabric. Then you don't need the rule book as much anymore.

Multiculturalism, as an official policy, is a bit like a set of training wheels. If it works properly, it will outlive its usefulness, because at some point you're not going to need it anymore. You have achieved your goal of spurring large waves of immigration to Canada, the immigrants have adapted to the local landscape, and the local landscape has adapted to the immigrants; now you have a self-sustaining system, though it may still have some hiccups and tension and racism. But overall, fifty years after the policy began, more and more immigrants want to come to Canada because it's a place that treats immigrants well, and more and more Canadians want immigrants to come to Canada because people have witnessed the ways in which immigration allows this tiny country, one-tenth the population size of America, to punch above its weight. Canada is now one of the top spots where immigrants want to settle.

Immigration works if you work it. In Canada, they worked it, and it worked so well that it became a virtuous cycle. There are lots of things about Canada that make Canada a good place to live—universal health care, a stable political system, a political spectrum narrowly anchored around the center—but it needed a kick-start, and multiculturalism was that kick-start. Today, the political system in Canada is filled with people like me and Mikey, people who grew up in this new reality. Our generation doesn't need the training wheels anymore because we've lived with each other and better understand one another. Which is precisely what Pierre Trudeau predicted would happen. He understood that if he allowed a certain flexibility and elasticity with the identity of the country, the center of gravity would hold. And it did.

What Trudeau did was a kind of cultural jiujitsu with the non-white immigrants the country needed in order to grow. This policy was brilliant. He said, "We're going to take this policy of multiculturalism and we're going to let you keep as much of your native language and culture as you want, but in respecting your right to be different, we're going to make you feel so welcome in Canadian society that you'll want to become Canadian and embrace everything good that Canada has to offer." And that's exactly what's happened. Today, the Ismaili kids and the Chinese kids and the Sikh kids feel less pressure to assimilate than I did forty years ago. They don't want to be called Judy or Dave. They're comfortable with their own ethnic names. They're not embarrassed to bring their leftover food to school. They're allowed to belong regardless of who they are. At the same time, all of those kids are drinking Tim Horton's coffee and going to hockey games and speaking the King's English and enjoying all the things that have always made the country what it is. It's evolved into something that is both entirely new and cosmopolitan and different and yet unmistakably, undeniably "Canadian" at its core. I can look across Toronto and Vancouver today at the growing, thriving cosmopolitan cities they've become and what I see, more than anything, is a country that looks a great deal like my mom and dad's living room at 42 Hoyle Avenue.

Which, by the way, is no longer there.

By the 1990s, my sister and I had moved out and my parents were traveling and there were plenty of places for new Indian immigrants to land, so our house stopped being such a way station for so many travelers. It had served its purpose in that regard. Then, by 2019, as my parents had grown older, two things had become true. One, my mother began insisting that my father was too old to be doing things like cleaning out the gutters and shoveling the snow, a fact he disputes to this day. And two, he was never going to pay $30 for someone else to do it, either. So it was time for them to downsize to an apartment.

Demand for real estate in central Toronto had exploded in the forty years since my parents bought, and on Hoyle Avenue the land under the 1,250-square-foot bungalows was worth far more than the old, cramped houses themselves, which nobody wants anymore. Everyone on the block was tearing them down, rebuilding with something double or triple the size, then selling and walking away with the profits. The street was transforming into something totally different. So my parents decided to do the same. My sister and I moved them into a nice place about fifteen minutes away. They've made friends in their building, which is walking distance to their jamatkhana and the buses. Then they tore down our old bungalow that they'd bought for $36,000 and built a stunningly beautiful new home in its place. The price they were able to get more than made up for what they'd lost when ABC Bakery was torn down and South Africa confiscated all the proceeds. Half a century after leaving Marabastad, thanks to their discipline, hard work, and countless small acts of courage, they were finally made whole again.

6

The Right Reasons

_____

Given that our bungalow at 42 Hoyle was only 1,250 square
feet, a space that included three bedrooms, a bathroom, a living room, a dining room, and a kitchen, it goes without saying that
the rooms were tiny, cramped. Yet my parents were always throwing
huge parties and having big political meetings. So one of the dominant memories of my childhood is that there were always too many
people and not enough chairs. Being the youngest, I was always sitting cross-legged on the floor with all these adults towering above
me, and that's exactly where I was the first time I heard about my
father's decision to run for office. I was eleven years old, and a bunch
of our Ismaili friends and several of my parents' political contacts
had crowded into our tiny living room, and I sat at their feet listening
quietly as my father sat everyone down and told them he was thinking about running for a seat in the provincial parliament of Ontario.

It was, to everyone assembled, a crazy idea. At that point, no Muslim or South Asian had ever been elected to any major political office anywhere in Canada, not at the provincial level and certainly not at the federal level. Even nonwhite people who'd been in the country for some time had enjoyed little success on that front. There was one Black man, Leonard Braithwaite, who'd been elected to the Ontario provincial parliament in 1963. He won by 443 votes.

That was *it*.

Most of my parents' friends tried to discourage him. "Why do you want to run?" they asked. "You're going to lose anyway." Which was understandable. At that point, it had been only ten years since we'd arrived from Kenya, and most of the Indians in the country hadn't even been there as long as we had. It's not uncommon for new immigrants to stay out of politics, in part because they don't feel that they're fully members of society when they first arrive, or because they don't speak the language or don't feel they have a big enough constituency. My parents were different. From the days my grandfather Rajabali spent growing up on Tolstoy Farm, our family had been steeped in a tradition that believed all people deserved full economic, civic, and political recognition in society, and like his father before him, my dad had never stopped fighting to see that reality come to pass. His aspirations had been crushed in Pretoria, and they'd failed to come to fruition in Kenya, but Canada was so open and inviting to my parents that they felt this was the place where their dreams would be possible. So my parents had a hunger to participate. They were champing at the bit to join in.

When they arrived, the first step was deciding which political party to join. In Canada at the time, as in America, we had a Liberal Party and a Conservative Party, only the ideological spectrum of the two parties was and still is about 10 percent of what the American spectrum is. Indeed, at the time the Conservative Party was actually known as the *Progressive* Conservative Party, which might sound like an oxymoron but is in fact a fairly accurate description of the party's views. The Conservatives were a bunch of normal people who you would define as marginally probusiness, and Liberals were a bunch of normal people who you would define as marginally pro-union. It all clustered around the middle, right to the left of where the middle is in America. Further to the left, there was a third party called the New Democratic Party, which was the closest thing we had to a socialist party, even though they weren't really socialists at all, just more pro-union and proworker. All that has changed somewhat in recent years as a small amount of polarization has pulled more people to the far right, and there have been other parties over the years, such as the Bloc Québécois, which has no representation outside of Quebec, and then there's always a couple of random parties that show up around the fringes. But in Ontario in 1981, you had the Conservatives and the Liberals and the New Democrats and that was about it.

After attending events for all three, my parents felt most comfortable with the Liberal Party. They didn't feel discomfort in the other ones; they just had more comfort with the Liberals. Having grown up in a place where politics was all about polarization and racism and identity, they liked the idea that the Liberal Party had a complex system of politics that straddled the middle. "It's not a party for the workers to the exclusion of capitalism and business," my dad used to say, "and it's not a party in favor of capitalism and business to the exclusion of the worker." Also, most immigrants at the time naturally gravitated to the Liberal Party anyway because they felt a natural affinity for its leader, Pierre Trudeau, who'd pushed for the policies that let them into Canada in the first place.

So after arriving and starting their travel agency business in 1971, they joined the Liberals in '72 and were already voting and volunteering out on the campaign trail, canvassing, putting up yard signs, whatever. They were all in the minute they hit the ground. They thrived in a society that said, "You're welcome to participate in the governance of your country." That was heaven to them.

Through their work with the Liberal Party and the Toronto business community, my parents' civic engagement soon went far beyond stuffing envelopes and handing out flyers. They started plugging into the established infrastructure outside of our community, taking on roles to serve the broader public. My dad was asked to serve on the board of the nearby Flemingdon Park Health Center; he eventually became chair. He was involved at various levels of the United Way and the North York Red Cross, also eventually becoming chairman of the latter organization.

My mother was right there with him. She became a member of the Canadian branch of the International Business and Professional Women's Foundation, a kind of Rotary Club for women, and she was eventually elected president for two terms. She was appointed to the Ontario Council for Citizenship and Multiculturalism, and after that to the Ontario Judicial Council, which was a council that took cases for people who had a complaint about how their case had been handled by the court system.

My parents had a dedication to this cause of building a civil society. They had a passion for it, and both of them have seemingly endless reserves of patience combined with a knack for paying tremendous attention to detail. There are certain kinds of people: you put them on a committee, and within six months they're running the damn thing. That was both of my parents. It's a sensibility that they have. Things have to get done, and things have to get done right. They weren't in it for social reasons, and they weren't in it for recognition. They were in it because they believed in it and because they thrived in the minutiae of it. They were equipped for the grind of it. So whether it was politics or social issues, they were involved all the time, nonstop. And as soon as my sister was old enough, she would enter that world as well.

Many people's reaction to my parents' civic engagement was, "Well, I don't have the time." But the way my parents saw it, even if politics isn't something you love to do, politics is something that needs to get done. The potholes don't fix themselves. The libraries and hospitals don't fund themselves. The garbage doesn't pick itself up. It's no different than running a household. Whether it's making dinner or mowing the lawn, it's got to get done. Either you can look at cooking and yard work as drudgery to be avoided, or you can make cooking and yard work your hobby and find joy in it. That's exactly how it was for my family and civic engagement. My parents didn't have other hobbies—no golf or card games. Politics was their hobby, and so as I grew older, it became mine, too. It was always my father who would speak in terms of something big that we needed to talk about. So we heard these tales about Martin Luther King Jr. and Nelson Mandela or Gandhi and my grandfather Rajabali. I was so young I wasn't always clear that these were real people. They were like fables to me, and there was always a moral to the story, about how to stand up and do the right thing and the importance of courage in the face of adversity. It was never a lecture. It was just a story about how things were in those days. That would be us on a typical Tuesday night.

We had the news on all the time, too. We watched election results on election night, back before the days of Steve Kornacki and his big map, when it was just two somber, serious guys at a desk. Whatever the issues of the day were, railroad strikes or inflation or unemployment figures, that's what we would talk about. It was always, "I'm going to get involved with this group." Or "I'm going to join this committee." I missed the boat on many of the normal things that kids did in those days, like scouting or sports. I didn't do any of that stuff because I was busy working with the Red Cross on a blood drive, or attending a political debate about a policy issue or some local ordinance that needed to be passed. That was our leisure time, and over time, I grew to love it.

Still, even as multiculturalism became the law of the land, there was a limit to what newly arrived immigrants could do in the public sphere, and that limit was elected office. From the moment my parents arrived, there was nothing about the political system that told them, "Your voice doesn't count here," and yet clearly there was this important platform that none of us had yet managed to attain. Why was that the case? You could say it was because the Canadian population wasn't ready to vote for people from our community. Or you could say it was because the people in our community simply weren't ready to run, let alone serve, in those offices. But the one impediment you couldn't point to was any form of legal discrimination. Those hurdles didn't exist in 1981 because what's really quite remarkable about the way elections work in Canada is that elections in Canada actually work *well*.

In America, depending on where you live and what color you are, voting requires as many headaches as possible. In Philadelphia, where I live some of the time, the nightmare of getting a mail-in ballot is like solving a weird logic puzzle in a video game. (In my county, at one point you had to mail a ballot back with a photocopy of your driver's license with one envelope properly inserted inside another envelope.) None of it makes any sense, and it's simply designed to have people make mistakes so that their votes don't count. Pennsylvania people figured out that a mail-in ballot has a greater chance of being a Democratic ballot than a Republican ballot, so the Republican state legislature decided, "OK, we're going to make mail-in balloting so complicated that eight out of ten people get it wrong." You see the same thing in Texas and Georgia. Last year we had drop-off ballots, this year we don't, next year we're closing half the polling places downtown. None of that shit exists in Canada.

In Canada, the whole thing's run by little old retired ladies who design it to be easy on purpose. For starters, we don't have fifty different election systems. Just the one. That's it. Whether it's municipal, provincial, or federal, it's fundamentally all the same.

Another blessing is that election periods are entirely, mercifully, prescribed. There's no permanent campaign where candidates bombard you with television commercials twenty-four hours a day for over a year before an election. In Canada, any election for any office is a six-week process, start to finish. You cannot begin publicly advertising or campaigning before that period begins, and then at the end of that period there's Election Day—that's it. Everybody go home.

There are tight limits on campaign finance, too. It's the opposite of America, where all these corporations and dark money groups are pouring millions of dollars into every race from senator to dog catcher. In Canada the formula is strict. You're not allowed to take money from any corporations or trade unions. Only individuals can donate, and there's a strict and low limit to what they can donate. The amount of money candidates can spend on advertising is directly proportional to how many registered voters there are in your district. If you are running to represent a district of one hundred thousand people, for example, you're allowed to spend $100,000 on your campaign. The same holds for your opponents. Is there "dark money" in Canadian elections? Sure. A bit. People do find ways to skirt the rules. But it's nowhere near the problem it is in America.

Your campaign is also responsible for all advertising that appears in your name, so there's none of this Super PAC nonsense, in which other people who are not part of your campaign advertise on your behalf. If you spend your allotted $100,000 and then another group spends $25,000 attacking your opponent on your behalf, you're now in violation of campaign finance laws, and you can even be disqualified for it. You can win the election and not be able to take office because you've overspent.

Even better than that, in Canada cheating isn't legal. Here in America, you've got all kinds of dirty tricks, like robo calls telling seniors to go vote the Tuesday after Election Day and all that. There's no quarter for that sort of thing in Canada, no allowance for misleading advertising to confuse people or suppress votes. All the big money and soft money and Nixonian trickery, it doesn't work. Or it didn't in 1981, at any rate.

Then, once the very simple campaigns run their very brief course, the actual voting couldn't be easier. Once you're registered to vote, you're presumed registered from that point forward unless you've moved. The voter rolls are kept up to date through a process called enumeration, which takes place before every election. Volunteers go door-to-door and ask you, "Are you David Smith?" And if you're not

David Smith you say, "No, that family moved out of here a year ago. I'm Ali Velshi." They'll take David Smith off the list and put Ali Velshi on the list. Now the registry is updated and when you show up to vote you just give them your name. You don't even have to show an ID, because you're already on the list. And wherever David Smith moved off to there's some other set of volunteers making sure he's on the rolls for whatever district he's moved into, so David Smith won't have any problems, either.

On Election Day, we do have poll watchers, called scrutineers, that either of the parties can appoint to watchdog the process and challenge someone's ballot. But the onus is squarely on them to prove that your registration is no good or that you're not who you say you are, and either way they can't stop you from voting in the moment. It is, generally speaking, not an adversarial process, and the whole system works so smoothly there's rarely anything to challenge.

Once you make it to the front of the queue, you're given a ballot that's folded a particular way, a trifold. You take it to a booth, open it up, take the pencil that's there in the booth, put an X next to the person you want to vote for, fold it back the way they gave it to you, and then you hand it to the poll worker, who initials it on the square that goes over the two parts of the fold. The poll worker hands it back to you, and you put it in the box. That's it, and it's the same everywhere, for everyone.

It really is that simple.

So, absent any legal barriers, the real force keeping South Asians and other immigrants out of office was simple inertia: The people who ran for office were the people who had always run for office—and identity was a huge piece of that. The Conservatives were always the English-speaking Protestants, and the Liberals were generally the Catholics, some English-speaking and some French-speaking. That's how it went.

So that system had worked and had kept everyone happy for years and years and years, but after the mass immigration of the 1970s changed the complexion of the country, it was increasingly obvious that it was no longer going to be a workable arrangement. My father was one of the people who spoke up at the time and said, "This has to change, because if we never break this power-sharing agreement that goes French/English, Catholic/Protestant, the rest of us—the Jews, the Muslims, the Indians, the Black people—are never getting into the system."

The French speakers, understandably, wanted to keep their status as the most-favored minority, with all the perks and privileges that it entailed. They wanted that status enshrined in the constitution. They wanted to be described as "a distinct society"; that was the language they used. But my father, while he fully supported their right to stand up for their language and their culture, believed that for a pluralistic society to work, no group could have an officially sanctioned status above any other group.

That was my father's hypothesis, anyway. This bipolar balance of power needed to evolve and become a multipolar balance of power, which was what Pierre Trudeau had promised. He hadn't brought brown people in to be undocumented, socially marginalized laborers, as South Africa had done and as America continues to do. Trudeau told my parents and all the other immigrants, "You will be welcome here as full citizens and full participants in society." And given the warm welcome we'd received, there was no reason to believe that wasn't true, except that virtually no one had ever run for office to actually *prove* that it was true. There was a point to be made, that you could run for office here without landing in jail or being shot by somebody, and it had to be done if for no other reason than to prove that it could be done.

Looking at my parents' lives in 1981, there was nothing to suggest that they should be the ones to do it. Their travel agency was barely on its feet and relied on both of them working full time to keep it running. Their experience in Canadian politics consisted largely of stuffing envelopes and knocking on doors. Add to that the fact that my dad is not what you'd call a natural retail politician. He loves politics, but he's more the guy you'd find with his nose in a policy paper than the guy you'd see out kissing babies at the mall. But after ten years of watching the system, my dad decided he would be the guy.

My father, Murad Velshi, announced he was running to be the Liberal Party nominee for the Don Mills riding of Toronto in the Ontario provincial parliament. (In Canada, a voting district is known as a "riding," and they're identified by names, not numbers.) If he won his party's nomination, he would be setting himself up to run against the incumbent Conservative Party representative, Dennis Timbrell. On paper, the matchup between Dennis Timbrell and my dad wasn't even a matchup at all. Timbrell looked unstoppable. First of all, he had the distinct advantage of being a Conservative incumbent in a district that had been held by a Conservative since its inception. Timbrell had the additional advantage of being the minister of health for the province. In Canada, where health care is universal and is the single biggest budget item for the government, the health minister is responsible for bringing funding into all the medical centers in the district. It's a position that's right up there with the finance minister and the attorney general in terms of prestige. If you're one of those people, unless there's a wave that sweeps your whole party out of power, the chances of you losing your election are approximately zero.

On top of those two substantial advantages was the fact that Timbrell looked every inch the Canadian politician. He was tall, white, clean-cut, and confident yet plainspoken. He seemed straight out of central casting. He couldn't have been a starker contrast to my father, this nice, quiet immigrant man who spoke with an accent and stood about five-foot-three.

Because my dad had been involved in so many local civic institutions, including his stint as chairman of the local health center, he wasn't a complete nobody. But when we ran the first polls to gauge local name recognition, where they put out the names of generic candidates and ask people who they'd vote for, my father had literally zero name recognition. In fact, some fake names that had been included in the poll polled higher than he did, simply because they were Anglo names that sounded more familiar to people than "Murad." A few people on the campaign staff half-jokingly suggested that my dad change his name to "Mike" to get better name recognition, a notion he didn't entertain even for a moment.

In 1981, Don Mills was an interesting collection of constituents. It was a typical riding in terms of its socioeconomic mix. Urban planning in Toronto was done fairly well; you don't have all the poor people concentrated in one area and all the rich people in another. What set Don Mills apart as a district was how uniquely multicultural it was. Seventy-three languages were spoken within its borders. So while it had this heavy ethnic concentration, there wasn't any one ethnicity other than white large enough to make an impact. So the older, whiter, more conservative Protestants in the area remained its political and economic center of gravity.

When my dad started his campaign, there were two parts to the process. First he had to win the Liberal Party nomination. The nomination process took place many months before the general election, and it felt much bigger than the election-night battle itself. Once you're in the election, everyone who's a partisan is on your side, but the nomination is a big in-fight. The way it works is like a caucus in the American primary system. The nomination is held on a particular night by members of the party in that constituency. To participate, you had to have registered with the Liberal Party of the Don Mills riding. If you had done so and were a member in good standing, you were then entitled to vote in it.

Getting the nomination was a numbers game. If you got more people to register for the party and show up for the night of the nomination, you got in. Because the Muslim and South Asian communities represented such a fresh crop of new voters, they gave my dad an advantage in securing the nomination. But it was a big undertaking. It took months of going door-to-door, having people sign carbon-copy triplicate forms, and you never knew when you signed somebody up if they were going to show up to vote for you. The night of the nomination was like a big convention, and getting people from where they lived to this auditorium was always a question of "Is there enough parking?" and "Can we bus people in?" It required a huge amount of resources just to get to that point in the process, which was partly why immigrants didn't often do it.

If you're in a heavily contested primary, the whole process is even more complicated, but luckily my father's primary that year wasn't contentious at all. Nobody wanted to run against Dennis Timbrell, and nobody cared about whoever did want to run against Dennis Timbrell, because running against Dennis Timbrell was a fool's errand. So with all the new Muslim and South Asian members my father was able to bring to the nomination contest, and because no one else wanted it, he took it fairly easily. And like everything else in Canada, the whole process is done instantly. You cast your ballot, they count it on the spot, it's administered by the party, and they declare the winner.

Once my dad secured the nomination, the general campaign began in earnest. Since we had no money, we had to rely on the campaign infrastructure we had inherited from the Don Mills Liberal Party, which, given that the Liberals had failed to hold this seat for forty-two consecutive years, was not much. Nonetheless, I can still remember walking into our campaign headquarters for the first time and thinking, "Wow, this is so neat!" It all felt wildly important to me, like I'd been invited into a secret world I didn't even know existed. Of course, I was eleven. Campaign offices, especially for local candidates, are nothing special, and they're all pretty much the same, some vacant storefront that you can rent for a short amount of time because H&R Block only needs it during tax season and the pop-up Christmas store hasn't opened yet. Inside there's nothing but bare-bones rooms with faded carpets and cheap desks and lots of boxes of donuts. This particular spot was in some random strip mall that wasn't on the way to anywhere, so it wasn't the best place to be, but it was what we could get.

Our staff was made up of the existing party regulars from Don Mills. They were all white people. We didn't have any immigrants on our staff because Toronto campaigns had never been populated by immigrants. They weren't in the system because they didn't have any campaign experience. What we got was a bunch of Liberal Party hacks who'd been around for a long, long time. People who are life-long devotees of political organizations are an odd bunch, much like chess fanatics or any other eccentrics who live and breathe whatever they're into. They tend to have time on their hands because they're either retired or don't work that much. You can always spot them. They're a type. They're also the most committed, determined kinds of people you'll ever meet.

Our campaign manager was an old Liberal from the area named Mike Kenny, one of the warmest guys I've ever met, one of those red-faced, hardworking Irishmen who always had a big smile when-ever he saw you. Then there was our yard sign guy, the woman who handled the phone canvass, the woman who organized the door-to-door canvass. None of them had ever staffed a winning campaign. They were quick to embrace us, because their losing streak was so long and hopeless, any novelty that might add a new dimension to the race was a welcome development. It was basically "Hey, let's give the brown guy a shot. What have we got to lose?"

Our staffers may have been the B team, but they proved to be dedicated and campaigned their hearts out. Those types of people may have their quirks, but they really do see themselves as warriors for democracy, and in our experience, that's what they were.

Once our six-week campaign began, we called as many people as we could call, knocking on every door possible and carpeting the area with pamphlets touting my dad's policy positions and strengths. Every campaign has the data from the last election of how every ward voted, so we knew where our built-in strengths were and where our weaknesses were. Out of the forty or so wards we had to canvass, we allocated resources where we thought we could turn the most votes around. If a particular ward had always voted Conservative by a margin of 90 percent, we weren't going to invest a lot of time in it. If a ward was 50–50, my dad would get out there himself as often as possible, shaking hands at the supermarket or meeting people at their homes.

Back then, politicking in local races was all about shaking hands and kissing babies. You didn't have enough money for TV or radio, so it was all a matter of knocking on doors and being at bus stops and subway stations in the morning and when people came home. Back then, people approached you and weren't scared of you. You could knock on people's doors in the evening, and while they would be annoyed if it was dinnertime, they wouldn't be annoyed at the mere fact that you had knocked on their door; they wouldn't think you were some weirdo.

I did all that door-to-door stuff with my dad. I was an extroverted, social kid, and a political campaign is, by definition, an attempt to meet as many people as possible as quickly as possible, so I loved it. There was nothing better to me than the freedom and the fun of knocking on a door to have people open it, look out at eye level, then look down and wonder why this kid had knocked at their door when it wasn't Halloween. I was an articulate kid for eleven, which people found compelling and precocious, or at least amusing. So I would give my very serious pitch about my dad and why he was running and then I'd say, "My dad's down the road if you want to meet him." I loved it so much that one time I got stuck talking to some lady at her house, and my dad got ahead of me and went and knocked on a door without me. I got upset with him and said, "Dad! I'm supposed to knock first!"—which he thought was great.

The best part about it was that a lot of people genuinely wanted
to talk to us. We'd get involved in these long, deep conversations.
Maybe that was a different time in Canada, but people would engage
and really talk to you, even when you randomly showed up on their
doorstep. We always had to juggle our enjoyment of these fun conversations with the fact that we still had eight thousand more doors
to go knock on.

There was nothing nasty about politics in Toronto in 1981, at
least not in Don Mills. We got to know the community and the
campaign workers. Once in a while at a street corner or bus stop,
we would run into Dennis Timbrell, and my father would chat with
him; I'd watch the two of them and think, "That's neat. This guy is
the opposition. This is the other team, and yet there's no hostility."

Watching my dad in the all-candidates debates was the best. I
loved seeing him up there debating. You wouldn't necessarily think
my soft-spoken dad would be the strongest debater, but he more
than held his own. He had a quiet strength that came from being
thoughtful, knowing the answers to all the questions, and having
firm convictions on all of the issues. He was disarmingly polite, too.
He didn't make enemies out of anyone. He enjoyed discourse and
dialogue with people, and that's something that I've gotten from
him. To see him onstage as a candidate, it looked like he was fulfilling a calling, which he was. I didn't know that at the time because I
hadn't fully connected my dad's story with the stories about Rajabali
and Gandhi and our family's history up to that point. I now understand what he was doing was a continuation of what had started in
Africa a century before.

I fell in love with politics during that campaign. I thought it was
the greatest thing in the world. The camaraderie, the interaction with

people, the sense of purpose. Spending all day out on the trail and then going back to the campaign office where the phones were ringing and the walls were covered with all these great maps showing the whole Don Mills riding broken down into color-coded wards. Eating cold pizza with staff and volunteers, recounting anything interesting that had happened to us that day, unified and energized by our shared sense of purpose. I liked the swag, too. In those days the party sent you a book with the designs and Pantone colors you could use for hats and pins and so forth. Because we were broke, it was the cheapest, worst-quality stuff money could buy. But it all had my dad's name emblazoned across it, and for an eleven-year-old kid, there's nothing cooler than that. The campaign was also a wonderful thing for us to share as a family. We were already close, but this became our full-time family activity.

It was also a notably civilized campaign. Any anti-Muslim rhetoric or backlash my parents might have expected to encounter simply failed to materialize. The ethnic factor was there, of course, in the background, and it did influence the race in certain ways. Dennis Timbrell went out of his way to get endorsements from people of color, to an extent that he had never done before. At the same time, it was apparent to everyone who wasn't white, whether they were Muslim, Chinese, Black, or whatever, that finally here was a chance to vote for someone who looked more like them than Dennis Timbrell did, a fact that might make my father more sympathetic to their needs and interests as constituents. So generally speaking, there was a bit of solidarity there, and my father certainly knew that. But at the end of the day, he ran as the candidate who would represent everyone.

Every now and then someone at the campaign office would jokingly call my dad "Mike," which was a reminder that we all understood the impact that his name and his background was having on the race, but that was about as far as it went. Ten years after this tectonic shift in Canada's racial and ethnic demographics, the big story was that it wasn't a big story at all.

The campaign was much more a logistical enterprise than anything else. The get-out-the-vote operation was a major piece of it. We knew there were Liberal Party voters who would support my dad, but we had to motivate them to go to the polls despite the fact that they'd lost the riding in every election cycle for forty-two years. People didn't vote because they didn't think their vote would affect the outcome. So we had a big push at the end not to convince people to like my dad but to get them to get up off their couches and go cast a ballot. We were calling everyone. "Do you have transportation? Do you know how to get there? What can we do for you? Are you working on that day?" That was the crazy, last-minute drama.

When Election Day finally came, we continued to work. We spent the morning rush hour at the busiest bus stop in the district, shaking hands and passing out flyers. Then we spent the rest of the day moving about to wherever the biggest crowds would be, and then for the evening rush hour we were all back at the bus station again, doing all the last-minute glad-handing we could.

Around 6:30 or so, rush hour slowed to a trickle. My dad said he wanted to go back to the house and change into the suit he was going to wear to watch the election returns come in at our campaign headquarters that night. So while everyone else went back to the office to eat and wait for the returns, I rode home with my dad.

After he changed and got his speeches ready, we left our house to return to headquarters just before the polls closed at eight. As we were driving, my father flicked on the radio right at 8:00 p.m., right as the station launched into the top of the next hour, which opened with news of the evening's election results. "The polls have closed across Ontario," the announcer said, "and it's too early to tell who will form the government tonight." He then continued, "But there is one race we can call, and we can declare Dennis Timbrell the victor in the riding of Don Mills, Toronto."

I couldn't believe it. It was literally 8:01. Over a hundred races had been run across the province that day, and my father had just suffered the biggest, swiftest, most resounding loss out of all of them. I didn't understand how they could have known who won right after the polls had closed. How could they have counted the votes already? I'd assumed it would take hours for the election to be called. I didn't understand anything about exit polling and projections or any of that. But they were able to call it based on nothing more than the fact that Dennis Timbrell was the safest incumbent running anywhere in the entire country. His victory was as inevitable and as obvious as the nose on my face.

I was shocked. I glanced up at my father, expecting him to be confused and angry as well, but the look on his face betrayed nothing but ease and contentment, which confused me.

"I can't believe we lost," I said.

"Of course we lost!" he said with the biggest smile. "We were never going to win."

"What?" I said. "Whaddya mean we were never going to win?! What was this all about?"

"We ran because we could," he said. "I stood for what I believed in, people had a chance to vote for me, and more people voted for the other guy than voted for me. That was always going to happen; I knew that. But I ran, and now that I've lost, our life goes on. We don't get arrested. We don't get shunned. Nothing bad happens."

It blew my mind. For the whole campaign, little eleven-year-old me had been looking up to my dad, seeing him onstage doing the debates, and thinking it was the coolest thing in the world. Not understanding politics at all, I'd honestly believed we were doing it because we had a shot and it was going to be so amazing when he won.

When we pulled into the campaign office, I was still trying to process it all. But then we walked in the front door and people started to clap and cheer. There weren't any tears. I thought, "What are you happy about? We lost." But I was the odd man out, because I was apparently the only one who thought we were going to win.

My dad promptly went in the back and called Dennis Timbrell and congratulated him on his victory. It was a cordial conversation that lasted under a minute. And that was that. My dad came out and thanked the staff, and what I remember about that moment is that everyone in the room was jubilant and ecstatic, except for my father. The staff were excited, because they thought we'd moved the needle. I would subsequently learn that they were celebrating because my dad had taken the Liberal Party from third place to second place, which was a difference of maybe a thousand votes. We'd made a solid dent in the district's Conservative majority, paving the way for a real victory in the future. My father, on the other hand, was at ease. That's how I would describe him. He had done what he needed to do, and he had a look of satisfaction that it had been done.

Thanks to my father, that was the night I learned that there is a deeper way to think about politics, which for so many people has become a dirty word. "Politicians are all crooks," they say. "The system is rigged. I don't trust any of them." And it's true that there's no shortage of politicians who provide reasons not to trust politicians. But the world is full of people who engage in politics for the right reasons. I know that because my immediate family is full of people who engage in politics for the right reasons, and on that night in 1981, that dingy old storefront campaign office was full of people celebrating, simply because they'd exercised their right to engage in politics for the right reasons. To this day, when I hear people run down politics and politicians, I recoil. Because cynicism about politics is actually a luxury of those who have never had to experience life without it, and if those people ever truly lost their ability to participate in the system, they'd never take it for granted again.

7

Murad Velshi Could Win

After my father's loss to Dennis Timbrell, as our election-night party wound down, most of the campaign staff went home and my parents and sister and I started cleaning up, throwing out the empty pizza boxes and packing up all the gear and supplies. If there's anything less glamorous than running a campaign for local office, it would have to be shutting down a campaign for local office, especially a losing one. It's twice the drudgery with none of the adrenaline. There were people who had pledged to donate that we still had to collect from in order to pay the bills that still needed to be paid. Somebody had to drive around and pick up all the yard signs. All the staplers and envelopes and the unused Post-its had to be boxed up to go and sit in some old Liberal's garage until the next go 'round. And on top of all of it, my parents had about a thousand phone calls to make and a thousand thank-you notes to write. Every person who'd donated or supported the campaign with even an ounce of their time had to be contacted and showered with appreciation. Because those were valuable relationships, and those relationships would be important if my father ever decided to run again.

Six years later, he did.

Shortly after his loss in 1981, my dad formed a committee called Federation of Ontario Liberal Satellites (FOLSAT). The goal of FOLSAT was to bring together leading members from all of the different ethnic communities of Ontario—Blacks, Japanese, Koreans, South Asians, and so on—identify credible candidates for office, and support their campaigns. FOLSAT played a major role in bringing nonwhites into the Liberal Party, which the party welcomed. One of my father's main jobs for FOLSAT was identifying the promising candidates. Their first success came with Alvin Curling, a Black college professor. Curling had no political experience, but in a district where most of the nonwhite and immigrant voters were working class, his academic credentials made him very appealing as a candidate. He was also a tall guy with a commanding presence and a great speaking voice. Curling's initial reaction to being asked to run for provincial parliament was "Why the hell would I do that?" But my parents convinced him; he ran in 1985 and won, becoming the representative for what was then the riding of Scarborough North. He later became the first Black Speaker of the Legislative Assembly.

Two years later, in 1987, six years after my father's first run for office, life seemed to be offering him the opportunity to run again. Two important developments took place in the Don Mills riding that year. The first major change was that the nonwhite and immigrant communities of Toronto had finally come of age. They were substantially larger in terms of sheer numbers, but more important, they had matured. The older, first-generation parents, many of whom had to work double-shift jobs to get by in the early days, finally had the time and means to do more than just survive.

Their children had come of age as well. Some were in college. Some were young professionals in their early twenties. All were fully Canadian, raised with the expectation that in this multicultural, pluralistic society, the doors of opportunity would be open to them. Many of those doors were open to varying degrees. University admissions in Canada are absurdly straightforward compared to the system in the United States. You graduate from high school with whatever grades and test scores you've got and you know within a few percentage points which universities you're qualified for. Then, when you apply, you get in.

So the children of all these immigrant groups were moving up and into different professions like law and medicine and what have you. But not into elected office. In 1987, that was still scarce. There had still never been a South Asian elected even at the provincial level anywhere in Canada. Both the older generation and the younger generation were ready for that aspirational candidate to come along, one who would represent people who didn't know that their sort could be elected to public office.

The second major development to come along that year was Dennis Timbrell's announcement that he would be retiring at the end of his term. Don Mills was still a Conservative area, but without the advantage of incumbency, winning would no longer be impossible for the Liberals. It would just be really, really hard. My dad, undaunted by the odds, energized by everything he'd learned last time, decided he would run again. And this time, he believed he had a shot to win.

So did I. By 1987, I had come of age, too. I was in high school, six years older, and I had what felt like a more grounded, realistic sense of optimism. My dad was able to raise meaningful money to fund a robust and viable campaign. We had a coalition that was waiting to be unleashed. Now it felt real because it was real. It wasn't a scrimmage. It wasn't "Let's support Murad Velshi because we support his ideas." It was "Murad Velshi could win." All we had to do was do it.

First up, again, came the Liberal Party nomination process. It was still a slog, but this time it was a much more organized slog because we knew what we were doing. Plus, we didn't have the name-recognition problem of "Who the heck is Murad Velshi." He faced four other candidates and won the nomination easily.

In the general election, my dad was up against a young Conservative named David Lindsay. Again, my father drew an opponent who was always cordial to him during the campaign, with my father responding in kind. There was never an ounce of acrimony during the campaign, no matter their significant differences on policy. Lindsay's genial nature notwithstanding, we were under no illusions about what we were up against. We didn't have to face Dennis Timbrell this time, but the fact that he was gone meant that the entire Conservative political machine had swung into action to focus on Don Mills. The Conservatives considered it one of their safe seats, and they were pouring resources into the race to make sure they didn't lose it.

We set up our campaign headquarters in a small three-office building in the parking lot of a shopping center in Flemingdon Park, right in the heart of the immigrant community we hoped to mobilize. It wasn't a large space. Same as with our last campaign office, every inch of every wall and every desk and even the floor was used for something, whether it was colored maps of all the wards or the spreadsheets of names and polling data or the boxes and boxes and boxes of pens and highlighters and paper clips.

Money made a huge difference. The combination of my dad's newfound skill as a fundraiser and the fact that the immigrant community, and particularly the Ismailis, had more resources from which to raise funds allowed us to up our game in certain ways. We still couldn't afford paid advertising, but we could afford extra runs of brochures and yard signs and T-shirts and hats—and the T-shirts didn't look like they'd been screen printed in somebody's basement. You could actually wash them and the ink wouldn't flake off.

But our greatest asset, the weapon in our arsenal that the opposition couldn't hope to match, was the enthusiasm of our coalition. The Conservatives probably had more voters, but we had more energized voters. In 1981, our campaign infrastructure was entirely inherited from the Don Mills Liberal Party of the past. In 1987, we built our own. We still had the old white Liberals in the constituency who'd worked on lots of campaigns and were coming out to use their experience in support of my dad the same way they had in '81. But this time, we had our own people, too. We attracted an army of volunteers. We had the entire Ismaili community that we were part of. They were the core. Then, beyond that, we had everyone else.

On any given day, our campaign office looked like a meeting of the General Assembly of the United Nations. We had Sikhs, Filipinos, and Jamaicans. We even had all the white-ethnic volunteers coming in, the Italians and the Portuguese and the eastern Europeans. There are all kinds of rivalries in and among ethnic groups, between Muslims and Hindus, Indians and Pakistanis. But all that was set aside for this common cause. They all took such deep pride in the fact that someone who didn't look like everyone else was running. Toronto had always been not just white but WASPy, and everyone in Don Mills who had ever felt like the power structure and the prevailing culture of the city didn't represent them flocked to the banner of Murad Velshi.

Over the course of the campaign, we even started amassing a coalition that stretched beyond our actual constituency. First it was the Ismailis who lived outside Don Mills who started showing up to volunteer, but then as word spread, people were coming from all over Toronto. They were catching buses and subway trains late after work, riding an hour across town to show up at our office. If you showed up at our campaign office during that campaign, we'd find something for you to do. It didn't matter what your skill level was. We would put you at a table with a phone bank. We'd give you envelopes to stuff. Whatever. People who couldn't afford babysitters brought their kids. I still meet people who tell me, "I remember coming with my parents to help your dad canvass and knock on doors and give out brochures."

Because it was a bunch of immigrants helping the campaign, tons of people would bring food. You'd walk into the office any time of day and it would be filled with the most wonderful smells from Tupperware and tinfoil containers filled with delicious curries and rice dishes from all the far-flung corners of the world.

For a city that had never had ethnic candidates, our office was quite a sight, all this different food and signs and brochures in different languages. It had a feeling. I wouldn't go so far as to call it a movement, but it was definitely a moment, a seminal moment for immigrants in their civic and democratic experience in Toronto. The idea that this five-foot-three brown man could be elected to the provincial legislature of Ontario—that didn't happen in our world, and the fact that it might happen was a big deal.

Being older, I was able to be much more involved myself. I wasn't hanging around as an appendage to my parents. I could drive. I got all my friends, among them Mikey and AJ, a high school dropout and kind of a ne'er-do-well mechanic we'd become friends with. Julian and Paul, a couple of upper-middle-class white kids I knew from school, were also regulars. They didn't have the same stake in my father's election that many in his core coalition had, but they were as into it as I was. It was hard not to be. We were making history. My friends and I did all kinds of stuff in that campaign, dropping brochures, knocking on doors, pressing the flesh at the bus stop. But the thing I was most proud of was our yard sign crew. We would load all the signs and stakes in the car and drive around to all the houses that had requested them. There's nothing more fun than pounding a stake into the ground and nothing more satisfying than a formerly empty patch of grass that now had our sign on it.

We didn't have enough money to do our own polling, but as the campaign gathered steam, we had access to polling that showed that the Liberal Party was leading across Ontario. There was a sense that a big shake-up was coming. The leader of the Liberal Party for the province once came through on his bus to visit our campaign, which we hadn't merited six years earlier. He would do these half-hour stops and see ten to fifteen candidates in a day, and they were a big deal because it would bring out constituents who wanted to meet this person who might become the premier of Ontario. Not all the candidates got that; the party only did it for the races where they felt the leader's time could affect the outcome. So the fact that he came to campaign with my dad said a great deal about how things were going.

Once Election Day arrived, we knew that it was going to be close and that the result would probably come down to turnout, so we knew we had to get as many as we could to the polls. Because Don Mills hadn't elected a Liberal in so long, the party didn't have a robust get-out-the-vote operation in the area. That shortcoming was further compounded by the fact that so many people in these immigrant enclaves were voting for the first time. They hadn't felt engaged by the system, so we had to engage them. We had to reach out and connect with thousands of people, get them to the polls and then get them home again, all before the polls closed 8:00 p.m.—a massive operation for a very small campaign in a very compressed window of time. We were going full tilt the whole day. Picking up groups of voters here and there, driving them to the polls, and driving them back home—the whole thing felt like a blur.

Luckily, we had an incredible source of help in this effort. In any city, there's a particular ethnicity that dominates the ranks of the taxi drivers, and in 1987, it seemed to me that every taxi driver in Toronto was Sikh. Outside our campaign office, there was literally an ocean of cabs lined up and waiting, like at the airport. None of them were running their meters. My mom's sister was the dispatcher. She'd run to the phone bank and get a voter on the line, then she'd come out and say, "This person at this address needs to go vote." The next driver in line would go, pick them up, take them to the polls, and return for more. If the voter didn't speak English properly, a volunteer who spoke their language would go along, get the person to the right polling location, make sure they voted, then get them back to their house. We had to make sure nobody had any excuse not to make it out to vote. We even had endless supplies of food for people who needed to eat. The taxi driver would pick them up, bring them to the campaign office to get a bite, then take them to vote, and drive them back home again. It went on all day. Nonstop.

This time, as the day wound down, my dad and I knew not to be in the car at 8:00 p.m. We were at the headquarters with everyone else, standing room only, everybody crammed into our tiny offices, clustered around the television watching the returns come in, standing on chairs to try to get a better view of the screen. The first good news was that our race wasn't called at 8:01. We watched and waited, taking calls from our people out in the field reporting on voter turnout and results at all the different polling locations.

At some point in the evening, as the exit polls and results started to come in, it became clear that it was going to be a big night for the Liberals. Part of it, I think, was that there was a general dissatisfaction with the Conservative government, which had been in power in Ontario forever. The pendulum always swings back the other way. But the other big part of it was that Toronto was a different place than it had been before. As the hours went on, the map started to color in a way that suggested that it would be unusual if we didn't win. The Liberal margins around Toronto were massive. But watching the returns come in, there's no way to know when your race is going to be called, so we waited and waited; at a certain point, I stepped out of the crowd and into my dad's office to get something, and right at that exact moment, there was a huge eruption of cheering and applause from the main campaign room behind me. I walked back out and everyone was smiling and high-fiving and by the time I jostled my way through up to the TV, it was already over. They'd called it and moved on to the next result. We had won. In the end, it wasn't even close. My dad got 10,973 votes, and the Conservative David Lindsay got 8,666 votes, which was a bigger margin than we ever imagined we would have won by. I started crying. My parents and my sister started crying. My friends soon joined us. We started hugging each other. It was emotional in a way that I wouldn't have understood when I was eleven.

The provincial parliament of Ontario is not that big a deal. In the grand scheme of things, it's actually a very small deal. But it was momentous to the people who were there in Don Mills that night. It was monumental that this little thing was happening, that it was the beginning of something, and that they got to have a piece of it. When I go back home and see people they still talk about it. "I remember the night your dad won in 1987," they say, always with a twinkle in their eye.

———————

On September 10, 1987, my father was sworn in as a member of the Legislative Assembly of Ontario to represent the district of Don Mills. For a swearing-in ceremony like his, typically you've got the candidate's family in attendance and that's it. His was packed. There must have been close to thirty people crowded into the room. When I look back at the picture of my dad taking the oath on that day, two things stand out. The first is that he's being sworn in on a Quran, another first in Ontario political history. But the second thing of note in the picture is who's not in the picture. My mom and my sister and I are there, and standing next to my dad is his mother, her hand resting gently on his back. The person missing is my grandfather, Rajabali, who had died twenty-six years earlier. That swearing in was the culmination of the journey he had begun eighty years before, riding on Gandhi's shoulders on the long walk from Tolstoy Farm to Johannesburg.

In the end, because my dad had come in on this big Liberal wave, he didn't get appointed as a minister. Every seat in Toronto was now held by a Liberal and all the plum assignments had to be spread around. So my dad became a parliamentary assistant, which is like a deputy to a minister. You don't have the full office of the ministry, but you do have some extra staff. You attend the events that the minister doesn't go to, the second-tier things where you present awards to people and stuff like that.

It was a busy life. As the first Muslim and South Asian elected to the body, he was invited to a lot of things and was endlessly giving speeches and serving on committees. He embraced what it meant to be an elected politician representing a constituency and not just the glad-handing for the cameras. That stuff he could take or leave. Those politico types are always trying to get some soundbite on the news, but that isn't my dad. He's happiest reading a policy book or having policy discussions. He is a quiet guy who loved his committee work and the research and the field trips they would go on and the things that he learned. He was that guy that you wanted to win because you thought he'd serve you well.

He cherished every mundane task that he had, and some weren't mundane at all. He served on the Committee for Soviet Jewry, helping Jews who couldn't get out of the Soviet Union; their liberation movement spoke to him as somebody who had lived under Apartheid. Probably the work my father cherished most of all was his involvement in the Afghanistan refugee situation. About 430 Ismaili Muslims had fled the country and were stateless. The United Nations wouldn't recognize them as refugees, so they were stuck. So my father organized this sophisticated program where they would take the refugees to camps in Pakistan where they would learn language skills, either French for Quebec or English for everywhere else, as well as Canadian social and cultural norms, which, needless to say, were quite different from those in Afghanistan.

Even from his relatively junior position in the parliament, my father was able to do meaningful, important work—and he loved doing it. He never squandered a moment of it. There was no event he was too tired to attend, no meeting too boring for him to sit through, no briefing book he wouldn't devour. He was driven by the thought that even if he was a junior backbencher, even if he was sitting off on the side of the table, he had a seat at the table, something that never would have been possible before we came to Canada. He loved it, and so did we. We all lived it through him and with him.

Then, in 1990, there was another election and another wave. This time it was the New Democrats routing the Liberals and pulling Ontario even further to the left, one of the first and only times that's happened in Canada's history. With that wave, my father got swept out the same way he'd been swept in, and then he was done. He'd taken his turn, and it was time to pass the torch.

To this day, I feel so much pride about what my dad accomplished. It was remarkable, but the most remarkable thing about it was that it paved the way for elections like his to be typical. After my dad, in short order there were many people who got elected to office—Ismailis, Muslims, South Asians—in Ontario and at the federal level across Canada. My dad's eighty-nine now, and for the past thirty years or so he's served as an elder statesman for all the Muslim, South Asian, immigrant, and nonwhite elected politicians in Toronto. He gets wheeled out as an exhibit every now and then at events where people will remember that he was the first. Every election, he gets called for his endorsement. On election night, he gets invited to watch the returns come in at somebody's victory party. It's fun.

Remarkably, it used to be that immigrants and nonwhites thought of themselves as de facto Liberals. Now you see second- and third-generation immigrants becoming members of all three major political parties, which is as it should be. There are elections in Canada today where you've got the three major candidates from the three major parties and none of them are white. They're all running against each other based on their qualities as candidates, not based on identity. In a world like that, my father's achievements become even less remarkable. They get left to the history books.

The last time I was visiting my parents, I saw a campaign brochure from a young South Asian woman running for office, and with a smile I thought, "I'm sure she's too young to have been influenced by my father. She probably knows who he is, but she's far enough removed that she's just a person with her own ideas running her own race. She can stand on her own." In many ways, that is the fulfillment of what my parents believed the promise of Canada would be. It was the demonstration of their belief that if you put yourself out there, it can happen. They grew up in a world where that was never going to be the case. In South Africa, you didn't get anything for putting yourself out there except possibly being arrested. But my parents put their faith in Canada. They believed that if you put into the system and trusted the system to be fair, then you could be part of the system. In the late '70s and early '80s, it wasn't clear that that was really true. You couldn't know that. There was no way to know it because nobody had tested it. So we tested it, and it worked—and Canadian politics have never been the same since.

8

The People Who Get Shit Done

———

I was an unusually scrawny infant who couldn't gain any weight. I was so tiny and gangly that my parents took me to the doctor to try to figure out how to put a few pounds on me. Just before leaving Kenya to immigrate to Canada, we took a trip to South Africa to visit my dad's brother. My parents had to spend the week sleeping in two twin beds pushed together. They each slept in one and put me in between, and in the middle of the night I slipped through the little crack between the two beds and fell on the floor. Luckily, I was fine, fast asleep on the floor under the bed.

That same trip was far more consequential for my sister, Ishrath, who was nine years old at the time. She'd been back to South Africa a couple of times before. People thought my parents were crazy, going back to a place like South Africa, but it was home, and they still had a lot of family there. My parents took her to see the room where she was born in the Holy Cross Home, run by white nuns in the Black township, Lady Selborne. She got to hang with Rehmtulla's kids, our cousins. They would run and play in the unpaved streets of Marabastad, which turned into one big mud puddle when it rained.

But the memory that really sticks out for her is from that last visit, right before we left for Canada. One of the adults decided to take the kids to the Pretoria Zoo. Right inside the entrance of the zoo that day they were offering the kids free horse rides, and a bunch of white kids were lined up to take a turn. Growing up in Nairobi, Ishrath had gone with my parents to agricultural shows, and whenever there was a horse ride, she'd loved doing it. Since nobody had told her she wasn't allowed to do what the white kids did, she marched right over to get her free pony ride, only to have the attendant brush her off with no explanation.

As fraught as the racial politics could be for the grown-ups in Kenya, most of that never trickled down to my sister's level. She went to a mixed, multicultural Catholic school in Nairobi that had Black kids from prominent political families, white kids from expat families, and lots of Muslims and Hindus. This was her first experience with being told she couldn't do something because she wasn't white. It knocked her for a loop. Years later, while studying Apartheid in high school in Canada, she was able to place the experience in its larger historical context, to understand what it had meant for our family to live as Indians in South Africa and, more importantly, what it meant that we'd had to leave South Africa.

It really pissed her off.

As my sister and I grew into adulthood, the gap between her experience of Africa and my experience of Africa would mark a decided difference between us. Being so young when we moved away, I got to grow up fully and completely Canadian, with no real sense of loss for what we left behind. I hit a few small bumps in the road, culturally speaking, being embarrassed to take samosas to school and not getting to play hockey. But overall it was a smooth landing. The Canada I grew up in was well on its way to accepting its new immigrant population. The Canada my sister grew up in was not. When she was dropped into a new school in Toronto at age nine, she was one of the first new brown kids in the country. None of Pierre Trudeau's multiculturalism policies had taken effect yet. All of her classmates were nice to her, in the way that Canadian people are generally nice about everything. But most of the kids probably couldn't even find Kenya on a map. Everything they knew about Africa came from nature documentaries, and they'd ask her things like "Did you live in a tree?" and "Is this your first time wearing clothes?"

For Ishrath, Canada was a much harder place to belong, and that was coming on top of her time in Kenya, where she never truly belonged. She wasn't Black, which meant she wasn't part of the dominant culture of the place. Culturally, my sister never felt like she fit in anywhere. None of the places she immigrated to ever felt entirely like home, and when you grow up like that, your only real "home" is the place you were born, even if that home is a place you never really knew. From the few memories she had of those brief trips as a kid, my sister developed a lifelong yearning for South Africa, a strong desire to go back and experience the smells and see the landscape; it was a kind of homesickness for a country in which she never actually lived.

When the first free elections in South Africa were held in 1994, as newly reinstated citizens, my parents, Ishrath, and I all had the right to vote in absentia at the South African consulate in Toronto.

For my parents, to be in their fifties and voting in a South African election for the first time marked an incredible milestone of a lifelong journey. For me, it was cool. It made me feel connected to events of historical importance. But for my sister the experience was cathartic. She went on her own and stood in line and cast her ballot and walked out feeling like she'd finally taken a step on a journey back home.

Two years later, my parents decided to go back to South Africa to live. Maybe, they thought, this whole thirty-five-year exile through Kenya and Canada had been a detour, and they should go back to where they should have been all along. South Africa was a wound they needed to heal. In their entrepreneurial hustle, they decided they would be the ones to bring bagels to South Africa, so they went back and opened a bagel shop. I decided to take a break from my career in journalism to go with them and help out. It ended up being a bust. The bagels sold well, but we were there during a period when the currency was collapsing and interest rates were skyrocketing. It was lucrative if you were South African, but if you were counting your money in dollars, it was terrible. The South African rand was losing so much value that it wasn't worth it. It was also a good lesson in the old adage "You can't go home again." Nobody there thought of us as South Africans. They looked at us like we were Canadians. Because we were Canadians. For decades, my parents had longed to be back home, and when finally given the opportunity, they found it wasn't back home anymore. It wasn't the closure they went looking for, but it was the closure they needed, and in the end we all went back to our lives as Canadians in Canada.

My sister had the exact opposite experience. Because of life and work, she wasn't able to uproot herself for the year and go back to live there. But she did visit with her husband, and in the time she spent there, she came away with a feeling of belonging that she'd never felt anywhere else, not in Kenya and not in Canada. She and her husband took a day to visit the zoo. She's not normally an emotional person, but it hit her like a ton of bricks, looking back on the experience of seeing the "For Whites Only" signs and being told where she could go and what horses she wasn't allowed to ride. She found she still harbored an incredible amount of anger about it.

Those feelings weren't about the horse ride, obviously. They were about loss. To her, South Africa was the place that should have been home. It was the place that *could* have been home, easily. Not letting a little girl have a pony ride is beyond petty and ridiculous. Apartheid was so senseless and unnecessary and cruel. None of it had to happen. None of it was inevitable. It was all a result of human beings, out of their own weakness and fear, making terrible choices when they could have made good choices. And in an alternate universe of better choices, ABC Bakery never had to close, my parents never had to leave, and my sister never had to live this nomadic existence of never being able to belong. Everything would have been fine. If only they'd let a nine-year-old Indian girl ride a stupid horse.

But they didn't.

By now, with only two chapters left to go, astute readers will have already picked up on one of the shortcomings of this book—namely, that it's biased. Other than a handful of anecdotes about my sister, mother, and grandmother, it's mostly been about the accomplishments of the men in my family. We've traced the narrative from a desperate jump into shark-infested waters to starting a bread war in

Pretoria to the thrill of political victory in Canada. We've followed a straight line from my great-grandfather Velshi to his son Rajabali to my father, Murad. Because that's how you write a good story. You find a compelling chain of events, and you lay out the cause and effect that led from one to the other. Then your editor slashes anything that isn't directly related to that chain of events, because that's how you edit a good story. But a good story isn't always the complete picture. In fact, it almost never is.

In cable TV news, as I've learned through much experience, the camera distorts as much as it reveals. The camera likes spectacle. It likes action, and as we saw in Minneapolis after George Floyd, depending on how you framed the footage, you could have made it look like the entire city was on fire when the truth was that the protests were overwhelmingly peaceful with a handful of bad actors causing a few outbreaks of violence. This potential for distortion is why, as I'm covering the news, I'm always consciously trying to compensate for the biases and limitations of the medium.

Similar distortions can happen on the page. The way history usually gets written is that if you do one amazing thing once, then there's usually a story there, as we've seen with (a) jumping into the Indian Ocean, (b) starting a bread war, and (c) becoming the first elected Muslim politician in Canadian history. But if you do a dozen amazing things, and you do them every single day for your entire life, then there's no story. There's just routine, which by its nature is repetitive, and who wants to read a story that's repetitive? So, counterintuitively, the people holding society together, the people actually in the trenches getting shit done day by day, are the ones who get left out of the story.

Given the patriarchal bent of most of human history, where men get their name on the marquee while all the women are busy toiling backstage, it's no surprise that the contributions of women too often get overlooked, and in large part that's what's happened to many of the women in this story. None of the men in my family would have been able to accomplish what they accomplished if the women hadn't been doing, well, everything else. As the decades have passed, people's memories of these women have started to fade, and little of what they did survives in the printed record, the kinds of business and legal documents that create the paper trail that makes it seem as if the men are the only drivers of the story.

Today, women play a large role in the Ismaili community. Generally speaking, all of the official roles in the community are equally distributed between men and women. We have officiants who serve as our equivalent to rabbis and priests, and in every jamatkhana there are two men and two women who hold that role. Even the presidents of Ismaili councils are often women. One hundred thirty years ago, that was certainly not the case. The first generation of Ismaili women who immigrated to South Africa were basically housewives, raising their kids and supporting their husbands, who were scraping by in a subsistence economy. Their opportunities for professional or personal fulfillment outside the home were basically nonexistent.

The next generation fared slightly better. As the community evolved, women stepped out of the home and into the limited roles that were available to them at the time. They were the schoolteachers who educated the children, the nurses who ran the health clinics. Any kind of social service program for the community they were generally in charge of. Some took up dressmaking and hairdressing. They took classes for cooking and embroidery and typing and things like that. They were the support staff, in other words, the backbone of the community's institutional structure. Without them, the whole operation would have fallen apart, but they were given little of the credit and even less opportunity.

The same was generally true in Gandhi's satyagraha campaign. For most of its duration, women weren't allowed on the front lines; it wasn't considered safe. It was only in 1912 that Gandhi's wife, Kasturba, and others stood up and demanded to be a part of the protests. After that, Gandhi had a change of heart, and women played a much different role in his efforts once he returned to India. But that is not how it was in the early days. The same dynamic played out in the ANC's freedom movement as well. Some women were directly involved in the struggle, but by and large, women provided the foundation of the movement in supporting domestic roles, which, in a country where Black people had practically no access to any institutional resources at all, served a vital function. But, again, their contributions lack the narrative zing that one gets from Nelson Mandela blowing up power stations and giving grand speeches.

I have one picture of Mithima, Keshavjee's wife in Chotila. She looks like she's four hundred years old, the way old people look in old photographs where you get the feeling they've seen hard times that people today could scarcely imagine. People talk about her like she was the real heart of the family operation back then, the most influential player, but without much in the way of specifics. It's the same with Jabu, Velshi's wife. In what you hear, she was all the stereotypes: the beloved matriarch, the bedrock of the family, the one who held everything together. But beyond those general descriptions, I have little information to go on.

It's only with my own memories of my grandmother Jena, the woman who raised me, that I'm able to start telling this part of the story in greater detail. In addition to being Rajabali's helpmate in raising the family and in running the business, when he died she took it upon herself to carry the mantle of passing on his wisdom, his mantras, and his stories to me and my sister. My grandmother was a woman ahead of her time: beautiful, witty, and for a woman with zero formal education, very worldly, a sharp and highly developed thinker. I can remember a time when my mother was at the dining room table talking about a friend who was getting divorced and how lamentable it was and how bad divorce was for the culture. Listening to her, my grandmother strongly but politely disagreed. "Divorce is the greatest thing that ever happened to women," she said. "In my day, if you got married to the wrong person, you stayed married to the wrong person."

"But getting divorced is so expensive," my mom said.

"Not as expensive as staying together," my grandmother replied.

When my grandparents were raising my dad and his brother and three sisters, the schooling for boys went all the way up to what South Africans call "matric," the equivalent of a high school diploma in America. For girls, it went up to only standard six, around middle school, at which point the girls were, as my mother puts it, "put on the chopping block" for marriage. Rajabali and Jena had a different philosophy. They didn't send my dad to university, because he already had a future in the family bakery. It was his two sisters, Gulbanoo and Goolshen, who were enrolled at Witwatersrand University to study. In the early 1950s, sending two daughters to college would have been radical even in America, but that's what my grandparents believed. At one point Rajabali served as the chairman of the education board at the jamatkhana, and during an address to the community he pressed everyone else to follow his example. "My two daughters are at university," he said. "They will each be marrying one of your sons, so you will have two educated girls in your families. Can you please educate your girls so that my sons can have educated wives, too?" That was his philosophy.

Across the street in my mother's family, my mother's mother, Koolsam, had a similar philosophy but for a long time lacked the means to carry it out. Where my father's upbringing was prosperous, defined by an austere, Gandhian work ethic, my mother's upbringing was the opposite. It was poor and raucous and sprawling. My mother says she doesn't remember a moment when her mother wasn't pregnant. They were like an old French Catholic family. By the time it was all said and done, her parents had thirteen children, one of whom died in childbirth, leaving twelve kids total.

There had to be that many children so they could get out there and work, because my mother's father didn't work much at all. His name was Nazrali Manji. People talk about him as being well-dressed and fashionable, a bit of a bon vivant and a charmer but less impactful in providing for his family. For my mom and her siblings, the whole operation was a matriarchy. While Nazrali was out on the town, Koolsam ran the whole show. In addition to rearing all those children, she ran a small café and concession stand in the back of the movie theater through which she was barely able to make ends meet month to month. For many years, the kids couldn't get much in the way of an education. As soon as they could spell and write and do some math, they had to go out and work. My mother's stories about growing up are much like what I saw in our ancestral village in Chotila—everybody selling stuff to everybody else. My mom was seven years old selling plastic bangles door-to-door. Sometimes she would go back to the same place too often, and they would say, "I bought plastic bangles from you last week. What do you think happens to them? Do you think we eat these things?"

In her schooling, my mother did manage to make it past standard six to standard eight, and she was a straight-A student in everything but Afrikaans. (Their teachers were Afrikaans, and the government compelled them to learn Afrikaans. So my mother, as a protest, never studied Afrikaans.) But that was as far as she got. After that she had to work and find a husband. But as the family scraped together a living, the younger siblings did better. Out of the twelve, everyone my mother's age and older got barely any education at all. Everybody younger went on to finish not only high school and college but some graduate school as well. Most have advanced degrees, PhDs, law degrees, medical degrees. That all came from one woman working a concession stand and all the older siblings working to support the younger ones.

I knew both of my mother's parents years later in Toronto; they followed the migration from Africa a few years after we did. Koolsam was still the matriarch. She didn't live with us like my father's mother did. She'd raised twelve children and sent half of them to college, and now they were taking good care of her in return. Nazrali, on the other hand, was living hand to mouth, holding odd jobs, which was unusual in my family, where everyone owned their own business or maintained steady employment. For a while he worked one of the newsstands in the subway, and despite the fact that he was flat broke, he was always giving me things like candy bars or buying me a camera. Everybody, including me, loved him. When he died, there was a huge funeral and everybody came and kept going on about what a great guy he was and how generous he was and how he'd bought them all this stuff over the years, which drove my grandmother up the wall because he'd never been able to do much for his own wife and kids.

Had my mother been able to go to college like her siblings, there's no telling what she might have accomplished. Luckily, as it turned out, once she found herself on the chopping block for marriage, she ended up with a husband who believed women should be equal partners with their own careers. They married the same year that ABC Bakery went under, and shortly after they landed in Kenya she enrolled in shorthand and typing classes to become a secretary. She hated doing that, so she took her natural exuberance and door-to-door bangle-selling experience and went to work as a saleswoman at the best perfume shop in Nairobi. She worked there for a year, and on one of her sales calls she met a manager from KLM airlines who was so impressed by her that he asked her to come and work at the airline as a reservation and ticketing agent, which she did.

When my parents arrived in Canada, it was not my father's experience in baking and real estate that gave them their foothold. It was my mother's expertise in the travel business. This was back before phone apps and the internet, when you still needed travel agents to navigate all the forms and the airport codes and all that. It required an incredibly specialized kind of knowledge, and my mother knew the system backward and forward. So that's what they decided to do, and it was her business. My dad managed the office and handled the books, but she was really the brains of the operation, and so she was the president of the company that owned the travel agencies, not him, and that was how my father wanted it, at a time when the politics of the era would have had it the other way around.

And if their success in business was largely attributable to my mother, their success in politics should have been as well. If you

looked at my parents and were asked which one ran for public office, you wouldn't guess my father. My father's the quieter guy. My
mother's the personality. She's rambunctious and boisterous and loud
and exactly what you'd think of someone who had to try to stand out
among twelve siblings. She was the salesperson, too, and a natural
politician. In 1981, when my parents decided to run for office, by all
rights it should have been her name on the yard signs. She didn't do
it because (a) she actually ran the travel agencies, which my father
couldn't do, and (b) at the time, Canadian politics was still too much
of a boys' club. There were barely any white women in public office,
never mind a brown woman with an unusual last name.

By 1993, circumstances had changed. Because my parents were
so active in the Liberal Party, the party leadership called up my
mother and asked her to run, not for the provincial legislature but
for a seat in the Canadian Parliament. She accepted and had started
putting her campaign together when my grandmother, her mother-
in-law, Jena, fell seriously ill. Having been my caregiver my whole
life, at eighty-six years old, Jena was now at the point of her life
where she needed a full-time caregiver of her own.

My father couldn't do it. He's a lovely man, but his beliefs about
the equality of the sexes didn't translate into his acquiring any practical domestic skills. He makes a mean cup of coffee, and he can
bake—the man ran a bakery, after all—but beyond that he couldn't
really take care of someone who was ill. I was barely out of college,
my sister had a full-time job, nobody wanted to put Jena in a nursing
home, and culturally it was tradition that the wife should step in
and take care of her aged mother-in-law. That was the role that my
mother felt she needed to play, and it's what my grandmother wanted
as well.

If my mother had run and won, it would have meant working

four hours away in Ottawa, unable to look after her mother-in-law, so in the end she decided to bow out of the race. She wrote a letter to the Liberal Party leader, Jean Chrétien, and told him that she was resigning from her campaign. When he phoned to ask her why, she explained the reasons, and he said, "I admire that you're willing to give up everything for your family. I wish you luck, but I would have loved to have you on my team."

So my mother passed up the opportunity of a lifetime for what turned out to be a very short-term obligation. My grandmother died a few months later, in March, and when the election took place in December the Liberal Party won ninety-nine of the one hundred seats in Ontario. Jean Chrétien was swept into the prime minister-ship in a landslide. My mother almost certainly would have been a member of Parliament and quite possibly would have been a minster in Chrétien's government as well. She would have gone much higher than my father had with his provincial victory in 1987.

Impressive as my father's accomplishments are, my mother should have been the big story in the family. The tale that begins in the shark-infested waters of Delagoa Bay shouldn't climax with the first Indian Muslim man elected to Canada's provincial parliament. It should climax with the first Indian Muslim woman serving in the Canadian national government. But it doesn't, and all because my mother had to make a choice that most men never have to make. And if I don't make a conscious effort to correct the narrative, then her part of it very easily gets left out.

If you ask my mother about giving up her chance to run for office, she'll express zero regrets or hard feelings on the subject. It was a choice she made that was necessary when she made it, and everything turned out fine in the end. That is not the perspective you'll get from my sister if you ask her about her life. To this day, she's still the girl who wasn't allowed to ride the pony at the zoo, and the wound that she carries from that experience has left her exquisitely attuned to the slightest measure of injustice in society. That's part of what has made her one of the best civil servants working in Canada today.

Because of our age difference, my childhood and my sister's childhood are so vastly dissimilar that it's like we were raised in different families. For starters, she had an entire African childhood full of cultural influences that I never experienced at all. When my mom and dad were busy building their business in Kenya, she was spending half her time with our aunts and uncles, in conservative immigrant homes where the parents would give you a good smack if you got out of line. She spoke Swahili and Gujarati. She spoke English with a British-inflected East African accent. When she got to Canada, she had to learn an entirely new cultural language, and she had to do it during those awkward middle school and high school years that are already difficult enough, even if you're not the brown kid with the unpronounceable name.

During the early, "struggling immigrant" years of our new Canadian life, while I was young enough not to have any real chores, Ishrath was old enough to be put to work. Any time my grandmother was busy, my sister was pulled in for free babysitting. The second she got her driver's license, she became the family chauffeur, shuttling my grandmother and me around on errands so that my parents could stay late at the travel agency or go to some political function. And the moment summer break came around, she found herself behind a desk at the travel agency, booking flights and hotels and Caribbean cruises. I didn't have to deal with any of that, not because my parents were unfair but more as a matter of circumstance. I didn't have any younger siblings that needed to be babysat or driven around, and by the time I was old enough to work, the travel agency had been sold.

The difference in our ages was compounded by the vast chasm in how the world treated our respective genders. Even liberal Indian families are more conservative with their daughters than they are with their sons, and my parents, being new to the country, didn't know how to raise a daughter in an open and relatively permissive world. So Ishrath grew up struggling between what Indian culture expected her to do and what Western culture allowed her to do. My parents would tell you that they were never overly restrictive; they were just doing what they thought they had to do. But they didn't let her go to high school parties with drinking and smoking. On the last day of class her senior year, she openly defied my parents for the first time and went with some kids to a bar. A half hour later, my dad showed up and stood over the table where she was sitting with the other students and made her get up and walk out.

By the time I was growing up, in addition to my being a boy, they'd relaxed about a lot of that stuff. So they mostly let me be. To this day, my sister will never let me forget how much easier I had it, and I do have to acknowledge that it wasn't the same. It wasn't fair, and as a consequence my sister has spent her life in a pitched battle against unfairness of any kind.

Like my parents, she caught the political bug early. She was only thirteen when she attended her first convention with the Ontario Young Liberals at the Don Valley Holiday Inn in 1974. It was a fascinating experience for her because back in Kenya, any time President Kenyatta was on the move through Nairobi there was a massive security apparatus around him. If he was driving down the road, everybody had to stop on the side of the street; you didn't breathe or move or do anything or else you'd be in trouble. But Prime Minister Pierre Trudeau was there at this Young Liberals meeting and with no obvious security; he was just walking around in his brown corduroy suit shaking hands. Less than four years after she was told she couldn't ride a horse at the zoo, here she was saying hello to the prime minister. It blew her mind that Canada was so open and democratic that a young immigrant girl like her could meet and interact with the most powerful man in the country in such a casual way.

After that, Ishrath was by my parents' side volunteering to work on any federal or provincial campaign she could. On at least one occasion my parents roped her into some protest where they were out in front of the US embassy with twenty or thirty people in the dead of winter, freezing their butts off and waving banners and chanting whatever was being chanted. She didn't necessarily love that part of it, but the thrill of the campaigns and elections themselves she was all in for.

When my dad ran for office the first time in 1981, Ishrath, while still in high school, spent the campaign running their travel agencies for them. She inherited from my father the qualities that I did not. She got his sense of organization and discipline, and she's a whiz at logistics, a problem solver, a tactician, the kind of person you give work to and the work gets done.

After my dad got elected in '87, my parents sold the travel business, which left my sister without a job, but at that point she fell right into political work and government service as if it were the most natural thing in the world. She started out working for the Liberal Party in Ontario. When the party swept into power on the wave that elected my dad, they suddenly had hundreds of staff positions that needed to be filled, and she started taking on various jobs in the offices of elected officials at the municipal and provincial levels.

From there, she segued into various civil service jobs. When we were growing up, our father had always talked about the importance of the civil service, how it was there to ensure that the government keeps functioning no matter which way the election goes. Civil servants and labor unions he talked about often, so we grew up believing that government work is noble work. Ishrath ultimately chose that path. She became a public servant, which often meant something different with each passing year. Every time a new government came in, it would have some major new initiative, like a job retraining program, and she typically found a way into it. She understood the nature of that kind of work—the relationship between a government and the people it serves.

Over time, she worked her way up to serve as executive aide to two different Toronto city councilors. "Executive aide" is a somewhat ambiguous title that translates to "the person who gets all the shit done while the politician raises money and kisses babies." With local politics, constituents come in looking for help with anything and everything, with absolutely no regard for whether the person they're speaking to has any jurisdiction over that particular issue. It could be a leaking roof in the public housing project, a cracked sidewalk, late garbage pickup—literally anything. Ishrath was the person they'd end up talking to in order to get it fixed. She took the skills that she learned in school and working for my parents' business and married them to an accumulated knowledge of local politics at an almost molecular level. Every department of every agency, every form you can fill out, every lever to pull, every button to press, she mastered every inch of it.

The way that you get things done on a local, city, or provincial level is all grunt work. If there were too many traffic accidents at a particular intersection, she'd put her head down to figure out what the problem was. Is it not enough crossing guards? Does it need a four-way stop? A street light? Should we add a crosswalk? She'd contact the experts, have the issue studied, and get a report written up. Then, once the problem was diagnosed, if the solution was to get a new traffic light, she'd be the one to get the new traffic light—which basically involves being a professional nuisance, because nobody wants to put up an extra traffic light because it costs money and requires maintenance. So you agitate people and call meetings and have hearings and stay at it for months and months until finally you get all the stakeholders together and get a consensus and then, voilà, the traffic light goes up. She's that person. That's what she does.

But more important than what she does are the people for whom she does it. Being from the glass-half-full side of the family, when I look at how Indians and other nonwhite immigrants have fared since Canada adopted its official multiculturalism policy, I see a new pluralistic nation that has flourished remarkably well. But naturally, even if the overwhelming majority of those people have gained a foothold of economic opportunity and social acceptance, that still leaves tens if not hundreds of thousands of people across the country who are stuck living on the margins of society. You can look at the immigrants who've succeeded and say, "Look how far we've come." Or you can look at the immigrants still struggling and say, "Look how far we have left to go."

The same thing goes for the country as a whole. Even if Canada's government functions remarkably well in terms of education and health care and other public services, which I would argue that it does, no system is perfect. People fall through the cracks every day. As in every country everywhere in the world, the rich and powerful find ways to work the system to their own ends at the expense of the less fortunate. So you can look at Canada as a paragon of good government, or you can see it as a place where the playing field will never be fully equal or fair.

My sister is one of those people who definitely thinks the system is rigged and somebody somewhere is somehow getting a raw deal. Because she's a person who's driven by a deep-rooted sense of grievance, she identifies well with people who have a grievance. She loves righting wrongs and taking up lost causes, and she's not afraid of anybody. She's also one of those people who cares, genuinely cares, about making people's lives better. Or, to put it more accurately, she can't *not* care. Ishrath often describes herself as a recovering public servant. Part of her is convinced that she'd be happier with some nice, comfortable job in the private sector, putting her own needs first for a change. She says she'd like to quit, but she probably never will because she sees injustice in the world and she can't not try to fix it.

In 2010, she ended up working for a Conservative city councilor, serving as his chief aide, and the whole thing turned out to be an extremely unpleasant experience. He'd hired her, it turned out, in large part to help get him the nonwhite votes that he needed to win, which she did. But then, once he was in office, she didn't sense any interest on his part to deliver any real change for those constituents. So she did a remarkable thing. In the next election, she ran against her own boss, which I think is amazing. It's everything that participating in a democracy should be. Don't like the status quo? Stand up and do something about it.

The people she most wanted to represent were recent immigrants who didn't know enough about what the government was able to do to help them. She didn't just want to help the people who showed up in her office asking for assistance. She wanted to help people who were so marginalized they didn't know there was assistance available to ask for. She wanted to go to those people and ask, "What's bugging you and what can I do about it?" because a lot of these people probably came from places where you don't get asked that. Their government didn't do it. If you needed a sidewalk fixed in the old country, who did you ask, the Taliban?

My sister ran as a Liberal, but hers was not an ideological campaign. It had nothing to do with right versus left. I mean, I assume my sister's politics are somewhat similar to mine, but she is not doctrinaire. She doesn't talk about that stuff. Generally speaking, in city politics, other than policing, that's how it goes. Everybody wants the same stuff, and everybody votes for their city councilor based on whether you can deliver on basic services; that was the gist of her message. "I'm the one who gets it all done." And she was, and on that basis, out of the six candidates running for the seat, she was endorsed by the *Toronto Star*, the biggest newspaper in the country.

She ran a good campaign, too. My mother had to be out of the country for work, but other than that it was a regular family affair. My dad helped out by lending his expertise to the campaign. I was living in New York by then. My life and schedule didn't give me the time to be as deeply involved as I would have liked, but I helped her write some speeches. And I came up as regularly as I could, including on Election Day to help get out the vote.

Unlike my father's first campaign where I thought he was going to win and nobody else did, most of us thought my sister would win and were genuinely surprised when she didn't. Hers was a municipal election, and as in the United States, turnout for municipal elections is tiny. Out of the six candidates vying for the seat, it was basically a three-way contest between her, her old boss, and another challenger. My sister ended up with around 3,500 votes, her old boss got around 6,000, and the other challenger who ended up winning got over 9,000. So she lost, which wasn't great. But her old boss lost, too; he was the only incumbent city councilor in Toronto to lose his seat. So in the end, even though my sister didn't win, her decision to participate had an impact on the outcome. At the end of the day, win or lose, that's really all you can ask for: the chance to participate and to have your participation matter.

After the race, she continued on in the civil service. The way it works in Canada is you reach a certain rank that qualifies you for a range of positions, and you can move between them based on what's available. During COVID, she was working for the government agency that performed contact tracing for people who'd come down with the virus. And just recently, in 2023, she went out on strike with her union, the Public Service Alliance of Canada, which represents more than 230,000 workers in every Canadian province and territory. They were striking over better pay and several other issues in what became the largest work action in Canadian history. On our family texts, my parents seemed almost jubilant that it was happening. They were pinging back and forth, giving her all sorts of advice and encouragement, thrilled to still be in the fight after all these years.

Not too long ago, I happened to see my sister's résumé, and she had her run for office listed way down under most of her other job experience. "That should be at the top," I said.

"But I lost," she said.

"Yeah," I replied, "but you put yourself up for public office. It's a big deal that you did that. There are always going to be people who lose in elections, but running and losing means that you subscribe to the process. That's what citizenship is."

I think that if we are worried about democracy dying—and I am worried about that—it will be saved by people like my sister. Most of us look around ourselves every day and see things that need to be fixed or could work better. Maybe you're worried about the whole society collapsing, or maybe you need a pothole fixed. Either way, your first question has to be "What can I do about it?" And the answer is, "Find someone like Ishrath Velshi." Or better yet, "Be someone like Ishrath Velshi." There is nothing about my sister that says career politician at all. She's not slick. She's a doer. She's in the arena. She was never looking to break a glass ceiling or become noteworthy in any way. She just thought that she could do a good job for people because she knew how to solve problems, and that's what society needs. We need fewer people posturing on social media about their politics, and we need more people in the trenches solving problems.

Democracy is the greatest form of government ever devised. Its Achilles' heel is that, at times, it can be stupendously boring. Good government doesn't move at the speed of social media. The tedious eighteen-month process to install a new traffic light may not make a great story—and even if it were a great story, increasingly, there wouldn't be any local news organization to cover it—but it's important nevertheless. We need society to function at every level, from the Supreme Court all the way down to the school board. Voting is fundamental. Activism and protest are necessary. We need legislators to make the laws and judges to enforce them. Journalism plays a vital role as well. But the gears in the machine that make democracy run are the civil servants like my sister. Without them, the whole thing breaks down and falls apart.

When my great-grandfather Velshi was hosting Gandhi during his visits to Pretoria back in the day, they didn't get into politics. Like many Indians of that generation, Velshi was more focused on surviving from day to day. Lofty ideas about free speech and equal representation and repairing the fabric of the world weren't going to put food on the family's table, at least not in the short term. But when Velshi got hit by a bus crossing Boom Street in 1952, what he really needed that day was a traffic light or at least a stop sign or a crosswalk. One simple improvement to the local municipal services and he might have lived happily for several more years. If South Africa had been the kind of place where a little brown girl were allowed to ride a pony at the zoo, it would have been the kind of place where that same girl could grow up to serve on the safety committee that oversees traffic lights and stop signs and crosswalks. It's all connected. That is why the grueling, thankless grunt work of citizenship is so important.

The Arc of History Bends
the Way You Bend It

As a kid growing up in Toronto, because we lived so close to the American border, we picked up the local stations out of Buffalo, New York. Because the American and Canadian TV stations sat side by side on the dial, I was initially confused as to what was Canadian and what was American. It took me a minute to grasp that we were one and not the other and that there was a difference. But once I grasped the distinction, the local five o'clock news out of Buffalo was where my education in all things American began, and one of my earliest impressions of America was that it was always on fire.

By the mid-1970s, in the wake of the civil rights movement and school busing and white flight, most major American cities were being torn apart, and that was certainly the case with Buffalo, which was also going into a steep industrial decline from which it's never fully recovered. It seemed like every night in Buffalo, the news would begin with a violent gang-related murder followed by footage of a house burning to the ground. We don't have guns in Canada, and Toronto's brick houses didn't often catch fire. So I started to form this very clear impression that America was different, a violent place that was forever burning. The other differentiating factor was that the American networks ran ads for Carvel ice cream, and we didn't have Carvel in Canada. So I was always kind of angry that I was being teased with these ads for this tasty, delicious ice cream, but I could never have any. That was probably the clearest example of how I knew I was not American. There wasn't any gun violence, my city wasn't on fire, and there was no Carvel.

As I grew up and began to see and understand America's political, cultural, and economic dominance on the world stage, I was in awe of it. Because how could you not be in awe of it? For most of my life, when I'd go back to Canada people would ask me, "What do Americans think of us?" And my answer was, "They don't. Americans are not thinking about you. At all." That has changed since the election of Donald Trump. Americans now look to their functional northern neighbor with a degree of envy that never existed before. But what hasn't changed is that the sheer size and scope of America makes its presence a fact of life that Canadians have to reckon with.

Like most of our countrymen, we took frequent trips to the United States, to Florida for winter sun and the Northeast for summer beauty. This was in the days before NAFTA, too, and back then Canada just didn't have as much stuff to buy. Fresh fruit was prohibitively expensive in the winter. You were pretty much stuck with a mealy red apple that had been sitting in an industrial fridge since October. You got cabbage instead of lettuce. And pretty much every imported consumer good had some kind of crazy markup. So to us

America was like one big mall, full of everything we wanted to buy, only cheaper. If you ever wanted something big like a camera or a Walkman, you waited for a trip to America to buy it.

The thing that stood out to me the most, even just crossing the border and pulling into a gas station convenience store, was the sheer volume of choices. At the Canadian convenience store, there might be one soda fridge with a few different sodas and maybe milk and eggs. At the American convenience store, there were nine or ten soda fridges with literally dozens of soda brands. And the toothpaste! In Canada we had a few brands of toothpaste. In America there would be sixty different brands of toothpaste. I understood that America was bigger, so it would need more soda and toothpaste, but I didn't understand why it needed ten times the number of choices of soda and toothpaste. Nor did I imagine that I would ever need to live in a place with that much soda and toothpaste, but then life turned out to have other ideas.

———————

In the movie *Gandhi*, Martin Sheen plays a fictional *New York Times* reporter, Vince Walker, inspired by United Press International reporter Webb Miller. A crucial scene in the movie depicts Walker in 1930 reporting on the gruesome violence unleashed against Gandhi-inspired protesters at the Dharasana saltworks in northwestern India, many of them women.

The description of Walker's big scene, as written in the script, goes as follows: "We see Walker, helping once or twice, turning, watching, torn between being an 'objective' journalist and a sentient human being." In the film itself, we see Walker, clothes matted with blood and dirt, finding a phone at a small shop to call in his article. "Goddammit, don't cut me off!" he yells into the receiver before dictating his report. "They walked with heads up," he says into the phone, "without music, or cheering, or any hope of escape from injury or death. It went on and on and on. Women carried the wounded bodies from the ditch until they dropped from exhaustion. But still it went on."

How accurate is the scene? Pretty accurate. Webb, on whom the Sheen character was based, did report live from Dharasana in dispatches closely followed all over the world, and he was the only Western reporter there. His report, widely published on May 22, 1930, after being delayed by censors, read in part: "More than 200 persons were injured in a massed advance on the Dharasana salt works today as (local) police beat unarmed volunteers. . . . The police kicked and prodded the non-violent raiders who swarmed the depot. I personally saw over 200 in a temporary hospital where they were carried on stretchers by volunteers. . . . Most of the injuries were head wounds, fractured arms and wrists. The (local) police lost their tempers. I saw them kick volunteers already lying on the ground. My clothes were splashed with mud when the police flung volunteers into ditches. The spectacle of them beating the unresisting volunteers was so painful I frequently was forced to turn away from the road."

When I saw that movie, despite all the Indian characters in it with whom I might have identified, Martin Sheen's reporter was the one who stood out for me. His big scene illustrates the reason I became a journalist in the first place: to bear witness. If a tree falls in the woods and there isn't a reporter there to record the moment, how will the world know that it fell? Gandhi understood the importance of journalists. From the beginning he was inviting reporters to come to Tolstoy Farm so he could explain to them the value of satyagraha and his movement. In the film, the next scene after the Dharasana saltworks shows Gandhi being summoned to London to discuss Indian independence. There's a direct cause and effect. Without the on-the-ground reporting, the story might have played out much differently.

I found myself on the road to becoming a reporter because it was clear from an early age that I had no interest in, or aptitude for, the family business. I wasn't destined to be a shopkeeper or entrepreneur. I don't think it was even discussed. My parents had the very immigrant idea that I would become a lawyer, and they pushed me pretty hard in that direction. Before being bitten by the journalism bug, I had some thoughts that I might eventually follow them into politics, given how inspired I'd been working on their campaigns. In high school, I was elected president of the student council. Then I went to Queens University and got involved in student government and campus activism there.

I had heard my family's stories about protesting and fighting for social justice for years, but college was a vastly different experience in that regard. I was not anything remotely like a social justice warrior when I got to college. I wasn't that guy. I understood people fighting for their own particular cause. I wasn't familiar with people coming together to fight for "causes." My parents had always been fighting to solve a very tangible set of problems that were right in front of them, that grew directly out of their own experiences as immigrants. I'd never lived in a world where people took up causes that weren't their own just because they wanted to be a part of the solution to those problems.

I also wasn't looking to make trouble. When I got into Queens University, I felt privileged to be able to go to this prestigious school.

I wasn't looking to tear the place down as soon as I arrived; I was just happy to be there. I wasn't looking to rock the boat, because it had never been my family's style to rock the boat. Indeed, my father's whole philosophy had been to try to get in the boat so you could help decide which way to steer it. So that's who I was when I got to college.

Many of my peers felt differently. Thirty years ago, Queen's University was a very white school in a very white place, Kingston, Ontario, and it was not quite what you would call progressive. It was quite common for people to be casually sexist and homophobic, and people didn't call you out for it. But by the late 1980s, groups of students were starting to stand up and say that those behaviors needed to change. Gay and lesbian students, Black students, international students—they were all coming into this environment that was potentially unwelcoming to them, and they were trying to change it. And they were doing so in an institutionalized, organized fashion. They did it by starting clubs and having debates and marching on campus, and I thought that was fascinating.

There was an anti–date rape campaign that launched soon after I arrived, a real effort to make people in general—and men, specifically—conscious of this as a problem. That triggered a reaction in which a group of ten or so boys in one of the boys' dorms put out banners from their balconies that were extremely misogynistic. They were generally some vulgar play on the slogan "No means no." So there was a lot of "No means yes" and "No means harder" and "No means kick her in the teeth." It turned into the biggest thing to happen on that campus in forty or fifty years. Many of these guys had connected families, so it turned into a big showdown over whether the boys were going to get expelled. The university's lawyers ended up sitting down across from the lawyers hired by all these families to decide the boys' fate. That was the atmosphere. It was all around us, and you were either one of the good guys or one of the bad guys.

Because of the way I'd been raised, I wanted to be one of the good guys, but the environment was completely new to me. At the start I was still the guy who wanted to be inside the boat. I ran for student government and got elected student rep so I could be the guy who sat down with the administration and discuss these things. But for many of my more liberal and more radical peers, that was a sellout move. That wasn't enough. They were agitators, and over the course of my four years they pulled me more and more in their direction. I joined the Liberal Party. I joined the debating society. The campus social justice movement became my extracurricular activity, and soon I was diving into it headlong off campus as well.

In 1992, when Reform Party leader Preston Manning arrived for an event at the Kingston Memorial Centre to tout his big "reforms" (i.e., lowering taxes for the rich and "getting tough" on crime), my roommate Paul Finch and I managed to get ourselves kicked out. Manning was only going to take written questions from the audience, which we thought was bullshit. So when Manning went to answer the written questions he had in his hand, we stood up in our chairs and started shouting questions at him, and security came and dragged us—literally dragged us like sacks of potatoes—out of the auditorium and tossed us onto the curb. Paul and I made the front page of the Kingston newspaper the next day. That was me in my youthful fervor, following in my family's protesting footsteps and marrying their traditions to the social justice movement of the era.

Still, politics and government didn't call to me as a vocation. It was my parents' thing. I enjoyed participating in it for them, but it

was not for me. What I realized in college was that I had an aptitude for writing and storytelling. That's what I enjoyed. I'd grown up
watching the news, and I believed the news was important. I wouldn't
be my grandfather marching to Johannesburg on Gandhi's shoulders or my uncle Rehmtulla manning the barricades of the Defiance
Campaign. I would be Webb Miller, the journalist with the notepad
and the typewriter—and, later, the iPhone, the news camera, and the
social-media feed—bearing witness to those events, bringing those
injustices to light, and using those tools to hold power to account.

When I informed my parents of this plan, they were horrified.
"You can't do that," they replied. "As hard as we've struggled, if
you're going to put effort into going to school, you need to be a lawyer." As with most immigrant parents, my future financial security
and social status were topmost in their minds. Back then, South
Asian kids could be a lawyer or a doctor, and that was it. Still, even
in the face of their disapproval, I persisted. In my mind, the work
I was pursuing was no less important than what they had done in
politics and community organization. I went after the sorts of jobs
I felt were important. My first internships were at *Crossfire* and then
at *60 Minutes*. My first paid job was as a producer on *Canada AM*, a
national show at CTV News. I produced several interviews with important people like South Africa's Archbishop Desmond Tutu and
Gerry Adams of Sinn Féin. I got a photograph with Tutu, which was
personally exciting for me but also felt like I was doing something
of outsized importance. With Gerry Adams—a terrorist to some, a
freedom fighter to others—I was even more excited. Because I had
no personal connection to the story of Irish independence, sitting
down with him felt even more like "I'm doing real, objective, hard-
hitting journalism. This is fantastic."

I was doing substantive work, which I enjoyed, but I wanted to make the jump from producer to reporter so that I could do what Webb Miller had done. I had found a number of professional mentors by this time, and all said the same thing: "If you want to be a reporter, go to local news." So that's what I did.

CTV News shared a building with the local Toronto affiliate, Channel 9. I applied and became a reporter. I hated it. There are rarely any world-changing moments of political violence to cover for local Canadian news, no opportunities for sit-downs with world leaders. I did car accidents, house fires, murders, and kittens stuck in trees. Sometimes we'd have three or four cameras on the kitten stuck in the tree, so you could get the fireman rescue from multiple angles. On one uniquely cold day, I was sent to the Toronto Zoo to do a story on how it was so cold that even the polar bears were trying to get back indoors. Stories about how cold and snowy it was in a place that is naturally cold and snowy always made me feel a bit dumb.

I was also uniquely bad at it. I was good at the minutiae of reporting, digging into facts and stories. But I was terrible on camera. The minute that little red light came on, all of my personality left me. I would learn to get better on camera over time, but only because I so desperately wanted to do the other part of it: bearing witness and uncovering the truth. Sadly, given my own disdain for the assignments I was given, I soured on the whole idea of local news rather than trying to make the job better. From my parents' work in civic organizations, I knew how critical local politics and community issues really are. Cracked sidewalks and potholes may seem like trivial matters, but depending on how bad the sidewalks and streets are, they actually tell an important story about whose needs are being prioritized and which zip codes have the power to get things done.

If I were a local news reporter today, I would go back with a completely different mindset. I would push to cover city council meetings like they mattered and hold politicians to account. As it happened, I only got to do that once. At one point during my local news tenure, there was a major subway accident in Toronto. Eleven people died. It was a massive scene, and I was the first reporter on it. I ended up covering it all the way up to the inquest that determined accountability for the crash. I was interviewing the witnesses and the victims, sitting down with the officials of the transit commission. That was my first and only real experience with using local news for accountability, and it was exhilarating. That experience only left me more disenchanted with kittens in trees and cold polar bears.

Fortunately, another opportunity would emerge, taking me into a corner of television news that I would not have imagined for myself. Hardcore business journalism didn't exist for us in Canada at the time, certainly not on television. The closest thing we had on TV were these old guys who would come on for a short segment on the local news and tell you really quickly what had gone down in the stock market and, because Canada was such a resource-dependent economy, they'd tell you about price fluctuations in oil and wheat and potash and things like that. Then in the late 1990s, the day trading and retail investing trend migrated to Canada from the United States. There was a local Toronto station, Citytv, and they decided, "Hey, we can do up our screen like Bloomberg's. Some of it will be news and weather and from nine to five every day we'll do the stock market because everybody's trading retail stocks."

They came to me and offered me a job, to which I said, "I know nothing about business. My degree is in religion."

"That's OK," they said. "You'll have your earpiece in, and the producer will tell you everything you need to know. He'll write the scripts and tell you the questions, and you'll say the stuff. That's how it's going to be."

So I took the job, solely as a means to get out of local news. It at least felt important. For the first year, I was wholly dependent on my producer, B. J. Del Conte, talking in my ear, but he was a wonderful guy and taught me everything. Even though I initially had no interest in the subject matter, I invested myself in it because I felt like it was something I could sink my teeth into. So I got better at it, and soon prime time came calling.

Canada's largest national newspaper is the *Globe and Mail*, and its business section, the Report on Business, is our equivalent of the *Wall Street Journal*. It's the most serious part of a serious paper. Riding the same trend of day trading that birthed Bloomberg and CNBC and FOX Business and CNNfn, the *Globe and Mail* decided to partner with a media company to create Report on Business Television, ROBTV, which has got to be the world's most awkward name for a television news network. In the small pond of Canadian business journalists, ROBTV quickly hired every last person it could find who could put together two sentences about business on camera. And that scramble to assemble a news network is how I became the first prime-time business anchor in Canada.

In the late 1990s, being in business journalism on cable TV was essentially no different than being in sports journalism on cable TV. Take away the network logos, and viewers could easily mistake most of the news desks for ESPN's *Sportscenter*, and that was by design. You were there to tell people what had happened during the game. You covered stock prices and commodities prices. You interviewed people about big industry shake-ups. You reported more about what happened than *why* it had happened. You didn't ask if that thing was the right thing to do, morally or ethically. You didn't interrogate much at all. There was no bearing witness or holding the powerful to account. It was color commentary for capitalism.

We were mostly big suck-ups to the hotshot CEOs, because those were the marquee guests we wanted to land for interviews, and if we wanted them to keep coming back, the interviews had to allow them to spout propaganda for their corporations. "Hey, it must feel great that you opened three hundred new stores last year. Which one is your favorite?" Those are the types of questions we would ask. I didn't press anyone inside the building, either. When I was a young brown Muslim journalist in Toronto, we did not talk about brown Muslim things at the editorial table. I was hardly ever at the table, and on the rare occasions I was, my goal was to be the whitest brown guy at the table, to stand out as little as possible so I wouldn't be asked to leave the table—and I wasn't asked to leave the table, nor did I accomplish anything meaningful while at the table.

I lasted two years, and I look back on that time now and think, "What a failure." I'd taken a wrong turn somewhere, and my dream of being Webb Miller recounting human rights atrocities outside the Dharasana saltworks was a million miles in the opposite direction. Both stops I'd made had made sense at the time I'd made them—go to local news to get experience, grab on to business journalism because it was a rung up from local news—but what it all added up to was a big, decade-long detour from the direction I'd intended to take.

Like a lot of naive young people, I wasn't even aware that I was taking the detour as I was taking it. Every year, I was getting bigger assignments, making more money, reaching a larger audience. All of the indicators told me "Ali, you're doing well. This is success." And I'll be honest, Toronto is a fun city in which to be a reporter. It's big enough to be cosmopolitan, yet small enough for you to make a splash. As a news anchor, you're kind of a big man around town. You get reservations at restaurants. You go places and get recognized. I had money in my pocket to spend, and I spent it. I bought a Honda Hawk motorcycle, a 750cc bike to tool around town on. There's a small island off Toronto that's home to what at the time was a piddly little private airport. I decided I wanted to get my pilot's license, so in what was almost certainly a subconscious desire to be Tom Cruise in *Top Gun*, I'd ride my motorcycle to the airport, fly a plane for a bit, then ride my bike to work and be on TV. I didn't see myself as a young man changing the world, and I wasn't going home every night lamenting that I wasn't changing the world. I was just being a guy, living life and enjoying it.

If it's the job of a journalist to comfort the afflicted and afflict the comfortable, as has been said many times before, I'd made the mistake of letting myself get comfortable very early in my career. That happened, in part, because of my own personal good fortune, but it was also a by-product of the era. The nineties were a bit of a fantasyland. Part of the reason our college crusades focused on solvable issues like date rape and diversity was because the big existential issues, like the nuclear stand-off that threatened to destroy all of humanity, seemed to have been dealt with. We'd seen the end of the Cold War and the death of Apartheid. We'd enjoyed a decade of no major military conflicts and nonstop economic growth, and many people believed, falsely, that this trajectory would only continue. In truth, the world's problems had not gone anywhere. The roots of our twenty-first-century crises were right there in front of us for anyone who was paying attention: the offshoring of jobs that would gut the small town of both America and Canada, the stirrings of right-wing fanaticism in the Ruby Ridge standoff and the Oklahoma City bombing, the rise of Muslim extremism in the first World Trade Center bombing and the attacks on the USS *Cole* and the US embassy in Nairobi. But as the 1990s came to a close and we rang in a new millennium, the overwhelming feeling in the West was to pat ourselves on the back for a job well done.

In that complacent, comfortable world, the idealistic fervor I'd developed on my dad's campaign and on my college campus had gone dormant. My parents and my grandmother had taught me many valuable lessons, but they'd also worked hard to give me a life where I wouldn't necessarily need to heed those lessons. My parents had to struggle. Even my sister, in her own way, had to struggle. I didn't. That wasn't my burden. My particular burden was that I had to *choose* to struggle, which is an entirely different problem from having no other option. My parents took the hard path because it was the only path for them to take. But life had offered me an easy path, and I'd taken it. I'd taken it without even consciously realizing that was what I was doing; I was always just trying to get the next job. I got wrapped up in my career, and it was only after twenty years in America that I would truly open my eyes again.

The first step I took toward becoming an American citizen was simply arriving, which in the end turned out to be no simple task at all. I'd never even imagined becoming an American, but then, during my tenure as the prime-time anchor for ROBTV, I became increasingly conscious of my neighbor to the south. Other than its

commodity exports, pretty much everything that happens in Canadian business is largely because of, and in response to, its biggest
trading partner and cultural influence. So I found myself reporting
on the New York Stock Exchange and interviewing CEOs of American companies as they passed through town.

Coincidentally, as America was more and more on my radar,
I was more and more on America's radar as well. From the time
ROBTV launched, because it was starting a brand-new channel and
because producing twenty-four hours of content a day is a challenge,
it was partnered with an American content provider, CNNfn. Having CNNfn as a partner was a fail-safe. If at any point anything went
wrong with our broadcast, we could hit a button and CNNfn would
be piped in to our audience. We could even air some of its program-
ming through the course of the day.

As a part of our contract, we were able to borrow a desk in
CNNfn's headquarters and staff it with two of our reporters, Amanda
Lang and Pat Kiernan, to whom we could go throughout the day
for live updates from New York. And since we had access to watch
CNNfn's feed all day, it had access to ours. So wholly unbeknownst
to me, CNNfn's executives and program directors were watching me
on the air and thinking, "We like this guy." Sometime in April 2001,
I got a call from a CNN senior executive with a classic broadcast
voice, a guy named Conway Cliff. He phoned me up and said, "Hey,
we've been watching your stuff, and we'd love for you to come down
and talk to us."

I flew down, and he took me to lunch with four other network
executives, including the president of CNNfn. We went to the steak-
house in Madison Square Garden, which was kitty-corner to CNN's
location at the time in the 5 Penn Plaza building. The five of them

spent most of the time catching up with one another. They didn't ask me anything. But we had a nice meal, and I must have made a good impression on them because right after that they called back and offered me a job. Up until that moment, America had never really been in my mind as a place to go. I had a good life in Toronto. I had a nice car. I'd just bought a house with a couple of friends. I didn't have any need to get out.

However, there's a sense among many Canadian professionals that when the Americans come knocking, you take the job. I'd seen successful Canadian journalists who had gone to America, Peter Jennings and people like that, and I'd thought, "Maybe that could work," though it hadn't been something I often thought about. In the end, being young enough to have a sense of adventure about these things, I decided to go for it, though it wasn't with any crazy dreams of making it big, and I certainly didn't envision myself becoming an American and staying. I just thought, "Well, I'll do this, and if it doesn't work out, I'll come back." I didn't give it much consideration beyond that. My heart was still in Canada. My life was there. My friends were there. I thought I would go to America, work for a bit, go home to Canada, and that would be it. That May, one month after my steak lunch in Manhattan, I accepted CNN's offer and started what would become a very involved process of securing my O-1 work visa and negotiating with CNN to sponsor me for a green card if everything worked and I decided to stay longer, and as all that was set in motion I was given an official start date: Monday, September 10, 2001.

While my work visa was being sorted out, I rented a place at the corner of Thirty-Third and Eighth, right next door to CNN; I think the distance between my front door and CNN's side door was about six feet. Then I went back home and packed up or sold off everything I had in Toronto, sending everything that was left down to the apartment in New York. The sole exception being my Honda Hawk motorcycle, which I parked in my parents' garage. That summer, with a few weeks off before starting my new gig, I flew down to spend some time with my parents in South Africa, where they were still wrapping up their less-than-successful adventure in the bagel business, and after a pleasant, uneventful visit, on Friday, September 7, 2001, I boarded a plane back to America to start my new job. Only when my flight from Johannesburg landed at JFK, there was some problem with my paperwork. I was told that I could enter as a tourist but not as a legal, working resident. The customs agents didn't tell me exactly what the problem was, just that some form was not yet processed or something. So I needed to go back to Toronto while they sorted out the issue and then re-enter the country from the Canadian side of the border. I still had a couple of days until I needed to report to the office, so it didn't seem like it was going to be any big deal. I flew back to Toronto, crashed at my parents' vacant house, and sat on the phone with CNN's lawyers to try to figure everything out.

Then, on the morning of September 11, the day I was expecting to return to New York, I woke up to a phone call from a friend. "Turn on your TV," he said. I did, and like nearly every other human being on the planet that day, I sat and stared at the screen in disbelief, watching the Twin Towers of the World Trade Center burst into flames and implode. Once the initial shock wore off, I found myself processing it on a number of levels. As a person, I was glued to the human drama unfolding before me, watching people leap from the towers and run screaming from the blast of smoke and debris from the tower's collapse and wondering, "What the hell just happened?

What's happening now? What's going to happen next?" Then, one step removed from that, as a television journalist, I was in awe of the coverage, how all the various news organizations were scrambling to cover the day's events and what an incredible job most of them were doing.

Thirdly, as someone who was supposed to have started at one of those news organizations the day before, I couldn't help but wonder how this was going to affect me. How was I going to get back to the United States? The last word I'd had from CNN's lawyers had come the day before, on the tenth, assuring me that everything was going to get sorted out today, on the date that would live in infamy as "9/11." Clearly, that wasn't going to happen. It was a mess. The people running the news desk at CNN didn't know all the ins and outs of the visa problems, and they didn't care. They were calling me and saying, "It's all hands on deck. We need you down here." To which I replied, "I can't get down there. My visa is not approved yet. Also, I sold my car, and there aren't any planes in the sky."

I don't recall who called whom, but by the morning of the twelfth, we had learned that my visa had in fact been approved before the planes hit the Twin Towers. However, the physical visa was stuck at a processing center in Vermont, so I had no way to get it. In the normal course of events, it would have been FedExed to CNN's law firm in Atlanta to get all the right signatures and then been FedExed straight to me in Toronto. Now, there was no normal course of business and no planes to FedEx, so I was stuck with no way into the country. Desperate, I did the only thing I could think of, which was to call the US consulate in Toronto, where I had some experience as a reporter, and explain my situation. When I finally got somebody on the phone, I laid everything out, and I was fully expecting them to say, "Yeah, there's nothing we can do for you. Our country's just been attacked." Instead, they were incredibly gracious and efficient. They said, "Hold on, we'll get back to you." Then they called me back and said, "The ability to admit somebody to the United States today is at the discretion of the person running that particular border crossing, and we happen to know the guy running the border crossing at Niagara Falls. We told him your story, and if you show up before midnight tonight with a copy of your visa, he'll let you in." And by "copy," they meant a fax, which they promptly sent over.

That was around noon. Now, with no cars to drive and no planes to catch, I had to get from midtown Toronto to the US-Canada border by midnight. That's when I remembered my 750cc Honda Hawk sitting in my parents' garage. This thing was a city bike. It wasn't something you'd take on the highway under any circumstances, certainly not for a 480-mile ride to New York City. The border was ninety minutes away by car. I had no idea how long it would take on the bike. Still, what other choice did I have?

Everything I owned was already in New York, so there wasn't a whole lot to pack. I printed a map from MapQuest, threw a change of clothes and a toothbrush into a backpack, got on the bike, and took off. It was a cool night, and any night is even colder on a bike going top speed on the highway. The bike shook going that fast as well. Between shivering from the cold and the vibration of the bike, I had to pull over and stop every forty minutes or so to stop shaking.

It was well past dark when I arrived at the border. What fascinated me most was that it was empty. I've crossed the Canada-US border at Niagara Falls many, many times, and one thing it has never been is empty. But on this night, there was no one else there. It was eerie, and it took me a moment to get my bearings, because there are three crossings at Niagara Falls and I had to make sure I went to the correct one, which was not the tourist crossing that most people typically go to.

I walked into the office and found the person who was supposed to be there. He knew I was coming. I reached into my backpack and pulled out my Canadian passport and the faxed copy of my visa, which was literally one of those curly, thermal-paper faxes we all used back in the day. Up to that moment, I'd been processing the 9/11 attacks as a human being and as a journalist, but it was only when I was standing in that office that I began to consider how the attacks might affect the way other people saw me. There I was, a brown Muslim guy who'd recently been training to get his pilot's license, sweet-talking my way into the country on the strength of a curled-up, faxed copy of a visa less than forty-eight hours after the worst terrorist attack on American soil, an attack perpetrated by a bunch of brown Muslim guys with box cutters who'd pulled off the crime of the century by training to get their pilot's licenses. But any apprehension I felt dissipated almost immediately, because the agent couldn't have been more genial and kind. I have literally never had a simpler, more pleasant time getting into the United States than on that night. There was no suspicion, no feeling of conflict or asking me a bunch of questions. The border guard did what he needed to do, stamped my passport, stamped my visa, welcomed me to the United States of America, and sent me on my way.

I rolled into Niagara Falls, New York, and had my pick of places to stay since all the tourists were at home. I found one of the honeymoon motels that litter the town. It looked clean enough, not that I was feeling particularly fussy at that point; I had been going on adrenaline and was wiped, and it was a place to lay my head.

The next morning, I got up and drove and drove and drove. Riding on a bike on the highway sucks because dirt and rocks are constantly getting kicked up by the big trucks, so you have to keep your visor down and I was breathing heavy from the exhaustion and the stress and it kept fogging up. So I kept having to lift the visor and let more air in, which left me breathing dust and exhaust. Plus, my hands were still freezing, and my whole body was shaking. I kept having to stop every forty-five minutes or so to fill up my tiny fuel tank and get coffee to warm up. The whole trip was hell, but I needed to get to work. I just kept going.

The trip took a whole day for what would have been only a seven-hour trip by car, and it was already dark by the time the skyscrapers of Manhattan appeared on the horizon. The normally awe-inspiring sight of that incredible skyline took on an entirely different cast from the smoke and the orange glow of flames. I drove over the George Washington Bridge and into Manhattan and the whole thing was like a scene out of a movie. There was some kind of cop or city official at nearly every intersection, especially in Midtown. You could tell they had pulled out everyone, even the newest cadets from the police academy, and they'd just put them in a uniform and dropped them on a street corner. As I rode down by Penn Station, everyone was out putting up their signs and posters for the family members who were missing.

I found a parking garage for my bike, parked it, headed up to my new apartment, and crashed hard. The next morning I woke up a resident of this new country for the first time. Though there was hardly time to sit with that fact, I couldn't help but pause for at least a moment to take in the view. My apartment looked out over Madison Square Garden and the Moynihan Post Office, straight down

Eighth Avenue to Ground Zero. There was this thick, acrid smoke hanging all over the city, and I could look right out my window down to the smoldering ruins of the World Trade Center, which at that point had been burning for over two days. But I couldn't pause for too long. America was on fire, and it was time to go to work.

The first shocks to the system followed swiftly thereafter. The business world plunged into the age of scandal, when companies like MCI and WorldCom and Enron were caught cooking their books to hide billions of dollars in losses from investors. We covered those stories ad nauseam, and it was the first time that we, as financial journalists, confronted the idea that some of the people who we are all excited to have on our TV stations were a bunch of crooks. Then came cascading crises of confidence in our institutions and leadership: the Iraq War, Hurricane Katrina, the 2008 financial meltdown. As I traveled the world reporting, going to places like Hong Kong and India, people would ask me, "Why can't you guys be more like Al Jazeera?" Meaning: "When are you guys going to stop being ESPN and really report the news and hold people to account?"

It would have been difficult for any reporter to remain a passive bystander with all of that going on, but the single biggest catalyst in my evolution as a journalist had nothing to do with world affairs. It was my wife, Lori, whom I met when she appeared as a guest on my show; a mutual fund portfolio manager, she'd come on to share her expertise in the consumer sector. Before I met her, I wasn't an ambitious guy. I didn't necessarily think I was anyone special who would accomplish anything great in this world. Without her, I might have been content to muddle through life, enjoying myself, making a decent living, having a good time. She was the one who said to me,

"You can do more than that." Most importantly, she was the one who made me believe it.

With her support, I ended up leaving CNN after twelve years and joining Al Jazeera for a spell, which proved to be the perfect transition for me. It's where I got in the trenches and learned the tradecraft of serious reporting that I'd been missing in my years behind the business anchor's desk. That was the proving ground. I had space for conversations with world figures that were an hour long. It was unheard of to have that kind of time at CNN. I went to Iran when the Obama administration was negotiating the nuclear deal, and I spent two full weeks on the ground reporting that story. I did a great story on people with disabilities who were being exploited in below-minimum-wage jobs. I did a big exposé on a traffic scam in Chicago, where this guy, in exchange for a kickback, had rigged the city's traffic lights to cause drivers to get more tickets and the city to generate more revenue. I got to do real stories holding real people to account. In twelve years at CNN, I got one Emmy nomination for a report about a terrorist attack. In two years at Al Jazeera, I got three. Becoming a more serious journalist and a more serious person, I also found the motivation to take the second step toward becoming an American citizen, completing the paperwork and the swearing-in ceremony at Lower Manhattan's Thurgood Marshall Courthouse.

Having made these radical changes in both my personal and professional lives, I was then hired by MSNBC in October 2016 on their broadly unchallenged expectation that Hillary Clinton was on a glide path to becoming the forty-fifth president of the United States of America (I wasn't so sure). After starting out in financial journalism as a talking head who read things off a teleprompter, I'd spent over fifteen years turning myself into a policy wonk, and

MSNBC wanted a guy with my knowledge and enjoyment of minu-tiae to parse what was going to be a very wonky presidency. I went home on election night and took an Ambien only to be wrenched out of a deep sleep by my boss Janelle Rodriguez calling to say, "I need you back in the office."

"Why?" I asked, bleary-eyed and stoned from the sleeping pill.

"Because markets are collapsing around the world."

"Whaddya mean markets are collapsing around the world?"

"Donald Trump is winning."

"OK, this is bullshit. I'm going back to sleep."

"Turn on your TV."

The fact that America allowed itself to sleepwalk into a Donald Trump presidency, the fact that so many otherwise knowledge-able people didn't see it coming, is testimony to how complacent we'd become about the hard work and extreme vigilance that true citizen-ship requires. I can remember being at CNN the night that Barack Obama was elected, back in the days when CNN had twenty people at a time in the newsroom in rows of desks. There wasn't a dry eye in the place. We were all caught up in watching history unfold, and I was thinking, "This is it. This was the big thing America needed to do that it hadn't done, and now we've broken through that." Even if you didn't buy into the absurdities about a "postracial America," there was a sense that we'd made a giant leap forward, and it was almost impossible to imagine things going backward from there.

Obama himself leaned hard on Martin Luther King Jr.'s famous formulation that "the arc of history is long but it bends toward jus-tice." But with all due respect to both of those men, that's not actually true. It's wishful thinking that people need to abandon because it breeds a complacency that things will just continue to get better on their own. Everything about my family's story tells me that the arc of history bends the way you bend it. That was true with the National Party in South Africa in 1948, it was true with Idi Amin in Uganda in 1972, and it's been true in America for quite some time. For the past fifty years, extremist right-wingers have been bending it the way they wanted, and with Trump's election, we finally got to the result of their efforts.

With Trump's victory, even though I was now an American citizen, I started making sure I always knew where my Canadian passport was. I thought about what the future would be like if things got bad here, but it was a back-of-my-mind sort of thing; my real moment of truth came only four years later, after the death of George Floyd, when the police and the National Guard pulled into that intersection in Minneapolis with their lights blazing and sirens blaring and rifles drawn. That was the moment everything finally clicked for me, and I truly understood the existential threat that America is up against. Because there was no reason for those officers to start shooting. The night after George Floyd's murder, people were overtaking the police station and burning buildings, and one can have a legitimate discussion about whether or not the police are justified in using force to intervene in that scenario. You may not like the police, and you may not sympathize with the mob or their grievances, but most reasonable people would probably say, "This is a bad scene. Somebody has to rein this in, and what is the best way to accomplish that?"

That's not what happened the night I got shot. There was zero violence that night. We were documenting a peaceful march. You wouldn't even call it a rally. It was more of a walk. It was a bunch of people walking through Minneapolis, their only crime being that they were in violation of a curfew. You want to arrest them for that? Get on the bullhorn and tell them to go home? Fine. Everyone knew they were breaking curfew and were subject to arrest. These people, thousands of them, had taken it upon themselves to take that risk. But they were just walking, and there was no threat that called for an armed response.

I've covered the G8 and the G20, these international conferences that draw all kinds of rock-throwing anarchists and the like, and every cop in every major city on earth learned years ago: if you're trying to control a crowd, you don't incite the crowd. It's never good. So the minute they opened fire, I knew it was the result of a deliberate choice. Subsequent recordings that came out indicated, especially when it came to journalists, cops were on a hunt that night. They were jacked up. They were pumped up to do this, and we were fair game. The Minneapolis police chief himself was a decent, honest official, but his power was hamstrung by the police union, and the head of the police union in Minneapolis was a big Trumper. So you had some cops who were juiced on this whole Trumpian mantra of "You need to rough people up a bit." Because other than that, there was no reason to do it. None. But they did it. They were excited to do it, and they continued to do it for hours all over the city. They chased people down. It was completely unnecessary, and it was wrong.

A few months later, the whole episode came up again because Trump started ranting about it on the campaign trail as part of his whole attack on the media. "I remember this guy Velshi," he said, recounting the incident. "He got hit in the knee with a canister of tear gas and he went down. He was down. 'My knee, my knee.'" He was wrong about every detail, by the way. It's all on video. But Trump makes up lies even when he doesn't need to.

But the truly disturbing part of Trump's speech was what came next, when he lavished praise on the police for attacking an American journalist. "It was the most beautiful thing," Trump said, "because after we take all that crap for weeks and weeks, and you finally see men get up there and go right through them, wasn't it really a beautiful sight? It's called *law* and *order*." Then the crowd erupted in cheers and applause.

The fact that I happened to be in the middle of that story isn't what makes it important. What makes it important is not only that armed agents of the state believe that it's OK to take unprovoked shots at both civilians and journalists but also that millions of American citizens are willing to cheer that on. It is chilling to realize there is a large and vocal faction in this country that is ready to burn it to the ground before they'll share it with anyone who doesn't look like them or doesn't think like them. They stand ready to tear down everything that makes America special—indeed, everything that makes America *possible*, like the right to vote and the right to a free and independent press.

Instagram-ready incursions against the US Capitol notwithstanding, what's become clear is that if American democracy dies, it will not be in a violent coup. It will be through the steady, deliberate erosion of our norms and laws and values: poll workers cowering in fear because of threats of violence, book bans and other attempts to evade and whitewash our nation's history, social media platforms that allow a complete retreat from any kind of shared reality and national identity. We are fighting a thousand different fights on a thousand different fronts.

As I've said, up until Minneapolis, I thought of myself as someone covering those fights. It was only when I got shot that I fully realized I was *in* the fight. That belated realization came, in part, simply because, even as a brown guy in Donald Trump's America, the system continued to work fine for me. It still works fine for me to this day. I make a good living. I go about my life without any real fears for my physical safety. I worry about larger societal problems, but day to day I'm good, which means I have a certain perspective on the promise of this land and I could easily go right on taking that promise as guaranteed. But I can't anymore, because I know that promise is not guaranteed. To any of us.

If the overturning of *Roe v. Wade* tells us anything, it's that none of the freedoms we enjoy in this society can be taken for granted, not even for a minute. The most marginalized groups in America have always understood that, the young Black man I met in Minneapolis on the night of the riots understood that, but those of us who remain relatively well-off need to understand it as well. It's not enough for society to be good enough for some of us. It has to be good enough for all of us. As has been said many times by those much wiser than me, if one of us is in chains, none of us are free. This is what my father and mother and sister knew. It's what my grandparents and great-grandparents knew, despite their total lack of a formal education. Justice isn't justice until it's universal. Equality isn't equality until it's universal. Democracy isn't democracy until it's universal.

Democracy also fails if you fail to work for it. It is not enough to stand on the street corner watching the liquor store burn and saying, "The system doesn't work for me." Because in a democracy, we are the system. We talk far too much about citizenship as the acquisition of rights when we ought to be talking about it as the assumption of responsibilities. When my parents first got the right to vote in Kenya and again ten years later in Canada, they were as excited about volunteering to drive people to the polls as they were about voting themselves. Their Canadian citizenship wasn't just something granted to them by Pierre Trudeau. It was something they created, something they built themselves out of the raw materials and opportunities that Pierre Trudeau gave them access to.

Citizenship is something you have to practice. It's a muscle that atrophies if you don't use it, and if it does, other people will be waiting to take advantage of its weakness. If the Trump presidency proved anything, it's that our institutions alone are not going to protect us. Our laws and social norms alone are not going to protect us. The booklet of the US Constitution that I read while waiting to take my citizenship oath, as foundational as that document is, that alone will not protect us.

Only we will protect us.

Only *you* will protect us.

We all have a role to play, and all of our roles are of equal importance. It was only when I understood that idea that I took the third and final step to become, in every sense of the word, a citizen of the United States of America.

Epilogue

Red Clay Boots

In the twenty years that have passed since my family's brief stretch in the South African bagel business, I've been back to the country a number of times. I try to make it every other year or so, to go on safari and to visit the friends that we've made there, and on those trips, I usually try to see some of the places and landmarks that were part of my family's history.

Over the years, my parents had taken me to a number of those spots. My father had shown me the site where ABC Bakery stood before it was torn down and replaced with a shopping mall. I had walked the crowded streets of Marabastad, no longer the residential ghetto it once was since the original Indian inhabitants were all moved out to different locations. Now it's a hawker's bazaar, people selling goods around a taxi stand, which is what a lot of South Africa is these days. You can still see shades of what it was when my parents lived there. There are still a few of the original Indian shops left, but it's no longer the place that it was.

Surprisingly, there was one place they'd never taken me, and that was Tolstoy Farm. Despite its instrumental place in our story, we'd never made the time to go. As I set out to research and write this book, I knew that Tolstoy Farm was going to be the starting point for my research on it, which meant it was time to visit. I wanted to go there for inspiration. Especially since I never knew my grandfather, I wanted to see if I could go and connect with his experience. I wanted to sit and look out and see what he saw as he learned about freedom and justice and democracy.

As it turns out, Tolstoy Farm is not the easiest place to get to. A normal Google search didn't turn up a whole lot of information, and it was only after I did some digging that I found a guy who found another guy who pointed me toward the guy I needed to talk to, Mohan Hira. Getting in touch with Mohan then proved to be its own challenge, as he doesn't have an email address and could only be messaged through WhatsApp, which I did and eventually got him to call me back.

Mohan Hira is a South African Indian guy in his eighties, and he's made it his life's work to preserve the memory of Tolstoy Farm and grow it into a real cultural landmark. It had been largely an uphill battle. Since Apartheid ended, the big cultural and historical push has been to commemorate the Freedom Movement led by Nelson Mandela, Oliver Tambo, and others. The 1952 Defiance Campaign, Mandela's galvanizing speech at the Rivonia trial, his tiny prison cell on Robben Island—these are the events and landmarks that the nation wants to commemorate and that tourists want to see. And this is entirely understandable, but as a result of that, the story of Gandhi and the satyagraha movement has become little more than an interesting footnote to the larger conversation. The Apartheid Museum is a world-class institution attracting tens of thousands of visitors a year, and it sits just thirty minutes up the road from Tolstoy Farm, which you have to dig to find on the internet.

After tracking Mohan down, I told him I wanted to visit, thinking that I would fly down to do some research and that he and I would spend an afternoon together at the farm. That's all I wanted to do: visit Tolstoy Farm. That was the only reason I contacted Mohan. But Mohan had a different plan. He proposed taking me on a ten-day journey. I would fly to Durban, and together we would follow Gandhi's footsteps on the same journey that he took during his years in South Africa. So that's what we did.

From the moment I landed in Durban, before I even had a chance to stop at a hotel and rest from my red-eye flight, Mohan picked me up, and despite his advanced age and the fact that he'd just been hospitalized from a bout with COVID so horrendous he'd lost twenty-five pounds, he was ready to go. Mohan, apparently, is a big karate guy, so he was in great physical shape for a man his age. Plus, this hobby meant he exclusively wore tracksuits with his name monogramed on the front. He was, however, too old to drive, so a third guy, Salim, a big Muslim dude with a big Muslim beard and a cowboy hat, had joined us to do the work behind the wheel.

Part of the Gandhian lesson of being with Mohan was patience. This trip was going to unfold at the pace he wanted it to. We started at the Pietermaritzburg train station where Gandhi got thrown off the train. There's a nice interpretive center there now. We also met with Gandhi's granddaughter, Ela, who still lives at the Phoenix settlement, the ashram that was Gandhi's prototype for Tolstoy Farm.

It sits just outside of Durban. From there, we stopped in every town that Gandhi had ever set foot in. We stopped at every courthouse he'd ever had a hearing in, every jail cell he'd ever been held in. We'd walk around and Mohan would tell me the story. There'd sometimes be commemorative markers to look at and read. In every town, he'd tell me about the history of the Indian community in that place. Or we'd meet with some Indian merchant who lived there and they'd talk about the olden times.

The six-hundred-kilometer journey from Durban to Johannesburg, a seven-hour drive, took us four days. I kept trying to make a plan, to figure out where we were staying each night so I could look it up on Trip Advisor to see if it had any bed bug warnings. Mohan would have none of it. He would just pick a place, and we'd pull in. Typically, it wouldn't have working WiFi, and there wouldn't be any restaurants nearby. So Salim would phone some auntie in Pretoria who would phone some auntie who lived nearby who'd cook us a meal and bring it to us, and we'd be sitting there eating Indian food in a dingy hotel room at 11:00 p.m. Then we'd wake up and do the same thing all over again. I never had any sense of when we were ever going to get to Tolstoy Farm, and Mohan wouldn't tell me anything. He wanted me to understand that (a) I wasn't going to find out any information any faster than he'd give it to me and (b) I should just be grateful we were making the journey by car, because every few years Mohan takes a handful of pilgrims and does the same six hundred kilometers on foot, to emulate how Gandhi actually got to Tolstoy Farm—not literally, of course, because it wasn't a direct journey. But the trek we were on was a representation of the long, exhausting slog that Gandhi took during his years in South Africa.

Finally, we made it. The big trick to Tolstoy Farm is that you can't find it on a map. It's adjacent to what's become a very industrialized area. You're going down a big street and you take a sharp turn into what looks like a patch of dirt that takes you down a really long road into the foothills outside Johannesburg. The first thing you pass is the railway station, Hobart Station, which is the train station that Gandhi didn't let his pupils use to go into town.

About a mile down this dirt road, we arrived at what's left of Tolstoy Farm. Of its original one thousand acres, about a hundred remain. At the center of the property there is the stone foundation of the main house. The tin shanties and everything else is gone. There's no museum documenting what happened or even a sign to tell you, "This is what it was like in Gandhi's time."

What hasn't changed, and what remains totally unspoiled, is the view. Johannesburg back then was nothing but industrial smokestacks and today it's high-rises, but otherwise it is all the same. The way the land slopes down, you can look out and see the city skyline, but all the suburban sprawl that stretches below is hidden from view. You'd never know it was there. It looks exactly like it did in my grandfather's day. I was quite taken by that. I could look out on the horizon and see what he saw, which was exactly what I'd originally come to see. But as I'd learned over the past four days, in any pilgrimage, the important part is not the destination but the journey, which was why Mohan had wanted to take me on the road. What felt like a random itinerary was actually done quite deliberately. Gandhi's journey wasn't linear. It was a constant struggle, forward and back, standing up, getting knocked down, and standing back up again. His time in South Africa was very Martin Luther King–esque. There was a lot of getting arrested, a lot of court hearings, a lot of jail time—and tiny bits of progress in between.

It's why Gandhi made his followers, including my seven-year-old grandfather, skip Hobart Station to walk that twenty miles over red clay dirt roads into town to get groceries and provisions. They had to learn that kind of endurance. It had to be second nature to them because the journey to a just and equal society is nothing if not an exercise in staying power. It's everyday people who are willing to say, "I'm going to keep at this. I'm going to keep marching, and you can't break me." That was what it took to build Tolstoy Farm, and Mohan wanted me to understand that. He wanted me to feel the actual, physical hardship of the struggle. And he was right. My moment of inspiration didn't come from sitting on a rock at Tolstoy Farm, gazing wistfully out over the horizon. It came from the aching knees and the sore feet.

Under the British Raj in India, my ancestors faced total political and economic dispossession. Taking a mad leap into the unknown, they landed in South Africa. There they enjoyed relative economic prosperity only to see it wiped out because they lacked the political and legal protections of citizenship. In Kenya, they managed a small step forward, rebuilding themselves financially and enjoying the legal rights of citizenship and full participation in the political process. Sadly, because of the nationalist backlash that came after East Africa's independence movements, as Kenyans, my parents were never able to enjoy those deeper, more intangible qualities of *true* citizenship, the feeling of acceptance and belonging that a truly open and pluralistic society provides. It was only in Canada and America that we were finally able to access the full spectrum of rights and privileges necessary to live life to our greatest potential— and, as proven by the experiences of my sister and millions of others, those rights and privileges are in no way evenly distributed, and they can be lost at any moment if we don't work and fight for them every single day.

When my great-grandfather Velshi left India, he was a poor emigrant with nothing but the clothes on his back. Making that leap from the ship was the riskiest, most daring thing he could do, and he did it. A decade later, sending his son to Tolstoy Farm to study with Gandhi was, by any measure, a radical, revolutionary thing for a Gujarati businessman to do, and he did it. Small acts of courage don't always bear fruit in their own time. Indeed, small, incremental successes can often look like failure until we get the chance to look at them from three generations down the road. Gandhi had no idea that the entire British Empire would collapse on the heels of his movement. He died. He didn't get to see it. But because of what Gandhi did and because of what Velshi did, the ideals of social activism, responsibility, and community were instilled in my grandfather Rajabali, who then passed them down to my father and his siblings and my mother and, ultimately, on to my sister and me.

We tend to think of an inheritance in strictly material terms. It's money, property, maybe a collection of family heirlooms. But the sum total of our choices and our actions constitutes a kind of inheritance as well. I look back at what Velshi did, and I think, "He had so little at his disposal, and yet he did something with it. So did my grandparents. So did my parents. Had any of them faltered, I would not be here today. The actions of this unknown, penniless migrant were responsible, ultimately, for the election of the first Muslim and first Indian representative in a Canadian parliament, over eighty years and eight thousand miles away in North America." It's become important to me to honor that. In addition to the onus that is placed on all of us to be the best neighbors and best citizens we can be, I feel an additional responsibility to make my forebears' sacrifices worthwhile. What is the biggest risk that I can take, and am I taking it? What is the most revolutionary thing that I can do, and am I doing it? Will I pass on to my children, Erica and Eli, the same inheritance of good choices and positive actions that was passed on to me?

I don't think I'll ever be called on to take a blind leap into the Indian Ocean—which comes as a huge relief since I still don't know how to swim—but for me, as a journalist, the most radical and revolutionary thing I can do is to simply use the platform that I'm so incredibly lucky to have. I can resolve to make journalism and the national dialogue better than they have been. I can promise to never again let go of my aspiration to be Webb Miller on that phone outside the Dharasana saltworks, using my camera to bear witness to injustice and using my microphone to hold power to account. But you don't have to be a television journalist to make a difference in this world. You don't have to be Mohandas Gandhi or Nelson Mandela or Pierre Trudeau or Barack Obama to do it, either. You can be a refugee on a boat. You can be an immigrant shopkeeper struggling to get by. You can be a working parent with barely five minutes to spare at the end of the week. All you have to do is make the greatest contribution you can make given what you have at that moment. Maybe it's running for local office, or maybe it's helping drive people to the polls. Maybe it's volunteering at the library. It can be anything. Your efforts may feel like a drop in the ocean. It may feel like change is impossible. Your actions may not even bear fruit until your children, your grandchildren, or your great-grandchildren come of age. But somehow, somewhere, your choices will leave their mark. They always do.

At the end of my pilgrimage to Tolstoy Farm, I marked my visit for any future visitors who make their way there. I planted a tree. That's one of the nice things Mohan Hira has done at the site. Every time someone visits, they plant a tree, and I got to plant one, too. I have these Wolverine 1,000 Mile boots that I wear on all my travels, and when I finished planting my tree, I looked down and saw that my boots had this red-clay dust all over them. "I don't want this dust to come off these shoes," I thought. "This is the same dirt that covered my grandfather's shoes when he worked on this farm and when he set out on his twenty-mile treks to Johannesburg. These boots are the proof that I've walked in my grandfather's footsteps and done my best to continue the journey he undertook a hundred years ago." So as Mohan and I wrapped up our time at Tolstoy Farm, I thanked him and said goodbye, then I went straight to the store to buy a new pair of boots to wear home. I put the old ones in a plastic bag, packed them up in a box, and shipped them home, where today they proudly sit in that same plastic bag in the back of a closet. Because there's no way Lori is going to let me make a display out of dirty boots in our living room.

And rightly so.

Acknowledgments

While I've been writing *some* sort of a book for years now, this particular incarnation was born during a COVID-19-era Zoom meeting
I had with my talent agent at UTA, Adam Leibner; his colleague,
Jennifer Rohrer; and my literary agent, also at UTA, Byrd Leavell.
Together, they gently explained to me that the book I'd wanted to
write—about how modern Western governments' distribution of the
spoils of unfettered trade was (a) inherently flawed and (b) a root
cause of economic inequality—was the wrong book for me to write
at this moment. I was annoyingly insistent, but they were right.
That's why this book exists.

Small Acts of Courage takes the form it does because the legendary
St. Martin's Press editor Tim Bartlett—who claims he was ready to
edit that *other* book I wanted to write—enthusiastically encouraged
me. Alongside his colleagues at St. Martin's, including Laura Clark

and Kevin Reilly, Tim employed remarkable patience and expertise to evolve this effort into the book a reader would actually want to read. My friend Steve Kettman started me traveling down this road, from Tolstoy Farm to today, helping me dive into the philosophical underpinnings of satyagraha and imparting both wisdom and optimism into my mission. Tanner Colby, my partner throughout this process, converted my somewhat disorderly approach to writing into the pages you read today.

MSNBC has given me the platform and the encouragement to do the work that has allowed me to fully comprehend the underpinnings of the current threat against, and fights to preserve, democracy. Rashida Jones, Greg Kordick, Yvette Miley, Omnika Thompson, David Verdi, and Betsy Korona have given me the freedom to travel America and the world, allowing me to see how this struggle manifests daily on the ground. Lorie Acio and Olivia Sieff, our expert communications team, help me spread the message far and wide. And my exceptionally dedicated and talented team at *Velshi*—led by my incredible executive producer, editorial partner, friend, and confidante Rebekah Dryden—shares my passion and provides me the space and the journalistic expertise to actively engage in the fight for democracy in my work.

My uncle Mohamed Keshavjee has literally put forty years into tracing our shared family history. He handed me the bones of this book in the form of his own 2015 volume, *Into This Heaven of Freedom*. As a British-trained South African Indian lawyer who immigrated first to Kenya and then to Canada, he has lived all of what I have written about. He spent many, many hours with me ensuring that this book captured the texture of the immigrant experience, of living as a colonial subject, and of surviving under Apartheid.

Hasan ChaCha, though not my biological uncle, is an uncle to everyone in my family. He is the keeper of our stories. There is virtually no surviving documentation of my family's history in India. All we know, we know from Hasan and his immensely generous family, who treat Lori and me as their own whenever we visit. Our last trip to Chotila was facilitated by Aman Halani, a superbly engaging Ismaili entrepreneur from Rajkot, who served as our guide, interpreter, and historian. Aman provided me with great context about the eroding state of democracy in India on our drives to Chotila and back to Rajkot.

In South Africa, Mohan Hira and Amien Osman took me, physically, on the road back to Tolstoy Farm and fed me well along that beautiful journey. May more people venture to that beautiful farm outside Johannesburg where my family's history, and the history of so many others, began.

Hiten Bawa, an architect and artist who is profoundly deaf with cochlear implants, returned to Tolstoy Farm with me and explained how much of what I was seeing resembled what my grandfather actually saw as the youngest student at that ashram. He then drew me a picture, literally, of what life on the farm would look like so that I could visualize it as accurately as possible.

My Afrikaner friends in South Africa, Jacques and Janine Botes, gave my parents and me great comfort in the effort to relocate "back home" in the mid-'90s. On my last trip to South Africa to research this book, Jacques presented me with a beautiful 1949 five-shilling coin with King George VI on the obverse and a springbok, the symbol of South Africa, on the reverse—1949 being the first full year of National Party control in South Africa, the year in which Apartheid went from an idea to an absurdly Byzantine labyrinth of laws that would mark the beginning of the end of my family's time there. I placed the coin in a holder next to my writing desk, a reminder of how the last seventy-five years played out, making this book a necessity.

Jan Boshoff—ostensibly our Afrikaner accountant for our business efforts in South Africa back in the nineties, in reality a true friend and fellow explorer—told me the stories of his people, the white tribe of Africa, during a two-week camping trip in the African hinterland in 2022. Jan showed me the call of the African *veld* and the almost spiritual appeal it held for the Boers before (and long after) they acknowledged and accepted that they would, in fact, need to share that land with *all* the tribes of Africa, especially those who came before them.

Back home, my son, Eli, the most driven human I know, provides the most consistent motivation in my life. Our weekly Sunday-night dinners give me the opportunity to float the trial balloons, discussions, and debates for the ideas about citizenship and democracy I discuss weekly on my show and now in this book.

My old buddy Rob Schroeder, my first American friend who interned with me at CNN in 1993, was my travel companion on my final eye-opening journey back to South Africa. He has been a fellow traveler and consistent supporter for my entire career.

And finally, Mikey. I call him a friend. But really, he's my brother.

Index

About the Author

Ali Velshi is an award-winning journalist, the host of *Velshi*, a chief correspondent for MSNBC, and a weekly economics contributor to NPR's *Here and Now*. He hosts the *Velshi Banned Book Club* on MSNBC, and the *Velshi Banned Book Club* podcast. Velshi is known for his immersive on-the-ground reporting and his inter-active discussions with small groups, which form part of his ongoing series *Velshi Across America*. He previously worked as an anchor and correspondent for Al Jazeera America and CNN.

Born in Nairobi and raised in Toronto, Velshi holds a degree in religion and an honorary doctorate of laws from Canada's Queen's University. He serves on the boards of the National Constitution Center, the Chicago History Museum, the X-Prize Foundation, and the *Philadelphia*

Citizen. Velshi is the author of *Gimme My Money Back* and *The Trump Indictments*, and coauthor of *How to Speak Money* and the upcoming *Open Space* (2025). Velshi has been nominated for multiple Emmy Awards, and is the recipient of two National Headliner Awards and a Society of Professional Journalists Sigma Delta Chi Award.